NER
press

ISLAMIZING EUROPE

Is the Conquest Inevitable?

ISLAMIZING EUROPE

Is the Conquest Inevitable?

HUGH FITZGERALD

Published by New English Review Press
a subsidiary of World Encounter Institute
PO Box 158397
Nashville, Tennessee 37215
&
27 Old Gloucester Street
London, England, WC1N 3AX

Cover Art and Design by Kendra Mallock

ISBN: 978-1-966833-01-7

Library of Congress Control Number: 2025938262

First Edition

NEW ENGLISH REVIEW PRESS
newenglishreview.org

To my wife

Shall Paper live, or Ink,
Since Brass and Marble can't withstand
This Iron Age's violating Hand?

Contents

The author wishes to thank for assistance of many kinds Robert Spencer, Ibn Warraq, and Rebecca Bynum.

FOREWORD

One For the Ages

OUR MISEDUCATED and absurd age doesn't lack for writers, but one ongoing source of consolation amid their windy and ill-informed pontifications is that their period of influence will, at least when one takes the long view, be mercifully brief. In a hundred years, and likely much sooner, immediately after their platforms have been given to no doubt even less worthy successors and they have passed, laden with honors, into a comfortable retirement, the likes of Thomas Friedman and Nicholas Kristof of the *New York Times*, and the BBC's John Simpson, will be forgotten.

If, meanwhile, any sanity is restored to the public discourse in future generations, one political and cultural analyst of the early twenty-first century will be read and studied, although he was almost completely unknown in his own day: Hugh Fitzgerald.

For twenty years, Hugh Fitzgerald has been writing on jihad, Islamization, and related issues at JihadWatch.org. The fact that nearly every young American can immediately identify who Taylor Swift is, but has never heard of Hugh Fitzgerald, is a symptom of the many maladies of the age. Yet when it comes to Swifts, Hugh is more Jonathan than Taylor. He writes with a depth and breadth of political, cultural, sociological and historical knowledge that is unparalleled today, even among those who are celebrated for their supposed mastery of the topic at hand. His erudition, eloquence and wit set a standard for analysts of the contemporary scene that is unlikely ever to be equaled.

Why, then, is Hugh Fitzgerald almost completely unknown, outside of a small but devoted following that preserves, treasures and circulates his writings as if they contained the lost wisdom of a vanished civilization — which, in a very real sense, they do. A chief reason is that this is an age of near-universal pusillanimity and cowardice, and Hugh Fitzgerald is neither pusillanimous nor cowardly. He has sounded the alarm about a phenomenon, the Islamization of Europe, that is at once world-historical and cataclysmic, with political, social and cultural effects that will reverberate for centuries. Yet as seismic as this transformation is, it has been nearly universally ignored, and where noted at all, has been dismissed as a conspiracy theory of the "far right."

Only now, with the demographic transformation of the European continent well underway and possibly irreversible, are the facts that Hugh Fitzgerald has been discussing and sounding the alarm about for two decades at last becoming obvious to the distracted and propagandized world. This volume contains many of Hugh's observations about this Islamization, and whether or not it was and is inevitable; had he been heeded earlier, the violence and strife that we now see across the continent with increasing frequency might have been avoided.

Another reason why Hugh Fitzgerald is today largely unknown is his unflinching honesty and laser-sharp accuracy in writing about the religion of Islam. The political and media elites long ago decided to blanket the West with fantasies about the "religion of peace," which was so completely compatible with secular pluralism that only bigots, racists, and other undesirables would dare suggest that it wasn't. It required of public intellectuals that they affirm that "Islamism," a fictional Western construct, was the problem, with Islam itself being totally benign and to be encouraged in every way. Those who declined to adhere publicly to this fantasy were ostracized, vilified, condemned, silenced and ignored.

Despite this, Hugh has never wavered in articulating the political, supremacist, aggressive, expansionist and violent aspects of this creed, and in stating unhesitatingly that if allowed to proliferate in Western countries, Islam would choke out, destroy and replace the existing civilization. His Cassandra-like warnings, many of which can be found in this book, have been ignored, but if history is written by free people, they will note that he was a watchman on the wall at a time when precious few dared to make such a stand, or were even aware that doing so was necessary.

And so this book collects many of Hugh Fitzgerald's choicest and most enduring observations about the Islamization of Europe, the Islamic imperatives that have given rise to this Islamization and the best efforts of vaunted "experts" to deny them or explain them away, and some practical guidance for a way forward if Europe as we have known it is to be preserved in whole or part. Although crafted in light of the tumultuous events of the first quarter of this century, Hugh's observations and analysis are timeless. His foundational assumptions are the keys to the health and success of any society; I look forward to the days when political science and sociology classes study this book, and other writings of Hugh Fitzgerald, for insight into the way forward.

I'm honored to have been able to call Hugh Fitzgerald a colleague at Jihad Watch for all these years. If Jihad Watch has contributed anything to the public discourse, surely one of its foremost and lasting contributions is making available the writings of Hugh Fitzgerald to the world. Yet while Internet sites have been and will be subject to censorship to the point of total erasure, and books can also be destroyed, once they are printed and distributed, at least some books can be hidden from the destroyers. The book you are holding may be the one that lights the way for a renewal of sane and humane civilization. Treasure it. Absorb its wisdom. Keep it in a safe place, so that you can return to it. As those who know nothing of Hugh Fitzgerald or his writings continue to wreak havoc upon our society, you will find yourself being drawn to do so more than once.

—*Robert Spencer*
July 2024

PART I

The Islamization of Europe

CHAPTER ONE

Douce France

I MAGINE THAT you are a cosseted member of the French elite. One child is doing the khâgne, aiming for rue d'Ulm. Another is now a politechnicien. You are very comfortable, working for the state. You and your spouse are journalists, or writers, or one of that vast tribe of people conducting "recherches," and life is comfortable, good, the way it should be. Yes, you do notice more and more Muslims about you as you walk, no longer in the banlieues, but in the center of Paris, or Toulouse, or Lyon. And you remember how uneasy you felt, four years ago, when you happened to be walking on the Canebière in Marseille. You decided, then and there, that you would not return.

And you have friends who live in the south. And they tell you that the — some call them maghrébins — make life hell for everyone. They attack French children on the way to school. They vandalize cars. They threaten, and do more than threaten, anyone who is still foolish enough to walk out wearing a kippah or a cross. Whole areas of cities in the south, as in the north, and east, and west, have become off-limits to non-Muslims. In the schools, the teachers have lost authority. They cannot even cover the subjects of World War II, the Resistance, and the murders of the Jews as the state prescribes; they fear, with reason, the violent reaction of the Muslim students.

And as the schools become more and more dangerous for non-Muslim students and teachers, with more time and resources devoted to discipline rather than to learning, French parents and would-be parents are now silently factoring into their childbearing plans the present value of the future cost of what, they see, will now have to be added: private school tuition. And that means, of course, that those French people will plan on smaller families. And they will also be factoring in the growing cost, paid by them, those French taxpayers, for the whole expanding edifice of security, the guards in the schools, the guards at the train stations and métro stations and airports and at government buildings everywhere, the costs of keeping the gravestones from being vandalized, the costs of protecting the synagogues and the churches, the costs for all those tapped phones and agents in mosques, and subsidies to lawyers and judges to hear charges and try cases against Muslims, and the costs of monitoring da'wa in the prisons (more than two-thirds of the inmates in France are now Muslim).

But the Muslims are indifferent to expenses incurred by the French state. France is part of the world; the world belongs to Allah, and to his Believers. That doctrine has remained immutable for 1400 years. Imam Bouziane, the one they keep trying to deport, had 16 children by two wives, all living on the French state: a representative Muslim man. Over time, the difference between average family size of Muslims and non-Muslims steadily increases. And, over time, the education system continues to disintegrate. Right now, perhaps, you cannot see it. Your children go to the best schools, followed by the best lycées. You vacation in Normandy, or Brittany, or the Île de Ré. And you do not take the metro often enough, or walk in the right districts, or work in the right factories or offices, to understand what tens of millions of your fellow Frenchmen now have to endure. You, for the moment, are still immune, still willfully unaware. You have spent the last few decades learning about the Muslim world from Eric Rouleau, and his epigones (after they silenced Jean-Pierre Peroncel-Hugoz, author of *Le radeau de Mahomet*, the one journalist who reported the truth) in *Le Monde*. You are deeply versed in the constantly reported-upon, endlessly dilated-upon, perfidy of the mighty empire of Israel. You know what we have all had dinned into us: that the Arab Muslims are reasonable people, with clearly justified grievances, grievances so reasonable and so limited in scope, that justice demands they be satisfied. Everyone agrees on the "solution." It is called a "two-state solution" and of course it is a "solution" for otherwise, of course, it would not have been called a "solution."

And everything looks the way it always has looked: the linden trees, the river, the bridges, the réverbères, the étalage in the neighborhood *boulangerie, avec ses baguettes à l'ancienne. Douce France, cher pays de mon enfance.* At the end of the school day, chic mothers still congregate in little towns, or small cities, outside the school — this or that Ecole Jules Ferry — waiting to pick up their children. Here come the littlest ones, from Maternelle, running up now — just look at how small they are. And here are the CE1 group, with those huge cartables on their tiny backs. Run, run, run, to Mommy. Oop-la. And then the years of study, study, study marked by ever-larger cahiers — "cahier" and "cartable" are the words that identify French DNA better than Piaf or gauloises, isn't that true? And now we will read the books, and study the subjects, set down so completely and precisely by the Ministry of Education. And now we are up to the final year, preparing for the Bac, with copies of blue-backed BALISES, guides to Les Châtiments and La Peau de Chagrin. And just look at the results listed in the newspaper: Claire-Alix has a mention très bien. Fantastic. Everything is fine, everything will always stay the same, whole countries cannot change. It's not possible.

But it is changing, coming apart, quietly, slowly – let's not look too closely, we mustn't pay too much attention — the streets, the schools, the hospitals, the ability to speak the truth about things, about life as it is lived, *la vita vissuta*, as they like to say in a neighboring country. Dominique de Villepin always knew there was nothing to worry about; he was born, after all, in Salé, next to Rabat, even spent a few years of his infancy there; of course he knows his Arabs, his Muslims. And surely Eric Rouleau, who for decades in *Le Monde* was the resident expert on the Middle East (he was so knowledgeable that he never had to so much as mention the teachings of the Qur'an and Sunna), knew everything that he needed to know for what Ionesco called "the newspaper everyone reads," didn't he? And those French translations of Edward Said that denounced with such passion the Islamophobia, and those vicious clichés with which the malevolent West has always caricatured the Arab Muslim world. Oh, we have been so terrible to the Arabs, we colonialists, we French, we Westerners. And then there is the never-ending outrage of Israel, that colonial-settler state and running sore that splits Arabdom in two. Of course, they have every right, those Muslims, to come here to France. We went to their countries once, now they come to ours. And they have every right to hate us, don't they?

So now we have decided not to understand, and to cut all ties of sympathy to, Israel — and how did we ever have any sympathy for it in the first place, the way some of our parents did back in 1948 or 1956 or 1967? How could they not have seen what the "Palestinian people" had to endure? Hanan, Yasser, Said, Saeb, Aziz, Walid, Rashid, Mohammed — you have won our hearts and minds. Take us, do with us what you will.

No one will mention what is happening or what kinds of things we must begin to think about doing to save ourselves. No one of any decency. And whatever Marine Le Pen and Jordan Bardella say, we must say, and think the opposite. Do not say those things, do not think them. Free thought is all very well in theory, but really — consider the consequences. Don't dare to think outside that box brimming with *idées reçues. Défense de sortir des sentiers battus.*

No, everything will be all right as you stroll down the Avenue Paule-Anne. Those Muslims will never be a match for us. Why, just look at those legionnaires marching *à pas lent* down the Champs-Elysées, think of that string of desert victories. Inside our heads, it is 1931 and over here is the Exposition coloniale. You remember, *tu t'en souviens,* that painting by le Douanier Rousseau, don't you, with the burnoosed Arab standing next to the black Senegalese? Or that song Georges Milton sang, "*La fille du Bédouin*"? I have it right, don't I? France will always be France. Nothing will ever change.

At a certain point, and despite everything that causes you not to see what is staring you in the face, you realize that something has gone irreparably wrong with your country, and you, and your children, are in danger of losing that country, down to every village and house, *qui m'est une province et beaucoup davantage.* And you do not know what to do, or how to explain this feeling to others, or in whom to confide your secret fears, or what can be done. It is so confusing, and so upsetting. Can you vote for the Right? And not tell anyone you did? You can't possibly endorse Bardella publicly. But you can vote for him. After all, you have no place else to go.

And then you learn what Jean-Luc Mélenchon and so many others in French political life, do not wish you to learn. For if you did, you might be very angry. You discover that one out of every five babies born in France today is a Muslim baby. And that means, in 20 years, one of every five 20-year-olds in France will be a Muslim twenty-year-old. And try to calculate just when, given the great disparity in the fertility rates of Muslim and non-Muslim women, and continued large-scale Muslim immigration from North Africa and the Middle East, and conversions to Islam by prison inmates and others on the mental fringes who are looking for a handy Answer to Everything, France will be one-third Muslim. But long before they are close to that, Muslims will be able, as a determined and single-minded bloc, to dominate political life. They have already made the far-left party, La France Insoumise, subject to their demands.

Where shall we hide the statues from Marly-le-roi? And the Venus de Milo? And what about all those paintings of animated life — all those portraits in the Louvre, and the Grand Palais, and the Musée Guimet down there in linden-lined Aix, and everywhere else in art-filled artful France, *mère des arts, des armes, et des loix* — that are absolutely forbidden according to the prohibition set out in a famous hadith found in the collections of Bukhari and Muslim. Should they be sent for safekeeping to those Americans across the seas?

By then most of the Jews in France will have left, gone across the oceans for their own safekeeping, to Israel or to English-speaking Canada (they were worried about the Muslim population of Quebec, you see, which had been allowed to grow under the Province of Quebec's policy of encouraging francophone immigrants, preferring North Africans to potential immigrants from Italy, Greece, Spain), and above all, to America. What luck those Americans have had. No more bequests to France by the likes of the Rothschilds, or Nissim Camondo. No more Donations from another Pierre Lévy. Enjoy the Kufic calligraphy; some find it endlessly fascinating.

For the moment, you allow yourself to believe that something will come up. Most likely, all those Muslims will simply convert. I mean, they do that, don't they, quite easily I'm told. Of course, why didn't I think of it, that is exactly what will happen. The situation is always saved in time. Just like during the war. Nothing to worry about. Nothing.

CHAPTER TWO

French Member of EU Parliament on What Muslim Immigration Has Meant for France

PATRICIA CHAGNON is a French politician, a member of the anti-Muslim immigrant National Rally party, and a member of the European Parliament. In a June 2024 interview, she said that Europe is torn between those who believe that each nation-state should be able to decide its own policy on immigration, and those who want the EU bureaucrats in Brussels, who favor mass migration, to decide such matters. More on Chagnon's views:

> The European Parliament elections represent an existential battle between the open borders agenda of elites in Brussels and those who wish to reclaim national sovereignty and save their countries and cultures from being subsumed by mass migration, a French MEP told Breitbart News.

> In an exclusive interview before the French public heads to the polls on Saturday to select their next representatives in the EU Parliament, National Rally Member of the European Parliament Patricia Chagnon said that the "crucial" vote will see people decide whether they want to continue being under the thumb of the centralised "imperialistic management" of EU technocrats or citizens taking back control of their own destinies.

> For Chagnon, one of the most glaring infringements on national sovereignty has been on immigration, with EU directives superseding national law and European courts enforcing the diktats, with the latest example coming in the form of the new Migration

Pact, which she said is an "absolute disaster" that "makes illegal immigration legal".

> If the Germans want to take in a million migrants from Africa, they can do whatever they like, but given the fact that we have Schengen [the EU's internal open borders system] and they can just walk right into France, there is a problem because that has not been decided by my country," she told Breitbart London.[1]

Once an immigrant lands in a European country that is a member of the Schengen Pact, that immigrant can then move freely everywhere in what is called "Schengenland." Thus an immigrant accepted by Germany under its more liberal immigration regime can then move, unhindered, to France.

"It is a country that should decide on its migration policy, definitely not a one-shoe-fits-all decided by some technocrats in Brussels," Chagnon said. "I profoundly believe that only the National Assembly, where the French people are represented, has sovereignty over my country."

The MEP said that she has personally experienced the negative ramifications of mass migration, saying that — especially as a woman — she felt the French way of life is slipping away.

Chagnon explained that even as a sixty-year-old woman, she "adapts" how she dresses when she goes to Paris, taking care to cover up when on the streets or public transport. She also said that her own daughter decided to leave the French capital and move to Australia after being attacked on the streets of Paris twice.

> "The whole way of life is being changed," she lamented. "People are adapting their way of life under the terrible pressure that we have from these Muslim gangs going around trying to enforce adherence to their Sharia Islamic laws. They have used the freedoms in Europe to curtail ours."...

> Meanwhile, the globalist project has been bolstered with support from the far-left, whom she argued have "lost their traditional labour [working class] electorate, and are purposefully looking at getting these new 'French citizens' to vote for them in opposition to 'bad, old colonial France.'"[2]

---

1   Kurt Zindulka, "Exclusive: From Brigitte Bardot to Burkinis, French 'Way of Life' Is Being Destroyed by Mass Migration, Says MEP," *Breitbart*, June 7, 2024.

2   Ibid.

The leftists in France have found themselves increasingly abandoned by their traditional base of working-class voters, but are intent on replacing those supporters with the new Muslim immigrants who have become citizens. Jean-Luc Mélenchon, head of La France Insoumise, is a perfect example of this: a Communist who appeals to Muslim voters for two reasons: he favors open borders and he hates Israel.

> However, Chagnon said that there is a burgeoning awakening in France of the need to curtail immigration, saying that people are coming to realise that "we can't integrate them, they are not going to school, they are dealing drugs, they are running wild," pointing to last year's race-inspired riots following the police killing of Algerian-heritage teen.... [3]

It is clear that when she refers to immigrants who "cannot integrate" into French society, she means Muslims. How can people who regard all non-Muslims as "the most vie of created beings" want to become part of a society created by those contemptible Infidels? It is Muslims from North Africa who have taken over most of the drug trade in France, who engage in street robberies, home burglaries, vandalism, as well as crimes of violence, such as rape and murder. Muslims now make up 10% of the French population, but 68% of its prison population.

Muslim immigration in France has led to steep rise in crime, leading to a general atmosphere of insecurity. Whole swathes of cities have been turned into No-Go areas where non-Muslims fear to enter. Even firemen enter these areas only when accompanied by a police guard, and the police, too, enter No-Go areas only in force.

The elections for seats in the European Parliament will from now on pit two world views against each other. There are members of that trans-national parliament in Brussels who are satisfied with the "project" of strengthening the EU's power over the individual nation-states, and who favor more, not less, immigration. And there are those who, such as Jordan Bardella of the National Rally Party in France, the party to which Patricia Chagnon also belongs, who want to decrease the power of the EU, in large part so as to be able to enforce their own anti-immigration policies at the national level. They have now seen the catastrophic effects of mass Muslim migration in their own countries and, mugged by reality, want to call for it to cease.

Can you blame them?

---

3 Ibid.

CHAPTER THREE

Pakistani Flag Flies Over Westminster Abbey

I N THE UNITED KINGDOM, as a way of taking part in the observance of Pakistan Day, a national holiday in Pakistan (and perhaps soon to be so in the U.K.), the Archbishop of Canterbury,
long a misunderstander and appeaser of Muslims, in 2024 decided to
fly the Pakistani flag over Westminster Abbey. For him, and for some
other equally obtuse Anglicans, this was no doubt seen as a gesture of
virtue-signaling ecumenical outreach. But for Muslims, that flag-rais-
ing will be interpreted as the highest religious authority in the United
Kingdom recognizing the supremacy of Islam, a vexing vexillological
sign of submission by the Infidels. After all, no Muslim country, least of
all Pakistan, would ever raise the flag of a non-Muslim country over any
mosque in its territory.

Ceremonies were conducted in various capitals worldwide to com-
memorate the 84th Pakistan Day, a significant national holiday in
Pakistan. This day primarily honors the adoption of Pakistan's first
Constitution, marking the transition of the Dominion of Pakistan
to the Islamic Republic of Pakistan on 23 March 1956. This established Pakistan as the world's first Islamic republic.

Among those who celebrated, Westminster Abbey's involvement
stands out as particularly disturbing. The United Kingdom's decision to fly the Pakistani flag above its most esteemed Anglican
church is a shocking display of submission to Islam.

According to reports from the Pakistan High Commission, the
flag was hoisted to celebrate Pakistan Day, a national holiday com-

memorating the adoption of the first Constitution of Pakistan. They claim that special prayers were offered during the event for the progress and prosperity of Pakistan, its leadership, its people, and for the continued friendship between the two countries....[1]

So the sign of submission was not merely that Pakistani flag on the top of Westminster Abbey. Apparently inside the Abbey, "special prayers were offered for the progress and prosperity of Pakistan, its leadership, its people." Really? Was it necessary for Anglican clergy to do this for a country where Hindus and Christians are persecuted, and sometimes murdered, a country whose scientist Dr. A.Q. Khan managed to steal nuclear secrets from Western countries where he had worked in research labs, allowing Pakistan to build its own bomb and proudly proclaim itself the "possessor of the Muslim nuclear weapon?" Was it necessary to celebrate "Pakistan Day" when tens of thousands of English girls have had their lives ruined by Pakistani men in Rochdale and Rotherham and Oxford and dozens of other cities in the UK, Pakistanis who engaged in "grooming" the girls, by seducing, drugging, raping them, and then passing them around to be used by their friends as sex slaves, sometimes over a period of years?

Hindu, Sikh, and Christian women in Pakistan can be kidnapped and subjected to forced marriages with Muslims, who also pressure them to convert to Islam. The government does nothing to stop this. And if the girls' families object, they then become the objects of persecution — and at times are even murdered — by Muslims enraged that non-Muslims might try to interfere.

Remember, any attempt by Christians to show entirely unmerited respect to Muslims or to attempt to befriend them is doomed to fail. The Qur'an warns Muslims not to take "Christians or Jews as friends." As with individuals, so with states: no Muslim state can truly be a "friend" to a non-Muslim polity. That Pakistani flag flying over Westminster will be interpreted not as a friendly gesture but as an act of submission to Islam. The Archbishop of Canterbury, representing the world's Anglicans, unwittingly has signaled submission to Islam — for that is what Muslims everywhere will take that flag flying over Westminster Abbey to mean — a fanatical faith at war with the non-Muslim world, and represented in this case by one of the most aggressive and dangerous of

1 "Islamization of London: Pakistan's Flag Hoisted On Top of Westminster Abbey's Rooftop, Child Sexual Exploitation Celebrated (Video)," RAIR Foundation, March 27, 2024.

Muslim states. A terrible decision, a surpassing disgrace.

CHAPTER FOUR

The Islamization of France

I N MAY 2024, a group of Muslims in France attacked a police van, and murdered two policemen in the course of freeing a Muslim prisoner — a gang leader — who was being transported. A week later, an Algerian who was illegally in France tried to burn down a synagogue; he was shot dead by the police.

French police have shot dead an armed man who allegedly set fire to a synagogue in the northwestern city of Rouen, officials said.

Interior Minister Gerald Darmanin posted on X that the armed man was "neutralized."

"In Rouen, national police officers neutralised early this morning an armed individual clearly wanting to set fire to the city's synagogue. I congratulate them for their reactivity and their courage," he said.

The synagogue is said to have suffered significant damage in the attack.

Local police responded at 6:45am to reports of a fire rising from the main Rouen synagogue.

The suspect exited the synagogue threatening police with a knife and an iron bar, according to the national police information service. An officer opened fire and fatally wounded the man, police said.

A source told Agence France-Presse the man "was armed with a knife and an iron bar, he approached police, who fired".

The Rouen synagogue sustained significant damage, including to its furniture, but no one was injured, mayor Nicolas Mayer-Rossignol said....

The fire has been brought under control, according to officials, but the attacker's identity and motive are still unclear....[1]

The story of Muslim mayhem and murder in just one French city — Rouen — represents what is going on all over the country. There Muslim criminals have murdered a priest, Father Jacques Hamel, 85, who was stabbed in his church in Saint-Etienne-du-Rouvray by two 19-year-old Muslims as he finished Mass. Two nuns and an elderly couple were held hostage before the assailants slashed the priest's throat and seriously injured another elderly churchgoer. His two attackers were shot dead by the police.

Muslim criminals in Rouen have also shot dead two prison officers in a successful attempt to free Muhammad Amra, a Muslim gang leader they were transporting. The police are still searching for Amra and the two other Muslims who freed him. Finally, a Muslim Algerian who was in the process of appealing an order for his expulsion from France tried to burn down a synagogue, causing considerable damage to the structure. He was shot dead.

That is what has happened in just one city in France. What is happening in all the other French cities where Muslim mayhem and murder have been taking place? What of the Bataclan nightclub massacre in 2015 in Paris, when Muslim shooters and suicide bombers left 80 people dead? What of the Muslim driver who in 2016 used a 19-ton truck to run down pedestrians in Nice, killing 86 and injuring 434? What of the Muslim gang in Paris that kidnapped and tortured over 24 days a young Jewish man, Ilan Halimi, who finally died of his wounds? What of the Muslim who beat to death and then defenestrated Sarah Halimi? What of the Muslim who stabbed Mireille Knoll eleven times and then set her on fire? What of the Muslim, Mohammed Merah, who murdered Rabbi Jonathan Sandler and his sons Aryeh, aged six, and Gavriel, aged three, and a little girl, eight-year-old Myriam Monsonego, at a Jewish school

---

1 Jane Prinsley, "Police shoot dead suspect who threw 'Molotov cocktail' into French synagogue," *The JC*, May 17, 2024.

in Toulouse? What of Merah's other victims, an off-duty French Army paratrooper he killed in Toulouse and two off-duty uniformed French soldiers he murdered in Montauban?

This is France today, where Muslims make up 12% of the general population, but 70% of the prison population. Their percentage of the population inexorably rises, both from legal and illegal immigration, and from the fact that the fertility rate of Muslims in France — 2.9 children — far outstrips that of the indigenous French, which at 1.9 children is below the replacement level. What will France be like in ten years? In twenty?

CHAPTER FIVE

Majority of Germans Want a Halt to Muslim Migration

I N 2015 FORMER German Chancellor Angela Merkel, opening wide the doors of her country to more than one million Muslim migrants that year, proudly proclaimed *"Wir schaffen das!,"* or "We Can Do This!" How wrong she was. Almost a decade has now passed, and the majority of Germans want to call a halt, not to migrants in general, but specifically to Muslim migrants. They now feel a sense of *dépaysement*, of no longer recognizing the neighborhood or city that they live in as part of Germany. They feel overwhelmed by Muslim migrants, who in some cities have carved out No-Go areas, where non-Muslims fear to tread. Some Germans are gloomily afraid that a demographic jihad — the result of the birthrates of Muslim women being much higher than those of the indigenous Germans — will inevitably lead to the "Great Replacement," that is, the replacement of Germans by a majority Muslim population.

> BERLIN. The rejection of immigrants from Islamic countries has increased in Germany. An absolute majority of 52 percent (somewhat) agrees with the statement that "Germany should fundamentally no longer accept refugees from Islamic countries." This is the result of a representative Insa survey commissioned by the Nius portal. 34 percent said "disagree" or "tend to disagree."[1]

---

1 "Mehrheit der Deutschen will keine muslimischen Zuwanderer mehr," *Junge Freiheit*, May 2, 2024.

The remaining 14 percent who offered "no opinion" are most likely people who are also opposed to admitting more Muslims to Germany, but are afraid of being thought to be "Islamophobes" or still worse, "racists," so prefer to remain publicly noncommittal. If we count them as opposed to more Muslim migrants, as I believe we should, then 66%, or two-thirds, of Germans, are against any more Muslim migration. That is an astonishing change from 2015, when a majority of Germans thought, with Merkel, that "we can do this."

> There is even greater agreement with this statement: "In certain areas of my city or village I have the feeling that I am no longer in Germany." 57 percent see it that way, 36 percent cannot share the feeling.[2]

A majority of Germans now declare that in parts of their towns or villages, the Muslim population is so overwhelmingly, even aggressively, present, that they no longer feel that they are still in Germany. The 7% who did not answer this question, though unwilling to publicly agree with that statement, lest they be seen as "Islamophobic," should be counted as sharing that sentiment — that is, of no longer feeling they belong in certain areas of their towns and villages. That would mean that nearly two-thirds of Germans, or 64%, share that feeling of no longer belonging, of *dépaysement*.

> This also leads to the fear of becoming a minority in one's own country. 54 percent of those surveyed said they were "afraid that Germans would become a minority in Germany." 37 percent see it differently.

> A relative majority supports the thesis of a population exchange [the "Great Replacement"], which the Office for the Protection of the Constitution classifies as right-wing extremist. 45 percent say: "I believe that Europeans are gradually being replaced by immigrants from Africa and the Middle East." 41 percent reject the sentence.[3]

Nearly half of Germans — 45% — now think that their progeny will eventually be replaced by Muslim migrants. Another 14% did not answer the question. I argue, just as I have above, that this was because

---

2 Ibid.
3 Ibid.

they didn't want to reveal their alarm, which some would attribute to "Islamophobia." That 14% ought logically to be counted in the column of those fearing that Muslims will become a majority in Germany. That means that 59% of Germans are worried about "the Great Replacement." An astounding number. And it rises, inexorably.

> The claim that there is racism against whites in Germany is also highly controversial. The CDU once suggested that former President of the Federal Office for the Protection of the Constitution Hans-Georg Maaßen leave the party because he had made statements in this direction. But the majority is on Maaßen's side. Two thirds (65 percent) confirm that there is "also racism against whites" in Germany. Only 22 percent think that's not true.

> The answer to the question of whether "migrants have largely integrated well into Germany" is also clear. 58 percent say no, 29 percent say the opposite.[4]

Here again, 13% answered "No Opinion," and again I think that means they were afraid to give an opinion unfavorable to Muslims, lest they be thought of as "Islamophobes." But we should count those 13% as believing "migrants" (overwhelmingly Muslims from North Africa and the Middle East) have not "integrated well in Germany." That means a total of 71% of Germans share that view.

> Germans agree most with the sentence "Current migration is overburdening the German school system". At 75 percent, three quarters of those surveyed are convinced that this is the case. 22 percent cannot detect overload.

> Insa interviewed a total of 2,004 representatively selected voters aged 18 and over for the survey from April 26th to 29th.[5]

Summary:

1. 66% of Germans now want a complete halt to Muslim immigration.

2. 64% of Germans have the sense that in their own towns and vil-

---

4 Ibid.
5 Ibid.

lages and cities there are places where they no longer belong — a troubling sense of *dépaysement.*

3. 59% of Germans believe that they will be "replaced" in their own country by Muslims — that is the "Great Replacement" that now haunts many in Europe.

4. 59% of Germans believe that Muslims "have not integrated well into Germany."

5. 3 out of 4 Germans agree that Muslim migrants are "overburdening the school system."

"Wir Schaffen Das!" "Wir Schaffen Das?"

No, Germany. Merkel was wrong. It turns out that you could not do it. But it was always a forlorn hope. And you are not alone. When it comes to integrating Muslims into your societies, no country in Europe has managed. It just can't be done. And the Great Replacement is no longer just a bad dream.

CHAPTER SIX

Swedish Lawmaker Who Once Favored Muslim Immigration Has Scales Fall From Her Eyes

M ANY OF THOSE in Europe who once supported immigration — and by that is meant immigration from Muslim lands, by far the largest source of immigrants arriving in Europe — have been mugged by reality. No one in Germany today would claim, as Chancellor Angela Merkel did in 2015 when she allowed into her country more than one million Muslim economic migrants, that *"Wir schaffen das!"* "We can do it!" With each passing year, more and more Germans are flocking to the anti-Muslim immigrant party, Alternative für Deutschland (AfD), and after the 2025 elections, it has become the second largest party in the Bundestag.

And it's not just the Germans who have lost whatever enthusiasm some once had for welcoming these migrants. Europeans in general are fed up with the Muslim migrants in their midst. They are tired of the vast sums that they spend on Muslim economic migrants now in the EU, with more of those migrants entering every year. These immigrants come not to contribute to the economies and societies of the countries they enter, but in order to batten on every benefit the generous welfare states of Europe offer: free or highly subsidized housing, free medical care, free education, unemployment benefits (even without a work history in Europe), family allowances, and more. In 2023, in Germany alone, those. migrants cost the government 30 billion euros. For 2024, the cost is estimated at 36 billion euros. Meanwhile, the German government is forced to cut welfare spending on its own citizens, including raising the age when social security can be claimed to 67.

Aside from the benefits these economic migrants receive from the government, some add to their incomes by engaging in illegal acts. There has been a steep rise in crimes of property — street muggings, robberies, house burglaries. And there has been a continent-wide increase, too, in crimes of violence — sexual assault, rape, and murder. In France, for example, Muslims make up 12% of the population but close to 70% of the prisoners. In German schools, Muslim pupils create disturbances in the schools, threaten non-Muslim classmates, show little respect for their teachers, and rebel at studying certain subjects, such as the history of Christianity, and the Holocaust. Schools now must spend time and resources to deal with the breakdown in classroom discipline that is caused by the Muslim student population.

As Europeans rethink their earlier, naïve support for Muslim migrants, they are giving their political support to such anti-Muslim parties as Marine Le Pen's Rassemblement Nationale, Giorgia Meloni's Fratelli d'Italia, and Alice Weidel's Alternative für Deutschland.

In March 2024, Louise Meijer, one of the lawmakers who stoutly supported Muslim immigration to Sweden in the past, announced: "I have changed my mind" about the matter.

> A Swedish lawmaker who previously advocated in favor of mass arrivals of asylum seekers during the migrant crisis of 2015 has admitted the influx of immigration has fundamentally changed the country and now wants to pull up the drawbridge.[1]

It is obvious that when she says the migrants have "fundamentally changed the country," she means Muslim migrants, because she mentions, among other problems they pose, their "Islamism."

> Louise Meijer of the now-governing Moderate Party penned her thoughts on the Swedish government's need to crack down on migration and signaled a U-turn from her previous desire to welcome an unprecedented number of new arrivals into the country.

> Writing in the *Expressen*, Meijer acknowledged that during the migrant crisis in 2015 she "took a stand for openness 'Refugees Wel-

---

1   Thomas Brooke, "'I have changed my mind!' — Pro-open borders MP undertakes spectacular U-turn and calls for strict immigration, deportations, and repatriation," *Remix News*, March 18, 2024.

come,'" opposing her party's call at the time for stricter rules to curb immigration.

"But I have changed my mind on the matter," she noted, adding she now supports "an even stricter migration policy than the one I opposed at the time."

Her reasoning is that "the change that Sweden has undergone and is undergoing is fundamentally changing the country" as she warns that "mass immigration has been followed by several major problems."

Among these, she highlights, is the fact that "serious, organized crime is committed to a large extent by people with foreign assets," that large groups of immigrants are "not self-sufficient," and that the "culture of honor, separatism, and Islamism is limiting and dangerous."

Organized crime and gang warfare have exploded across the Scandinavian country in the past decade, and the nation has now experienced a record number of shootings for the past three years....[2]

These criminals are Muslims. They control the drug trade in Sweden as they do most everywhere else in Europe, except for Italy. They commit street robberies, home burglaries, shoplifting, arson. They sexually assault, and rape, Swedish girls and women, whose manner of dress for Muslims signifies come-hither looseness — "they had it coming to them." The Muslim criminal gangs carry out their vendettas in the middle of cities, endangering the indigenous passersby as they shoot at one another.

---

2 Ibid.

CHAPTER SEVEN

The Saracen's Head

A S OF 2024, THERE are still many pubs throughout Britain named the Saracen's Head. The late medieval buildings in Kings Norton, Birmingham, however, including an eighteenth-century pub that bore that name, were renamed in 2004. Canon Rob Morris wanted the ancient pub renamed so as not to offend Muslims.

Why does one harbor the suspicion that Canon Rob Morris has never, in his life, been troubled by such terms as "Jew's harp" or "Jewfish" or lifted a finger to have them changed? As for questioning lower-school performances of "The Merchant of Venice" or the big sign at "The Swastika and Bells" that may still be visible just off St. Stephen's Green in Dublin — my god, some people are hypersensitive, aren't they?

Well, let us be charitable, and take Canon Morris at his word. If he was agitated at the name of his local "Saracen's Head" pub, should he not have been equally agitated at the hundreds or thousands of similarly named pubs, inns, taverns, coffeehouses, that still to this day dot the landscape of England and Canada, and Australia, and New Zealand, and America? And then there are the hundreds, or thousands, of pubs, inns, taverns named "Turk's Head" throughout the English-speaking world. (Even in Cambridge, Massachusetts there was recently a "Turk's Head Grill.")

Dickens mentions a "Saracen's Head" pub in *Pickwick Papers*. And to make matters worse, one of the most memorable characters in that same *Pickwick Papers*, The Fat Boy ("I wants to make your flesh creep") was based on an overweight boot boy Dickens noticed at a pub in Devon, in Exeter. And that pub was called — The Turk's Head. Well, Mr.

Charles Dickens, you ought to be ashamed of yourself.

Yet Canon Morris was on to something. We need to rethink, and remove, words and phrases in books written in the cruel and careless past, words and phrases that now might offend the new Muslim populations of Europe. Just because the Jews have had to endure, for centuries, all sorts of truly unpleasant words — *vide supra* — that is no reason why Muslims should have to do the same, now is it? And what is so winning about Muslims is that they don't just sit cowering meekly in a corner trying not to be noticed, like some other minorities I could name. No, they express their grievances forthrightly, with a refreshing candor and directness.

In the U.K., Rafiq Baqa, a convicted Muslim terrorist, has even sued a pub in Buckinghamshire called "The Saracen's Head" for its sign depicting a turbaned Turk, which he alleges is "clearly xenophobic, racist, and inciting violence." He did not add that the "violence incited" would come from Muslims. In Italy Muslims have called for the banning of Dante in Italian schools, because he wrote some mean things about Muhammad. That's not chutzpah. That willingness of Muslims, in Catholic Italy, to call for banning texts and paintings inimical to Islam should make a deep impression. And when some Muslims belonging to Al Qaeda noticed that a 15th-century fresco by Giovanni da Modena in the Basilica of San Petronio in Bologna showed Muhammad in an undignified light — he is being devoured by demons, in the Ninth Circle of Hell, as described by Dante, they decided to subject that fresco to severe art criticism, Muslim-style, and planned to blow up the church. Their plans were caught on tape by the Italian police, who showed themselves to be singularly obstinate in refusing to view the whole problem globally and compassionately, from the offended Muslims' point of view. For now, that offending fresco is still intact on the wall of the Basilica but, alas, the security that was installed to safeguard the fresco makes it impossible for visitors to see it clearly.

In northern France, at Floing, a Jesus and Mary were both decapitated by Muslims who were offended by Christian statuary. They have a point. Why must they be subject to such sights? Why are those statues, whether placed just outside, or in churches where any curious person including Muslims, might walk in and see them, still not hidden away?

Fifty million Muslims now live in Europe; for them every statue is a source of anxiety and anguish. They know that Muhammad, the Perfect Man (*al-insan al-kamil*), refused to enter a dwelling that had paintings or statues of living creatures in it. That explains the Muslim detestation of statues. But if a statue is vandalized, with the head or nose or members cut off, it is no longer a depiction of a living thing and thus does not offend Muslim sensibilities. In Rome's Piazza del Popolo, three statues had their noses, ears, hands, and feet cut off. by Muslim art critics. In fact outdoor statuary all over Europe is at risk,. But at least the torsos were left at the Piazza del Popolo,, and as we know from much Roman statuary, and from the famous Venus de Milo itself, it's not necessary for all parts to be present to appreciate the essential beauty of the sculpture.

Again, I put it to you: if the authorities in the Western world, who know full well how many Muslims live in their countries, and how deeply offensive such displays are, refuse to act to remove those works of so-called art, what should Muslims do? Just accept the mental torture? Or do something about it, in as quick and painless a manner as possible? Aren't human feelings more important than carvings in stone, or than oil on canvas?

And it is the same with words. In a world where different ethnicities and religious beliefs jostle one another, we have to learn to be acutely sensitive. We cannot fall back on the tired excuse that "this is art." Art, like "truth," is a culture-bound category. And boundaries shift, and change. The boundaries of dar al-harb, for example, are shifting and changing. And in all this healthy recognition of changes that have to be made, surely it is Shakespeare who presents the greatest obstacle to a new, more sensitive, healthier cultural environment. And this is because he is Shakespeare, and we have grown up thinking he is untouchable and immutable. No, he isn't. And the Bible isn't, as all those lovely new editions that keep coming out demonstrate. There is, of course, only one work in the history of the world that is immutable — and, as all Muslims know, it isn't by Shakespeare.

No, it is nonsense to think that Shakespeare just sits there, silently, and abides our question. He has to answer for his words, just like everyone else. Why, it was a famous Russian fighter for social justice in the nineteenth century who wrote that a good carpenter was worth more than all the works of Pushkin. Or maybe it was a shoemaker. Whatever. But he was right, wasn't he? What is Pushkin worth compared to a good pair of slippers, or Timberland boots in winter time, or canvas boat shoes for a trip to Europe on the S.S. Naufragium? Surely, the higher good of creating a world where we can all get along must take precedence over treating like some sacred text a few words set down by a mere mortal — yes, granted, a very great mere mortal — centuries ago, writing as furiously on foolscap as some of us type on a keyboard, posting into the ether. No, Shakespeare does not get a bye, not if one cares about one's fellow man.

Consider those famous lines in *Othello*:

Say that in Aleppo once,
Where a malignant and a turbaned Turk,
Beat a Venetian and traduced the state,
I took by the throat the circumcised dog
And smote him — thus!

"Malignant?" "Traduced the state?" "Circumcised dog?" This will never do. Thomas Bowdler, by turns a Londoner, a Vectensian, and finally a resident of New South Wales, had his famous way with the classics in the nineteenth century, excising words and rewriting passages that might make a maiden blush. He is easily mocked, but it should be remembered that his Family Shakespeare appeared at a time when young girls and boys were reading Shakespeare at the same age that girls and boys nowadays read Garfield the Cat. Muslims may not blush like nineteenth century maidens, but they are sensitive people, and if we Infidels have a drop of decency left in us, we will want to emend the texts of those who in the benighted past of our own arrogant civilization, were insufficiently fair to Islam. Unlike us, with our modern communications, they just didn't know enough about Islam to fully appreciate it.

It would be unfeeling, even cruel, to subject the millions of Muslim pupils now in European public schools to the task of reading assigned texts by Diderot, or Francis Bacon, or Montaigne (especially *The Apology for Raymond Sebond*), or Hugo Grotius, or Pascal, or Spinoza, or Montesquieu, or Jeremy Bentham, or John Stuart Mill, not one of whom was favorable toward Islam. And it would be demeaning, and divisive, to assign works by such historians as Edward Gibbon, who shuddered in print as he considered what Europe would have become had Charles Martel not defeated the Muslims at Poitiers in 745 A.D., or Jacob Burckhardt, with his pronounced animus toward Islam, or Henri Pirenne who in his *Muhammad and Charlemagne* rejected the notion that barbarian invasions in the 4th and 5th centuries caused the collapse of the Roman Empire. Pirenne instead pointed the finger at the Muslims, and their conquest of North Africa that made the Mediterranean, not a bridge but a barrier, and cut western Europe off from the east.

Are these authors really essential to the curriculum?

Why cause extra problems for Muslim students? Why bring to their attention the prejudices of the past that can only increase their resentment of their non-Muslim hosts? A good teacher tries to establish a good learning environment, and a good learning environment may require that certain texts and writers should just be ignored, perhaps not even mentioned. If someone really insists on reading Spinoza, or Pascal, or Montaigne, or Gibbon, or Bentham, or Spinoza — well, the non-Muslim students can, if they feel inclined, do that reading outside of school, on their own.

No one should be off-limits to the need to rewrite or remove passages that can prove hurtful or wounding. No one is sacred, not even Shakespeare. Perhaps especially Shakespeare. So here's a stab at turning that malignant Turk into a heartwarming easygoing innkeeper in Aleppo (Haleb). Just picture in your mind's eye a kind of Muslim version of *Fawlty Towers*, a turbaned Basil Fawlty acting agreeably as Mine Host. In the off-season, when well-heeled Muslims make the hajj and business falls off, this Turkish Fawlty offers special rates to Christian tourists who, of course, will not go on the hajj, and will not offend any Muslims by staying in the same inn, because for that period there won't be any Muslims at the inn.

And what a delightful surprise to see, in one's mind's eye, a group of intrepid Venetians spill out of their carriage, led by their Tour Guide, a youthful Othello, in his first summer job before he found his military calling, herding them firmly toward the Registration Desk. The Venetians are already bustling with excitement, ready to take full advantage of the advertised "Turkish Delight Great Getaways Package" (those were the early days of advertising, and the art of compression was still in its infancy) — just imagine their reaction when their Turkish Host announces to his assembled guests that, because they are the first to arrive from outside the confines of the Ottoman Empire, he wishes to give them a special discount.

Recalling that moment, that early example of kindnesses offered and accepted across the silly and essentially false barriers of culture and belief, remembering that perfect early exemplar of the "Dialogue of Civilisations," Othello — instead of uttering the violent and hateful words that Shakespeare puts in his mouth — recalls that moment as anyone nowadays would recall the kindness, say, of an Arab in a souk, who has given one a special price on a prayer rug because he loves you, he explains, effendi, more than he loves his father, more than he loves his mother:

> Say that in Aleppo once,
> Where a dignified and a turbaned Turk
> Greeting Venetians, did reduce their rates,
> I took by the arm my openhearted friend,
> And hugged him — thus!

Yes, I know what you are going to say. It's not enough that I managed to preserve most of the meter. You want to complain that the rewrite fails to preserve the sense of the original. So what? That "sense of the original" was cruel. You know that as well as I. What are you trying to do — make Shakespeare accessible, make him kinder and gentler, or just throw his texts unchanged in the face of tens of millions of European Muslims who did nothing to deserve that? I went in, located the diseased lexical tissue, cut it right out and put in a replacement, and sewed up the incision, quickly and cleanly. Not a line, not a word, in the rest of the play was touched. I don't know about you, but at my graduation I actually listened to the commencement speakers. I took their sentiments to heart. I'm trying to make the world a better place. I'm trying to make a difference. I'm trying to give something back. But I can't do everything. I've made a start at preparing a Shakespeare fit for the Age of Eurabia. The alternative is likely to be no Shakespeare at all. If you have a better idea, then go ahead.

And of course the problem doesn't stop there. Even Mother Goose rhymes can cause trouble. Here you are, reading to your sleepy two-year-old, and the innocent mind of a he or a not impossible she takes in a phrase, just before the spider comes along to sit down beside Miss Muffet, about "curds and whey." A young child might not understand, might take the phrase in the wrong way, with the wrong Kurds. And even atlases pose problems, with their funny toponyms that don't sound quite right in English. Surely I'm not the only one who finds that the "Shatt al-Arab" can be cause for misplaced merriment. Perhaps Canon Morris can lead devout toponomasiologists, in solemn conclave assembled, to invent new place-names to replace those likely to be objects of mockery in the o'erweening, arrogant, English-speaking world. No one should have to suffer because a perfectly respectable word or phrase or place-name in one's native language or dialect serves as a source of amusement to speakers of another. Canon Morris is probably the man to do this — he should be saluted, for consistently displaying such spunk.

And please, in undertaking these Good Works that compensate

for so Little Faith, national borders should be treated as irrelevant. In this new Europe, where so many are hell-bent on melting down and blending into one gooey mass market their past national histories, and languages, and literatures (perhaps to be traded in for a pidgin English more appropriate to the grunt-and-squeak of the two worlds of business and entertainment, which soon will be all we know on earth, anyway, and all we will need to know): One folk, one market, one world. It has a certain ring. Farewell narrow parochialism, and farewell parishes!

So Canon Morris, sally forth beyond the bourne of Kings Norton, and the diversity program at your church. Your light must not be left to shine under English unofficial rose bushes or bushels. Fresh fields, and pastures new. The Italians have an exclamative that expresses fright (at times comical fright): *mamma, li turchi!* — Mamma, the Turks! (are here, or on the way). Not very nice, is it? And the word "Turk" here means a generic "Muslim," which makes it worse; the phrase originates from the fears stirred everywhere in Italy by centuries of Arab raids, with local inhabitants killed or kidnapped, their women raped, their houses and churches plundered and destroyed. Sort of like Darfur. But that was then, and this is now. We live in a new age, and everything is fine in Europe today. The descendants of those very raiders live smack dab among the descendants of the survivors of those raids, and there have been no raids, no kidnappings or killings, no burning down of churches, no seizing of hostages, as far as I know, anywhere in Europe. So bygones should be bygones. There is nothing to worry about. That nasty little phrase deserves to be drowned in the lexical Lethe.

And history books need to be rewritten, with the new facts and new insights supplied by members of the Euro-Mediterranean Dialogue, or by the Anna Lindh Foundation, located in Alexandria, Egypt. Every age needs to have the past rewritten, so that the history one learns in school is fit to meet the challenges and requirements of the day. Did you know, for example, that the Renaissance was practically a Muslim invention? Jacob Burckhardt may not have agreed, but then, when was he writing? 1970? 1880? Did you know that almost all of modern Western science, Newton, Einstein, Watson and Crick, and Rosalind Franklin, quantum theory and fractals and neurobiology and the structure of DNA, owes its flourishing to Al-Khwarizmi and Al-Rhazi a thousand years ago? Yes, it's going into the revised textbooks right now.

I once believed that the most useful thing Muslims did for Western civilization in Europe was, over several centuries, to conquer Byzantium, and in the process driving out the Christian scholars of the Eastern Empire. They fled West, was how the story went, taking with them their books, and their manuscripts dating back to classical antiquity, and their own vast learning inside their heads. Old history books used to explain that this flight from Byzantium had something to do with the Revival of Learning and, therefore, with the Renaissance.

And they used to tell us that a second major achievement of Islamic (i.e., mostly Persian and Mughal) civilization was to act as a conduit between Europe and the East (since the former movement between the two was now blocked by Islam itself). Thus, paper-making invented in China (see Dard Hunter) came to Europe, as geographically it had to, via the Islamic world. The same was true for the Hindu zero, and algebra. We used to be taught that major credit for Chinese and Indian discoveries ought to be given to the Chinese and the Indians. But we were wrong; without Federal Express, the package is not delivered. Without the delivery truck of Islam, where would Europe be today?

And we were also told that certain Greek texts, above all those of Aristotle, were translated into Arabic, and somehow "preserved" for Western consumption and use. Yet history books used to point out that the translators, from Greek into Syriac and thence into Arabic, were mostly Christians and Jews, and that in any case Aristotle, though translated, was made much of only in the Christian world, not — save for Averroes — in the Muslim one.

Needless to say, all of these attempts to diminish Islam will have to be removed from the history books. And it might help, as well, just to give a little less attention to the Chinese (let's get copies of Joseph Needham's *Science and Civilisation in China* out of school libraries, shall we? They may prove embarrassing to Muslims) and to the greatly overrated West itself.

It must be hard to be a clergyman, nowadays, if in reality one falls within the category of "Ye of Little Faith." In what some call the post-Christian era, one compensates for Little Faith with a superflux of Good Works, hoping no one notices the old switcheroo. And even the Little Faith that remains is faith in a wan and etiolated brand of Christianity, instead of that muscular old-time religion. And that old-time religion need not be that of a holy-roller's twists and shouts. John Donne, thundering from the pulpit at St. Paul's, Jeremy Taylor, Lancelot Andrewes, the Mather boys of New England, George Whitfield of the Great Awakening,will all do nicely, with their King James Bible, and their mastery of rhetoric, and their passionate delivery — all of which could command belief, even from a non-believer.

Canon Morris may be one of those who spends his post-Christian hours Christianly meeting the needs, not of the Christians who are under assault from Muslims in a thousand places, and in a thousand displays of hate, but those of his newfound Muslim brothers and sisters. One in doubt may find the exhibition of such certainty, even uncompromising rigidity, not frightening, but heartening. Perhaps some admire the True Believer no matter the substance of those beliefs. And many more Muslims than Christians are True Believers. It is the strength of that Belief that some Christians find impressive. And there is one way to be a super-Christian, and doing that "love your enemies" stuff one better. Just force yourself to believe, and try to get others to believe, that those Muslim enemies do not really mean what they say, and thus were never your enemies in the first place.

Perhaps Canon Morris, or others like him, will find themselves thinking — does the path we take to God really matter? If Christianity will no longer work, then on the any-port-in-a-storm theory, perhaps we must take the path in the way of Allah. Tariq Ramadan, the propagandist for da'wa who, before his trials for multiple rapes, was referred to as "the world's leading Muslim intellectual," thought hapless Westerners secretly longed to trod that path. He was not alone. Many Muslims insist that the decadent West, as they see it, is confused and at the end of its civilizational tether. All they need do is to wait; the Call to Islam, and not Combat — da'wa not qital — will make the whole world one vast Islamic domain. And the pax Islamica will reign, and the world will look like — well, like the Muslim countries today, such as Saudi Arabia, or Pakistan, or Iran, or the Sudan. Something to look forward to.

It's true. The Western world, with almost everyone in it fixed firmly on their phones, may sometimes appear to have a diminished interest in literature, art, and philosophy. Unlike the Muslims, who can do without them all as long as they can hold onto the Qur'an and hadith, Westerners need all of those. But the king of kitman, Tariq Ramadan, does not really know the West, despite having lived in it, or rather in a Muslim cocoon within it, where he has become adept at delivering himself of self-assured and soothing pronouncements designed for Western ears. His books, once examined, appear to be those of a mediocre graduate student in philosophy, gainfully employed through the fluke of being a Muslim, and no doubt having a genuine live Muslim on the faculty, lending an authentic air to the business of "dialogues" and "we all have so much to learn from each other" and so on, was just too good to pass up. Tariq Ramadan's ultimate aims were the same as those of Osama Bin

Laden; only their views of the most effective methods differed.

What could Ramadan have told us that had not been told, much better, much more piercingly, by others? William James, Ortega y Gasset, Nicholas Berdyaev, Lev Shestov, Wladimir Weidle, Josef Pieper, Christopher Dawson, Jacques Ellul, Raymond Aron, Jacques Barzun, Ian Robinson, Richard Hoggart, in the past century, have diagnosed various mental and cultural woes of the decadent West. The prescription of Islam, a belief-system that meets most of the criteria, as Ibn Warraq has said, to be considered fascism, is the disease for which it is supposed to be a cure. We've been there before, with Fascism; we really need not try it, in Italy or Germany or Spain or anywhere else, again. Some Muslims seem to believe that the European equivalents of "Access Hollywood" and "Entertainment Tonight" represent the West's cultural level. Some of them consider Bernard Henri-Levy to be an "intellectual" (whatever that is). No wonder they underestimate the West. There is life in the old boy yet — that talented, exasperating, often silly old West of ours. But the survival of that West will depend on whether Europe further succumbs to the blandishments of the Euro-Arab Dialogue, and heeds the Euro-Arab siren song that plays variations on the themes of anti-Americanism, antisemitism, and outright fear of the local Muslims, so as to encourage inattention and drift.

The inhabitants of the Western world can demonstrate the will, and the ability, to repel the attacks being launched, at every level, with every means, against it by the adherents of a belief-system that could not possibly have produced any of those who created that civilization. Over there, in that corner of the ring, in the white trunks, representing Western civilization — here list 500 or 1000 names perhaps taken from the list in Jacques Barzun's *From Dawn to Decadence*, and over there, in the black trunks, representing Islamic civilization are — well, who would you list?

It may be time, Canon Morris, to trade your flaccid faith for something that will prove more satisfactorily rigid. For you, it may be getting close to Da'wa Time. It worked for John Walker Lindh, and Richard Reid, and José Padilla. And not just for them. It worked for Jemima Goldsmith after she married that good-looking Pakistani (from that family of squash players, wasn't he?), at least she says so, and for that French physicist, Bruno Guiderdoni, and for a recent Italian ambassador to Saudi Arabia whose name I forget, and for Tim Winter (who when he claws at F. E. Peters in the pages of the *TLS* takes care to use his non-Muslim name). The Faith That Provides Everything. An Unshakeable Sense of Community, Exclusive Loyalty Given, and Taken, Unreservedly, To Muslims, From Muslims, For Muslims. An end to anomie. Unreserved Hostility Toward All Those Who Are Unbelievers. A scapegoat offered for every occasion. A Clear Set of Defined Goals. Just like a winning business plan. A Faith With a Lifetime Guarantee — your life is the guarantee of your faith. Certainty. A Total Explanation of the Universe, unlike some of those wishy-washy religions that at critical moments may seem to leave you in the lurch. Complete Regulations For Absolutely Everything, from bathroom behavior to bouffant hairdos to the do's and don't's of beating your wife, all in one handy guide. No need for trying to find yourself, because you hardly matter.

And if you can't find the answer to something, you can always ask for a mufti's fatwa. Do I pay taxes to an Infidel state? Can I inherit from an Infidel relative even if he can't inherit from me? Can I marry an Infidel girl while I'm a student in the Bilad al-kufr, and dump her when my studies are done? Depends. Yes. Yes. No doubts, no uncertainties, no troubling directeur de conscience. Just the Holy Law of Islam. It's all in the Rules and Regulations, the Believer's Handbook. Wasn't it Villiers de l'Isle Adam who famously said, "[A]s for living, our servants will do that for us?" As for thinking, the texts of Islam, and the muftis, are prepared to do that for us.

As a bonus, if you sign up for our comforting and attractive belief-system, we will include absolutely free in your Da'wa New Members Kit a special gift: a sheet of cream-colored bond, richly embossed in the center with a single word: The Name To Blame For Every Occasion. Think of it as a Special Answer to the Riddle of a Confusing Universe, the all-purpose hysterical shriek of fury when you confront That World You Never Made. Yes, it will be the centerpiece and aide-memoire of your very own Blame Game. It's the Blame Game Name. Fun for the whole family.

Perhaps you don't feel like waiting for that kit to arrive in the mail. You want to know that special name right now. All right, here's a hint for all you lovers of old-fashioned charades: My first is where you go whenever you enter. My second is the name of the former dictator of Cuba. My all is the source of every evil that has ever afflicted the world.

Entries must be received, postmarked no later than 12 o'clock midnight, Eastern Standard Time. There may be a valuable, or invaluable, award, depending on the whim of the judges.

Get cracking, Canon Rob Morris. You too can play this game. But I forgot — you already are.

CHAPTER EIGHT

The Persistent Myth of Andalusia

MANY HAVE the naive hope that an Islamized Europe may turn into a "new Andalusia."

The myths about Islamic Spain (known collectively as the "myth of Andalusia") have their origins in the romantic writers of the early nineteenth century. Just as Sir Walter Scott, venturing beyond Scotland, painted a completely fictional portrait of the "noble Saracens" tutoring the Christians in chivalrous behavior, so the myths of wonderful tolerant Andalusia owe their existence to two highly imaginative works by celebrated writers: *Tales of the Alhambra* by Washington Irving and *Le Dernier des Abencérages* by François-René de Chateaubriand. The latter, of course, thought nothing of making things up even about his own life — some of his entirely fictional trips are set down as fact in *Mémoires d'Outre-Tombe*. He writes, for example, that while traveling through the young American Republic in 1791, he visited the town of Lexington: "*J'ai vu les champs de Lexington.*" He never did. And his account of Muslim Spain was equally fictional.

The apotheosis of this is the dreamy effort of Maria Rosa Menocal, entitled *Ornament of the World*, which purports to be about Cordoba, where "three faiths" worked harmoniously blah-blah-blah a lesson and hope for our age blah-blah-blah Maimonides blah-blah-blah. Now the first thing to know about this impressionistic fantasy is that it completely ignores, does not even mention in its bibliography, any of the major scholarly works on Muslim Spain — including those of Evariste Levi-Provencal, of Dufourcq, of Bousquet, of many others. It ignores a good deal else as well, including Maimonides' own words: "...the Arabs have persecuted us severely, and passed baneful and discriminatory legislation against us…Never did a nation molest, degrade, debase, and hate us as much as they…"

This is particularly disturbing because this book received all sorts of praise, including some uncharacteristic guff and nonsense from the late Fouad Ajami. Maria Rosa Menocal, now dead, was a "professor at Yale" and the "Director of the Whitney Humanities Center." Well, no one takes academic standards very seriously anymore, what with Cornel West being snapped up at Princeton, and Rashid Khalidi offering his PLO propaganda at Columbia, and the "post-colonial hegemonic discourse" still apparently in full swing. And one cannot here resist the temptation to notice that more than one teacher of literature has publicly expressed his long-past-receiving-of-tenure version of a deathbed conversion, and publicly admits that all that theory, that post-hegemonic discourse, whether of the Derrida-delirium, or Saidian swamp variety, was a monstrous error, and that one would do better to teach students in this audiovisual age to read books with attention, affection, and a well-stocked mind. (See Frank Lenticchia, et al., who have attempted to express more or less the same thing).

Oh, al-Andaluz, al-Andaluz. Cordoba, and the red gitanillas flowing over the balconies above the whitewashed walls flanking the narrow alleys, and from outside one can hear the pleasing plash of fountains in the inside hidden courtyards, and one can see, in one's imaginative mind's eye, venerable old scholars, one Muslim, one Jew, one Christian (in a kind of backdated Benetton ad), walking together, talking animatedly of philosophy and spiritual manners, in an atmosphere of the highest mutual regard and understanding — for that was Al-Andaluz, according to Professor Menocal — and the smell of the orange blossoms (the whole city *holiendo a azahar*), and in the distance a glimpse of the Guadalquivir, and….fill in the rest yourself, courtesy of the Tourist Board of Spain or Menocal's book or your own imagination.

Islamic Spain was far from being a paradise. Cordoba was no "ornament of the world." Maimonides had to flee the city because of the persecution by the fanatical Almohads, but even before the Alhomads, the treatment of non-Muslims was dismal. When the Jewish viziers Samuel ibn Naghrela and his son Joseph were both murdered, and then the entire Jewish community of Granada was massacred as well in 1066 — yes, in Granada, home of the "Alhambra" of which Washington Irving sung — it was not something without deep Islamic roots.

Richard Fletcher's *Moorish Spain* and the scholarship of Levi-Provencal and others all show that this "tolerance" was born from

the Romantic poets-in-prose mentioned above and is directly contradicted by the historical evidence. The records of the Muslim jurists, such
as Ibn Abdun, confirm that the tolerance of Muslim Spain is a myth. In
his opinion on the treatment of the Christians and Jews of Seville, Ibn
Abdun insisted that "No…Jew or Christian may be allowed to wear the
dress of an aristocrat, nor of a jurist, nor of a wealthy individual; on the
contrary they must be detested and avoided. It is forbidden to accost
them with the greeting, 'Peace be upon you'…In effect, 'Satan has gained
possession of them, and caused them to forget God's warning. They are
the confederates of Satan's path; Satan's confederates will surely be the
losers!' (Quran 58:19). A distinct sign must be imposed upon them in
order that they may be recognized and this will be for them a form of
disgrace."

A well-known jurist and poet of Muslim Spain, Abu Ishaq al-El-
biri, may have helped to promote the Granada massacres in his famous
anti-Jewish poem:

> Bring them [the Jews] down to their place and Return them to the
> most abject station. They used to roam around us in tatters Cov-
> ered with contempt, humiliation, and scorn. They used to rum-
> mage amongst the dungheaps for a bit of a filthy rag To serve as
> a shroud for a man to be buried in…Do not consider that killing
> them is treachery. Nay, it would be treachery to leave them scoffing.

This has not prevented Muslim apologists from starting their own
little "Cordoba Dialogues" and suchlike; it will not prevent many Europeans from wanting so desperately to believe that once upon a time, in
an ancient land called Andalusia, Muslims, Jews, and Christians lived
happily together. Nor does it prevent the sentimental and sloppy, such as
Menocal, from adding their embarrassing mites. If Andalusia was such
a wonderful example of "Convivencia" under wise Muslim rulers, why
did the Christians in Spain spend 700 years trying to topple Muslim
rule?

The Myth of Andalusia originates in the Western Romantic movement. And it is also linked with the human need to believe in a Golden
Age. In the Western world, this myth has been summed up by Harry
Levin in his essay on "The Myth of the Golden Age in the Renaissance."
(The same "myth of the Golden Age" has a Muslim version — the Sunna, a record of the words and deeds of Muhammad and the kind of life
the Prophet and the Companions led, which was perfect in all respects.)

And nowadays, in an age which we think of as tough-minded, re-alistic, skeptical, and so on, the dreamily romantic mythmaking about Islam lives on for geopolitical reasons. It is difficult to face reality and a threat that will not disappear — not through word-conjuring, nor log-ic-chopping, nor further protesting-too-much that Islam is a "religion of peace and tolerance." Too much evidence, and more of it every day, suggests the opposite.

So we are left with a myth of the "convivencia" in Islamic Spain that requires ignorance of the facts to survive, and many — Menocal was hardly alone, and hardly the worst offender — are happy to oblige. Yet even these romanticizers who write of Al-Andaluz as the great ex-emplar of tolerance also consider it to be, at best, a unique example in the long 1400-year history of Islam — which already is a way of admit-ting that the treatment of non-Muslims under Islam in general was not a paradise of "tolerance" and fruitful mutual accommodation. In all of the history of Islam, the story of Muslim Spain is the only one where there is even a colorable claim for "tolerance."

How pleasant it would be to make of history what it was not. How wonderful to think that at least once, just once, in the whole long histo-ry of Muslim conquest, there really was one spot where there was real tolerance — not the tolerance that is purchased by the Christians and Jews through payment of the jizya and submission in a hundred ways to a crushing regime of permanent degradation, humiliation, and physical insecurity. No wonder it is not only non-Muslims who like to imagine such a world, but also those Muslims who feel they must stick with Is-lam and cannot jettison that belief-system with which their entire civili-zation, their ancestors, and they themselves are so identified. These be-lievers must create, or must believe in, a mythical world of past tolerance that is now being "ruined" by these Bin Ladens and the others who have "hijacked a great religion."

Oh, the Will to Believe is strong. One wants to believe in Eden, and Santa Claus, and Endless Peace (*das ewige Frieden*), and once upon a time living happily ever after, in the thrice-nine kingdom, over hill and down dale, and the princesse lointaine awakened by her prince, and in the "buzzin'" of the bees/In the cigarette trees/Near the soda water foun-tain/At the lemonade springs/Where the bluebird sings/On the big rock candy mountain."

Dream-worlds do no harm — except in cases of civilizational peril. If dreams about the past or the present prevent sensible measures from being taken to prevent mass war, and to prevent the disappearance of one's own imperfect, silly, but still-worth-defending Infidel civilization, then the hollowness of those dream-worlds, whether the creation of Romantic writers or of slapdash historians, aided by a publishing industry without standards, must be exposed.

The reality of Muslim Spain should be based on a familiarity with Levi-Provencal and other scholars of that period. One's views should not consist of repeating phrases about "how wonderfully people of all faiths got along in Andalusia — gosh, why can't we just do that again?" Schoolgirl gush is not permissible in our current grim circumstances. Some "congress of dialogue." Some "springwell [sic] for the enlightement." Some convivencia.

CHAPTER NINE

The Marriage Game

"**I** WAS JUST A stepping stone to a green card," said one victim of visa fraud. "I married a terrorist. I married somebody who did not like America, who didn't like Americans."

I have known one or two of these stepping-stones. Some are complete innocents, others don't want to know. But it is not always the Green Card alone. Sometimes it is the Green Card, and the stepping-stone's property, or even a possible future inheritance, as well.

And it happens all over Europe and in North America and Australia. Indeed, one can find guides on Muslim websites for the "muhajiroun" as to the advantages of marrying an Infidel woman. And since women are essentially chattel, who really cares what happens to them?

The advantages are clear:

1. If you are a Muslim student and enter into this "temporary" (from your Muslim point of view, the only point of view that counts) union, you will have a source of steady sex — and all that cooking and cleaning are not to be sneezed at, either.

2. Protection against expulsion or against visa-expiration (at least until recently). If you can father a child, or six, while in the particular Infidel country you happen to be in, that polyphiloprogenitive activity may get you in, like Flynn.

3. Economic benefits — those Infidel women sometimes own property, and why not enjoy the Infidel loot, or at least some of it, by waiting around for it to drop from your wife's inheritance into your lap. Several spectacular cases of such come to mind.

4. While Arab and Muslim apologists now enjoy dismissing any realistic assessment of Islam, of its tenets, as merely the result of the West's,

or America's, supposed "need" to "create the 'Other'" (funny since Islam itself is based entirely on the need to subjugate, push back, destroy "the Other" — i.e., the Infidel), in fact the Arabs and Muslims who manage to inveigle Infidels into marrying them often exploit their own seeming outward exoticness, their physical "otherness": shades of the Sheik of Araby and other cliches that linger in the substratum of some incurably Emma-Bovaryish minds, intrigued by the liquid brown eyes, and soft speech — in short, by the tariqramadanish come-hither that ought to be so transparent, and to which one must now add that frisson of societal and political transgression that can now be derived from sleeping with someone who, in ways the foolish Infidel does not understand — is in the deepest sense, the enemy.

But before becoming so entangled, Infidel women should pay a visit to their nearest art museum. And look around, and think about the paintings on the walls of the museum, and what art would be permitted in, or could have come out of, the world that your would-be Muslilm husband comes from. Are you aware of how women are treated in the Qur'an? Do you know that it tells men they can beat their wives if they even suspect them of disobedience? Or that in Islam, a woman's testimony is worth half that of a man, and a daughter's inheritance is half that of a son? Do you know that a Muslim man can divorce his wife merely by uttering the triple-talaq — saying "talaq, talaq, talaq?"

No one should enter into any such liaison without reading the extensive testimonies of women who married into Islam and "reverted" — that is, became Muslim — and then, little by little, saw what they took to be the underside, but turned out to be the beating heart, of Islam. And they left their husbands, and abandoned Islam. There used to be a category of literature for children called "cautionary tales." Those tales need to be updated for the naïve non-Muslim adults about to marry Muslims.

But your naivete affects, in the main, you, and your children. The naivete about Islam of American policymakers, who after the fiascos of Iraq and Afghanistan, now realize that "democracy" cannot be imposed on Muslim peoples, that only one of the twenty-two existing Arab states — Lebanon — can claim to. be a democracy, and that it has been difficult even in Turkey after a century since the end of the caliphate and the rise of Kemalism, to create a secular class sufficient in size to keep that secularist orthodoxy in power. The West failed to create in Iraq, as policymakers in Washington had once hoped would be possible, a Light-Unto-the-Muslim-Nations. The best we can hope for is regimes that by slow degrees become ever less despotic, less cruel, less corrupt.

Besides, for 80 years there has already been a Light Unto the Muslim Nations. It is called Turkey. Ataturk did what he could to constrain Islam, step by systematic step, beginning in 1924, when the caliphate was officially dissolved. And in those eighty years not one circumjacent or distant Muslim state emulated Turkey (except Afghanistan, where the semi-enlightened King Amanullah Khan introduced some Kemalist reforms). In the past 20 years, Erdogan has been eviscerating the Kemalist system. He has purged the army's officer corps of secular supporters of Kemalism. He has built between 20,000 and 32,000 new mosques. He has constructed a vast network of Iman Hatip schools which are focused on training new imams; it's vocational training with a religious focus.

Turkey is in constant danger of what, from the Infidel point of view, would be a complete relapse, as Erdogan, that male sparrowhawk, chirpily pecks, pecks, pecks away at the foundations and protections of Kemalism, disguising his tying down the Turkish army, the last bastion of secularism, as merely "complying with the requirements of the E.U." And who can object to that?

A futile policy, based on ignorance of Islam, or on the continued dreamy belief that Islam itself is not a problem, or that the idea of jihad is a recent invention — see the "Army War College study," put out some years ago by one Lt.-Commander Aboul-Enein, and wonder just who thinks this sort of thing, full of misstatements about Islamic tenets and what Muslim attitudes really are, was worth sponsoring. It's just one more attempt by someone who, while no doubt a reasonably fine fellow and decent lieutenant commander in the Navy, either has no idea what Islam is all about, because even bearing the name Aboul-Enein, and calling yourself a "Muslim" does not make you an instant expert on what is uttered in khutbas all over the Middle East, especially if you have yourself been raised in Mississippi. Or perhaps he does know, but out of fear or filial piety or a desire to deceive the Infidels, will not allow himself to say.

There was recently in the news the story of a lady who realized that her husband saw her only as a way to get a Green Card, while he continued to hate America (where he could now live safely). She had the courage to publicly explain how silly and trusting and innocent of Islam she had once been. She now has been thoroughly disabused of her previous belief in the goodness of Islam.

If she can do it, so can the highest-ranking officers in the American army, and so can the officials in the Pentagon.

And they had better.

CHAPTER TEN

On Integrating Muslims in the West

ONCE ON AN NPR STATION I heard a very smooth-talking Muslim from Holland, like Hirsi Ali only in that she is, apparently, also a member of the Dutch Parliament, speak about how there is "fear on both sides" — Dutch and Muslim — and that Muslims who feel problems of "identity" embrace "Islamism" because, she said, they simply cannot go back to Turkey or Morocco (why not?) because they are now "Dutch."

In what sense, exactly, are they Dutch? What is it about the Dutch laws, customs, manners, or history that they comprehend and fully identify with? Anything? Or is their "Dutchness" merely a matter of where they are, geographic happenstance — and then also a matter of knowing Dutch, or possibly a bastardized form of it, which will not do as a definition of "Dutchness" that should satisfy any of the Dutch themselves, even if at one time it seemed to?

She did not explain this, this plausible sounding Muslim lady, who spoke excellent English and who no doubt would welcome the "integration" of other Muslims — that is, their becoming fluent in the local language of whatever Infidel country they happen to have settled in, and well- versed enough in the way the local Infidels think to better conduct propaganda and apologetics, to deflect any criticism of Islam and Muslims, and to successfully conduct da'wa among the Infidels.

And the height of absurdity was reached — though apparently the interviewer, on a program called "The World," did not find it absurd — when the lady said that the poor Muslims were being asked to choose between their Dutch identity and their Muslim identity. This, she insisted, was like asking someone to choose between his mother and his father. But the analogy is false. In this case, Islam is not the loyal wedded spouse of Holland and the Dutch. Islam, rather, is an alien creed. To be sure, plenty of Believers in exotic creeds alien or new to the West have managed to fit in perfectly well, and be friendly neighbors and loyal citizens, even if they came from Vietnam or India or China. Only one group, only one belief-system, distinguishes itself by appearing incapable of fitting in. And that is Muslims, and Islam. For their belief-system does not envision a Holland, an Italy, an England, a France. Islam does not distinguish between the various components of one single unit, the dar al-harb, the regions of the world where Islam does not yet reign and Muslims do not yet dominate. The analogy, while it may have fooled some and won sympathy for local Muslims in the Netherlands who are "forced to choose between their mother and their father," is ridiculous.

Now there is a problem in France. Will government-funded monitored mosques, language teaching, and affirmative-action programs for Muslims (but not for all those non-troublemaking Vietnamese, and Chinese, and non-Muslim blacks from sub-Saharan Africa or the Caribbean, Hindus and Sikhs, since these people can integrate, and so there is no need to have special programs for them) solve the problem? It will not.

Endless attempts by Europeans to "integrate" the Muslims in their midst will only lead to a loss of precious time, time that ought to be spent figuring out how to both halt all further Muslim migration into Europe, and to remove many of those already in Europe back to their countries of origin. These efforts will misleadingly continue to hold out hope, when there is no hope for real integration. What is in the Qur'an, the hadith, and the sira, though their contents may not always be fully comprehended, remains unaltered and unalterable, and can always be appealed to by any Muslim who wishes to bring "moderate" Muslims back into the fold. Those we call "extremist" Muslims are simply True Believers; it is the "moderate" Muslims who have deviated from the texts and teachings of Islam. The "extremist" Muslims are not untrue to the faith. They are are perfectly loyal Muslims, good and righteous followers of that exemplar Muhammad. No Muslim can honestly contend otherwise, although of course that is what many Muslims are doing — attempting to make Infidels believe that there is no problem for Muslims to integrate into Western societies, but it just takes time. Yet they never tell us exactly how they are going to change those texts, those passages in the Qur'an, the hadith, the sira that stand in the way of such integration. How can a Muslim cease to believe, as the Qur'an says, that

Muslims are "the best of peoples?" Or ignore the Qur'anic description of non-Muslims as "the most vile of created beings?" How can Muslims ignore the instruction "not to take Jews or Christians as friends, for they are friends only with each other?" And how can Muslims not heed the many Qur'anic verses about violently attacking Infidels?

And Muslims today cannot truthfully discuss the real history of the Muslim conquest of many lands and many peoples, and the subsequent mistreatment of non-Muslims who were presented with three possibilities after such conquest: either conversion to Islam, or death, or the permanent status of dhimmi, allowed to the People of the Book (Christians and Jews), who may remain alive and practice their religion if they submit to a host of economic, social, and political disabilities, the most onerous of which was the imposition of a capitation tax, the jizyah. None of that is mentioned by Muslims conducting outreach among the Infidels. Instead, these Muslim apologists repeat, ad nauseam, that Islam is a religion of "peace and tolerance." And by dint of constant repetition, there are many Infidels who believe such nonsense. The world's Muslims cannot explain, and refuse to discuss, the treatment of Christians, Jews, Hindus, Sikhs, Zoroastrians (Zoroastrianism was once the state religion of Persia; now fewer than 15,000 remain in Iran), and all other non-Muslims who have endured, in some cases, nearly 1400 years of Muslim rule.. Why won't they? Aside from the by-now absurd claim that "Islam is a religion of peace" — the kind of absurdity only the former Archbishop of Canterbury, Justin Welby, and the late Pope Francis could believe — what else can they say?

If integration can't work, except to benefit Muslims and keep the day of Infidel comprehension from arriving in time, and if non-integration can't work, what then?

At this point some will prefer — since there is no solution that we find "thinkable" — not to think about anything, and to go back to the previous state of denial. Just pretend that somehow things will work out. Pretend that Islam is not what it is. Pretend that the spicy lamb with cumin you were served at a Mosque Outreach Iftar is all ye know about Islam, and all ye need to know. Umm, the food. Umm, Muslims can be so nice, so soft-spoken, so hospitable. And that chicken with pita! No, there will have to be something a bit more substantive about the tenets of Islam. But if one really knew what Islam contained, as not all Muslims born or raised in the West may quite realize, then how could any decent person remain a Muslim? Hard to explain the hold of this belief-system on so many who cannot, out of some kind of diseased loyalty, insist on standing up for it. They needn't.

The solution is to stop all Muslim migration to the Lands of the Infidels, and, wherever possible, to reverse it. This can be done by taking care to ruthlessly enforce the immigration laws when it comes to those who, by virtue of their beliefs, are not unreasonably deemed to constitute a group that supports, actively or passively, those who do not wish this or any Infidel country well, in its laws, customs, manners, understandings, and will work, are required as a duty to work, for the triumph of Islam — and hence for changing those laws, those customs, those manners, those understandings.

And along with it, in ways little and big, the country can be Islam-proofed the way a house is child-proofed. Instead of letting the Saudis buy land and build mosques, and paying for the upkeep and the staffing of those mosques, let them be monitored so that no foreign money, or any money judged tainted, can be used to pay for mosques or madrasas. Monitor what is said in khutbas. At the first sign of hate-preaching, do not merely be satisfied if a congregation removes the current imam. Close the mosque. Put everyone on notice that this kind of thing cannot go on. Nor can it be allowed in any of the textbooks used in madrasas. Close any madrasa that makes allusion to smiting the Unbelievers. Since the division between Believer and Infidel is so central to Islam, and since the jihad is a virtual "sixth pillar" of Islam, it should not be hard to find ways to limit the spread or practice of Islam. In addition to whatever local, state and federal government officials do, private parties can simply conduct their own boycott of goods and services offered by Muslims, in the same way that they would have refused to buy, in 1938, a German Voigtlander camera, or in 1953, to buy Baltic amber from the Soviet government's official ministry for trading-with-the-West, Vneshtorg.

Why should one buy an oriental rug, or dates, or curry powder, from people whose presence, in merely swelling Muslim ranks, will inevitably swell Muslim political power — which, in turn, makes the lives of Infidels, in the end, more insecure?

If people born into Islam are at long last free to investigate fully what Islam is all about, and having done so, they still insist on remaining loyal to Islam, there is no reason for Infidels to support or indulge them on some specious theory that Islam cannot really teach what it teaches, and that adherents of Islam cannot possibly want what they are taught, according to Islam, to want: the spread of Islam, and the submission of all non-Muslims to, at best, the status assigned them in Islam of dhimmi.

Why should we tolerate this? On what theory? On what grounds?

CHAPTER ELEVEN

Why Don't Muslims Integrate into Western Societies?

ISLAM ITSELF IS entirely responsible for the failure of Muslims in Infidel lands to integrate.

And here is why:

1. Islam itself teaches Muslims to be suspicious of, to hate, to refuse to trust, to offer only feigned friendship to, all non-Muslims. There are passages all over the Qur'an and hadith about this: "Take not the Christians and Jews for friends, for they are friends only with each other." "Smite the Unbelievers wherever you find them." Not much room for nuance there. The stories in the hadith about the triumph over, and the killing of, and the seizure of women and property from, non-Muslims whom Muhammad believed he and his men were entitled to attack (even if those in question had done nothing to them) further encourages such an attitude.

Then there are all the stories about Muhammad himself. What does it mean to someone to learn that Muhammad watched with satisfaction as 600-800 members of the Banu Qurayza, bound and helpless, were decapitated one by one? Does that encourage peaceful co-existence, or that famous "convivencia" that supposedly was such a heart-warming feature of Islamic Spain — which for some has become the model of what they apparently see as an inevitably-islamized Europe? If so, they should delve more deeply into the history of Islamic Spain (that is, read the historians Richard Fletcher and Evariste Levi-Provencal rather than Maria Rosa Menocal)

It may be quite difficult for Muslims to take orders from non-Muslims, knowing as they do that they are the "best of peoples" and non-Muslims "the most vile of created beings, or to get along well with Infidel fellow-workers, if one is constantly offering only ill-concealed — or at times well-concealed — hostility. Nor does the Muslim sense of Muslim entitlement make it easy for Muslims to endure, or to endure with good grace, such an arrangement: Islam by right should dominate, Muslims should rule, it is contra naturam, against all that is right and just, for Muslims to have to accommodate themselves to non-Muslim customs and laws and ways of behaving. If they must, they should only do so temporarily — until Muslims are sufficiently numerous to dominate a society, which can happen long before they are an absolute majority. Just look at all the demands made constantly by Muslims in Europe, so that Infidels begin to behave, even when they need not, as dhimmis: willing to placate, to make excuses for, to bend over backwards for, Muslim outrages in word, in deed, or in attitude — outrages that should be obvious to those who have kept their wits about them. Think of the Musim demands, for example, for changes in school lunches to make them strictly halal, or for prayer rooms set aside in schools, airports, factories, and offices, for Muslims only. Or the ever-more frequent demands to allow electronic loudspeakers on mosques that will blast prayers across a quiet neighborhood of non-Muslims. Or the Muslim demand for municipal pools where same-sex swimming hours are imposed. If they do this when they now constitute at most, in European countries, 10% of the population, what will they demand in ten years, or in twenty, when they are far more numerous?

2. Inshallah-fatalism. The deep belief in the will of Allah, of Allah ta'ala (Allah Knows Best), of references to Allah's foreknowledge in every greeting, in every prediction, in every discussion; the invoking of Allah ta'ala reminds Muslims that Allah knows what will happen, and there is nothing we mortals can do about it. This inshallah fatalism dampens personal effort that has economic consequences; why try so hard, when what will happen is already known to Allah?

3. The habit of submission — of mental submission to the authority of the Qur'an and sunna— does not encourage skepticism, liveliness, "thinking outside the box" and so on. This can limit entrepreneurial activity and innovation, just as the sullen dislike of one's status felt by Muslims who do not lord it over non-Muslims but in the West often have non-Muslim bosses, helps to explain the difficulty of employing Muslims in a non-Muslim workplace.

4. Why should Infidels wish to employ Muslims? Why should they

wish to create an unpleasant work environment for themselves? Fetish-worshippers of diversity may wish to do so. And think of the media outlets that assume that the best way to cover stories involving Muslims is to hire a Muslim reporter (which is, in fact, probably the worst way, if it amounts to the usual apologetics and misinformation). Sometimes, of course, one is dealing with those who either hide very well, or may in fact not feel — as "Muslim-for-identification-purposes-only" Muslims — the hostility toward non-Muslims that Islam inculcates. But even those who never go to a mosque may at times engage in a sudden flaring-up, a sudden note of hysteria, when the subject of Islam is even tangentially raised — as if it is simply a subject completely off-limits for discussion by Infidels. And nowadays, how can one discuss anything in the world's news without discussing Islam? One sees this reaction even in some of the seemingly most Westernized, most sophisticated, and suavest of Muslims — a sudden rage, a sudden rush of furious defensiveness that overcomes the truth, that makes even someone who a minute ago was so calm, so rational, so seemingly part of the same moral and intellectual universe as non-Muslims, and might even have been attacking the behavior of Muslims himself, reacts defensively if an Infidel agrees with the attack, or dares to add his own two-cents' worth of critical analysis to the discussion, and withdraws into a circling-the-wagons mode.

5. Muslims through time and space lived in the lands they conquered on the loot they seized from non-Muslims, and they continued to exploit those non-Muslims through the jizyah, and in other ways. As historians of India well know, the Hindus were initially subject to mass execution and mass enslavement. Some of those enslaved converted. Others did not wait to be enslaved, but converted after witnessing the realities of life under Muslim rule. But the Mughal rulers soon realized that if the only possible choices open to Hindus — as non-People of the Book (*ahl al-kitab*), they were not permitted to live and practice openly their religion — were death or conversion, then there would ultimately be few non-Muslims left to be exploited economically for the purposes of the Muslim state.

This could end the fabled Mughal luxury, the famed Mughal magnificence that so entrances certain writers (as the upscale, and more scholarly, Barbara Cartland of Mughal India, William Dalrymple). Hindus were accorded "honorary" status as dhimmis, not because of Muslim mercy, but because by so doing, the ruling Muslims could economically exploit them through the jizyah (which the tolerant, syncretistic Akbar managed to temporarily suspend — one more reason why Akbar is remembered fondly by Hindus, and despised by Muslims).

Another way of finding loot, or slaves to exploit, were the constant series of slaving raids. Islam created slave societies — slaves on horseback, slaves in the harem, slaves to build the palace of Moulay Hasan or the Taj Mahal. Everywhere, slaves from non-Muslim lands — from black Africa by the tens of millions, slaves from the Slavic lands and Georgia and Circassia, by the many millions, and slaves taken over centuries by raiding parties that landed, destroyed villages, and seized villagers up and down the coasts of Western Europe. This too was a source of wealth, and in fact the corsairs that left ports in North Africa, especially Algiers, continued to raid Christian shipping until two things happened — the American military response to the Barbary Pirates, and then the seizure, by the exasperated French, of Algiers in 1830, which put an end to the corsairs and their officially-sanctioned raids on Christian cargoes and enslavement of Infidel sailors.

The corsair-piracy has stopped, or found new means of expression, but the jizyah, in disguised forms, has continued. Arab and Muslim states have economies that depend heavily on one of two things:

1. The oil and gas-rich Muslim states depend on this manna from Allah — which is exactly how they see it. They do not regard these fabulous oil-and-gas riches as an accident of geology, but as a sign of Allah's favor — why else should so much of the world's oil lie under the lands of dar al-Islam?

2. The Arab and Muslim states that do not possess oil wealth, instead of having the oil-rich Muslim states share that wealth, have managed to get on the Infidel list of countries deserving of foreign aid. Suddenly that supposed loyalty of the umma al-islamiyya seems to disappear when it comes to oil money, save for the sums given to reward suicide bombers among the "Palestinians," and of course for any significant arms projects. No matter how corrupt, how full of anti-Americanism and antisemitism these societies may be, Western money keeps pouring in: to Egypt ($80 billion from America alone), to Pakistan, to Jordan, and to the shock troops of the jihad against Israel, the local Arabs who, beginning in the late 1960s, were carefully renamed as the "Palestinian people" so as to disguise the essential nature, and ultimate aims (not exactly concealed, by the way) of the Arab war on Israel, an Infidel sovereign state in the midst of dar al-Islam that must, in Arab and Muslim eyes, disappear — sooner or later. It is a matter of pride. It is a matter of self-esteem. It is a matter of how the Arabs and the Muslims see themselves. What else could possibly matter?

Billions have been spent by the U.S. and Europe to keep afloat a statelet-in-posse, the hoped-for-"state of Palestine," a 23rd Arab state that could only exist if the territory of the tiny Jewish state is diminished still further. Israel would again be squeezed back within the now-indefensible 1949 armistice lines. Such an outcome can only be supported if one ignores the 3500-year claim of Jews to that area, the demographics, the land ownership, and the long-settled rules of war about the legitimacy of retaining territory captured from an aggressor. For how else did Italy acquire the Alto Adige, which, when it was handed over had a population that was 97% German-speaking and ethnically part of Deutschtum? Yet who among us thinks Italy was not entitled to, and should return to Austria, the Sudtirol it possesses? And what of all the changes in borders after World War II, and the expulsion of ethnic Germans from Czechoslovakia (three million Sudeteners), from Poland, and elsewhere, not to mention land taken from the loser, Germany, by one of the victors, the Soviet Union, turning Kant's city of Koenigsberg into Putin's city of Kaliningrad?

Yet, the Americans and Europeans continue to pay this disguised jizyah to the "Palestinians" and are fearful of stopping their massive aid to Ramallah. They also continue to provide aid to Pakistan, the supporter of the Taliban, that provided Osama Bin Laden with a refuge, and made a national hero of Dr. A. Q. Khan, who, while working in a Dutch laboratory, stole nuclear secrets that allowed Pakistan to build a nuclear weapon. A. Q. Khan also sold nuclear secrets to North Korea. Yet America continued long after that to give Pakistan about $2 billion a year in aid. Only in the last few years have the Americans reduced that aid to $300 million a year. Which still leaves one puzzled: why is America still giving any aid to malevolent Muslim Pakistan? We continue to engage in bribery, albeit at a lower level than before, instead of reading Pakistan the riot-act, threatening first, to damage its military by refusing to export necessary spare parts, second, to harm its economy by preventing Pakistan from selling textiles and rugs that are produced by child labor, and third, to put a large tariff on all imports from Pakistan, which in 2024 were valued at more than $5 billion. These acts will get the attention of generals and zamindars alike. Within Europe, the Muslims have the same attitude toward non-Muslims as they do in their own lands. The property and women of the Infidels belongs to them. There is nothing wrong with taking Infidel property. There is nothing wrong with raping Infidel women. It is not an accident that almost 70% of the prison population in France is Muslim; that 70% of the rapes of women in Scandinavia are by Muslims; that the drug traffickers in the Netherlands, and the *spacciatori di droga* in Italy, are Muslims — no, this should not surprise.

What does surprise is the failure of the non-Muslim world to understand that this all fits into, and can be explained by, a coherent ideology that makes it virtually impossible for Muslims — to the extent that they remain full believers, or turn into full believers — to ever comfortably fit into, or ever accept, Western or other non-Muslim societies, mores, manners, laws, or ever to accept the idea of living in a society where the Infidel ways, the Infidel understandings, are to be permanent. This rankles Muslims. This is not right. The world belongs in the end to Allah, and to his people. It is to them that the property and women of others belongs. Not every Believer feels this, but in the canonical texts, and the tenets logically derived from them, and in the attitudes and atmospherics to which those tenets and the whole system of Islam gives rise, these views are not strange but natural and familiar.

And then there is another problem: the problem of the "moderate" Muslim — which is to say, the relaxed, or unobservant Muslim, the Muslim who may not act according to the tenets of Islam today, but may suddenly acquire a deep psychic need to return to Islam, for whatever reasons. When one is in mental disarray, and happens to be a Muslim, provided with a Total Explanation of the Universe, and a Complete Regulation of Existence, one can quite easily come to view the universe through the prism of Islam.

And it need be nothing political — nothing in the newspapers — that sets one off. A death in the family, the loss of a job, the failure to get into a certain school, the perception that others do not share one's worldview and see no reason to accommodate themselves to you, and of course the depression that can come upon so many of us, Muslim and non-Muslim, at any time — are all cause for alarm. But non-Muslims provide their own answers, their own home remedies, as they can, and those answers, and their affixing of blame for their problems, can be as various as their parents, their spouses, their children, their siblings, their employer, The System, the stars, Fate, their cholesterol level, their serotonin level, even — at times — themselves. Muslims have only to look to the one thing that always presents itself to be blamed: the Infidels. Their wiles, their whisperings of Shaytan, their decadence, their bland and maddening indifference to the commands of Allah, and for which non-Muslims must be held to account. And once a non-Muslim Muslim, a "Muslim-for-identification-purposes-only" Muslim, begins to rediscover Islam, to return to Islam, he can turn into that other thing — a Muslim Muslim. And that is the problem, the permanent problem for Infidels, who have done nothing to deserve this ever-ready, this omnipresent, blame.

There is no solution. Reducing Muslim numbers, and Muslim power, and ensuring that the Infidel lands do not engage in some kind of attempt to win Muslims by changing their own laws and customs, but remain implacably themselves, or even better, deliberately Islam-hostile rather than Islam-friendly, so that those who now claim that they are "thinking of leaving" really do leave — would anyone wish to stop them? — should be the goal of Infidels, engaged only in defending themselves against the carriers of jihad, all over the world.

CHAPTER TWELVE

The Other Jihad

J IHAD TO SPREAD Islam does not rely on military conquest alone. Where outright military conquest has not been possible, the fruits of da'wa and demographic conquest (migration to Lands of the Infidels, and then outbreeding them) certainly can lead and has led to Muslim dominance. "Migration" as a new weapon of jihad is in fact discussed explicitly in the most mainstream publications — e.g., the newspaper *Dawn* in Pakistan.

Immigrants may move to the West for all sorts of reasons. But there is no reason why Infidels should not wonder if, whatever their other reasons, as long as they remain Believers, the Muslims in their midst will lend their support, direct or indirect, to the jihad — even if only by helping to misinform unwary Infidels. Furthermore, the first-generation economic immigrant can be transformed from a "moderate," who seems fully integrated, to an "immoderate" Muslim" — that is, one who takes Islam's texts and teachings fully to heart — who is prepared to kill Infidels. For example, see the case of Intel engineer Mike Hawash, who was a smashing American success story until he got that old-time religion and prepared to go off to western China, hoping to join the Taliban and Al Qaeda in Afghanistan and kill his fellow Americans. And still another problem is that of "My Son the Fanatic" — the second or third-generation Muslim who, for all sorts of reasons (personal setbacks or depression, which can strike anyone, and which may have certain consequences if one views the universe through the prism of Islam) may embrace completely what the Qur'an, hadith, and sira teach — rather than ignore those teachings, or the most dangerous of them. Again, how can Infidels separate out those who come and will never be a threat from those who come and seem harmless but can change, or from those whose children may, at some Manchurian-Candidate point in the future, be set off?

The answer is: those helpless Infidels cannot. Surely that is worth pointing out.

For all these reasons and more, da'wa and demographic conquest from within are far more dangerous than outright terrorism, and it will require a change in mental makeup for the Infidels to deal with them properly. Yet such a change is not forthcoming. So far the rulers of Infidel lands have foolishly focused their efforts not on addressing and defeating this da'wa and demographic conquest, but on allowing Muslims in large numbers to settle within their lands, behind what many of those Muslims themselves consider to be enemy lines. This has created a situation unprecedented in human history, and one which everyone is pretending is not what it is, because they lack the wit and imagination to figure out how to deal with this peril. But it can and must be dealt with, in ways that may not require mass expulsions.

The tendency to recoil in horror at the prospect of mass expulsions is a modern development; they have, after all, been a feature of Middle Eastern life forever. Mass expulsions are nothing new in the Middle East. One million Yemenis were expelled from Saudi Arabia in 1990, because the Yemeni government had supported Saddam Hussein's seizure of Kuwait, and hundreds of thousands more expelled in 2021, as part of Mohammad bin Salman's policy of increasing Saudi participation in the labor force; more than 300,000 "Palestinians" were booted out of Kuwait in 1991 after they had sided with the Iraqi invaders, hundreds of thousands of Egyptians and other non-Libyans were expelled from Libya by Qaddafi; six million Sunnis in Syria were forced to flee the country during the civil war, and seven million Syrians of different sects and ethnicities were internally displaced, thousands of Palestinians were expelled from Jordan, from Syria, and from Lebanon at different times and for different reasons; from 1948 to the early 1950s, 850,000 Jews were expelled from Arab lands where their families had lived for centuries— all these show that this kind of mass displacement is routine in the Arab Muslim world.

No, it is not only, and not mainly, Islamic "terrorism" that is the threat in Europe today, but the slow and steady takeover, simply through numbers, that can do the trick where military force cannot. But this can only be recognized by those who are willing to study, and re-study, and study even more, the doctrines of Islam, and the history of Islamic conquest and subjugation of non-Muslims, and the persistence and immutability of those teachings, those attitudes, those atmospherics that make even the most "moderate" of Muslims essentially part of the problem, for we do not know when, and why, such a "moderate" may change, or when, or why, his progeny may do so.

Yet Westerners continue to act against their own best interests. Oriana Fallaci's *La Forza della Ragione* details just how fully many in the Vatican, and individual bishops and priests, have collaborated in making Italy, and other parts of Europe, welcoming for Muslims, even handing over churches for use by Muslims as living quarters. Her long indictment is overwhelming. The submission Fallaci describes goes far beyond the desire to placate Muslims because otherwise they may harm Christians in the Middle East, and has become a vehicle for those left-wing priests who have grown weary of their own civilization, and exhibit a diseased sympathy for Muslims who would not, were they to prevail in Europe, tolerate those priests or their diminishing flocks.

We cannot bet our own civilization on some concocted and mostly exaggerated notion of "moderate" Islam. The stakes are too high for mistakes, for feelgood niceness, for assuming the best in everyone, for refusing to believe that those who make the most terrible threats and plans really do mean it.

See the history of World War II — not the war itself, but the run-up to that war. We had ample warning then. We have ample warning now.

CHAPTER THIRTEEN

Normal Muslim Kids in the West

VIRTUALLY EVERY TIME a Muslim terrorist is arrested we hear it: "He was a quiet, soft-spoken young man." "He was a normal young kid like all his peers...A normal kid, very polite but secluded. He didn't mingle much with people...We never felt that or noticed any changes in his attitude."

Terrorists, in murdering Infidels, do not necessarily start out as fire-breathers. They may, in outward aspect, seem to be just like any "normal young kid." But that "normal young kid" is a normal young Muslim kid — and that makes all the difference.

Indeed, they need not have been concealing, all this time, a particularly fervent and murderous faith at all, as some have suggested. There are Muslim "moderates" but we cannot always distinguish the feigned from the true. Nor do we have any way to detect those moderates who change over time, becoming deeper in their belief, and hence more dangerous for us, the Infidels. It is also possible that rising high in various Western governments are Muslim moles, concealing their real feelings until such time as they are able to exploit their positions, or perhaps even now are exploiting them. But there is a much larger problem. It is not the fervent Muslim who is hiding his fervency. It is the Muslim who is not fervent, but for whom changes in his personal life transform the merely observant into the fanatic and the protector or supporter of killers, or even a killer himself.

And if Muslims themselves, in Iraq, in Israel, in Egypt, in Morocco, in Tunisia, in Algeria, and elsewhere, have expressed great surprise, not in all but in many cases, at the son or brother who ended up as a suicide killer, how much more difficult, how impossible, really, for Infidels, innocent of Muslim ways, innocent of the fantastic ability of Muslims to conceal, overwhelmed and confused by Muslim apologetics and rhetoric, disinclined to see the scope or nature of the menace because to recognize it is simply too upsetting, then how nearly impossible it must be for those Infidels to avoid being deceived. And this happens all the time, individually, and collectively, about all sorts of Muslim matters.

Shall all Muslims be monitored for sudden changes in their personal lives? Shall we have a National Register to record when that Muslim someone's father or mother dies, when a child becomes mortally ill, a husband or wife leaves, a job is lost, a stock investment sours, or bipolar disorder sets in — for every last Muslim?

Of course we cannot. We must recognize that with the System of Islam already accepted, any Believer might, potentially, be set off by these purely personal setbacks. Apologists for Islam keep stressing the idiotic idea that Muslims behave as they do only because of perceived injustice by the "colonialist" or "imperialist" West. You know what the Arabs and Muslims mean — they mean such outrages as the United States of America stealing all of Iraq's oil. No such theft took place. In fact, the U.S. spent more than two trillion dollars trying, and failing, to make Iraq into a Western-style democracy. Nor did America "steal all" or, indeed, any of Saudi Arabia's oil, but has always paid the market price. In fact, the Americans have provided more than $400 billion in aid ($80 billion went to Egypt alone) to the MENA countries since 1946 — a fact no Arab or Muslim has ever mentioned publicly.

Through the prism of Islam, one views the Universe as divided into two camps: the Believers and the Infidels. It does not matter if the Infidels are white or black, rich or poor, whether they have rescued you from a tyrant, or rushed to help you when a tsunami, or an earthquake struck. It does not matter if they are Infidel Americans in the United States, or in Iraq training the national army, or walking down a street to see a tourist site in Cairo or Beirut, or taking the metro in London, or Madrid. It does not matter if they are Hindus celebrating a wedding in Kashmir, or a poor tiffin-wallah who happens to be walking by a mosque at the end of Friday Prayers in Dacca, who is then beaten to death by the excited worshippers, eager to take care of at least one Hindu that day. It does not matter if those Infidels happen to be Dinka and Nuer tribesmen in the south of the Sudan, who never posed a threat to the Arabs, who have over the past century gone from being a mere 10% of the country, to slowly taking it over, demographically and geographically. It does not matter whether they are Christian villagers, who are ethnically identical to Muslims in northern Nigeria, or in the Moluccas, or the southern Philippines, or whether they are Buddhists villagers in southern Thailand. All that matters is that they are Infidels, non-Muslims. They can be targeted for any reason — or no reason.

Not all Muslims feel their Islam in that way. But we, the Infidels, cannot detect who receives Islam in what way. And the insistent blend of nonsense and lies, the taqiyya (concealment) and tu quoque (the defense of "you do it too"), that we receive from Muslim spokesmen, some smoother and more plausible than others, does not inspire our confidence. And we have no way of detecting the changes, over time, that can occur for no other reason than personal ones. Mohamed Atta felt keenly his loss of status, and the usual graduate student angst, and loneliness, while in Hamburg. All of that led him to more, and more fanatical, Islam. It was his consolation. Ayman al-Zawahiri and Bin Laden were children of very prominent and rich families, but had always taken their religious obligations more seriously. Their disgust at the circum-ambient society necessarily had to take on a religious cast, had to locate the enemy not in the corruption and swinish behavior of the Egyptian and Saudi elites, but in Infidels. And they responded by attacking those elites for being, precisely, insufficiently Islamic, and tied to the Infidels.

When will this government, when will other Western governments, when will the media, manage to understand that ideas matter, and that Islam is essentially an idea, a very primitive Idea, but an Idea, a geopolitical Idea, with an admixture of bits and pieces of pagan Arab lore, and stories appropriated in distorted fashion from Judaism and Christianity?

These ideas must be taken seriously. One cannot blandly assert that "only a few" Muslims are a problem. How does one know this? How does one know which Muslim, perhaps both outwardly and inwardly content with his life, will never prove susceptible, not to some wild extra-Islamic doctrine, but to Islam itself? All the technological "progress" that has been made has helped to dry up those pockets of innocent village Islam, where illiterate peasants go to a ramshackle mosque and are pious, content, and know nothing of the outside world. Now those same villagers, like the Iranian peasants who listened to Khomeini's tapes, can see the videos of decapitations of Nicholas Berg and Kenneth Bigley, and can hear the chants — Qur'anic chants, war chants, consisting only of Qur'anic verses (nothing made up, for nothing need be made up).

Let us assume that the estimate, commonly cited, though no source is provided, that 10-15% of Muslims are terrorists or potential terrorists.

One does not know how this figure is arrived at. Ali Sina and other defectors from Islam, whom I trust, consider it to have the percentages backwards, for they suggest that 85-90% of Muslims might become potential terrorists, or supporters of similar acts, or would be ready to harm non-Muslims in other ways, in the conduct of jihad. Who knows, really — and how could we ever be certain? But even the gleeful behavior of masses of Muslims all over the world after learning of 9/11, or the sudden increase in the numbers of Muslims naming their sons "Osama," or the kinds of things routinely said and applauded at meetings of Muslim nations, or the kinds of demands made on Infidel societies by Muslims now living in their midst, or the behavior of Muslim pressure groups to limit the power of Infidels to undertake reasonable security measures (including, precisely, profiling to target not a race, or an ethnic group, but the adherents or potential adherents of the ideology of Islam), and to undermine the enormous efforts by Muslims to conduct da'wa by every conceivable and sly means, including the rewriting of textbooks to transform the history of Infidel lands, and to target the most vulnerable members of society (prisoners, non-Mulsim immigrants, young people) for the conduct of da'wa — all of this should give any Infidel who has studied the theory and practice of Islam, considerable pause.

But suppose that the lowest estimate — 10% of all Muslims — were in fact somehow true? No, let us make that figure 5% — only 5% are potential terrorists. There are 1.9 billion Muslims in the world. That means, at a minimum, 95 million Muslims are potential terrorists. It's a staggering number. If one out of 20 Muslims allowed into the Western world holds to these ideas, where are we then? Or what if one of the other 19 picks them up from that one? We have no way of insuring that every single Muslim will forever and ever be immune to such appeals.

That being the case, it is a matter of obvious prudence for Western governments to study carefully the question of Muslims migration to the Western world. Even if the figure of "only" 10% is accurate, we would be mad to continue to allow in and give citizenship to such a pool of people without a moment's hesitation or examination or consideration. Infidel governments should not allow their policies to be dictated by fear of offending, or by believing their own nonsense — no one should continue to mouth the kind of absurdities about the religion of "peace" and "tolerance" that we have had to endure in the past.

Prudence demands that risks be minimized. And time is running out.

CHAPTER FOURTEEN

The Cultural Imperialism of the Arabs

As EUROPE ISLAMIZES, it will become more Arab.

Within Islam, a supposedly universalist religion where all Muslims in the ummah are equal, there is a special place for the Arabs. But how could it be otherwise? Islam itself, a mishmash of pagan Arab lore, Judaism and Christianity, has its origins in the attempt to take what was available and construct out of it something, a belief-system, that would both promote, and justify, Arab attacks on, and Arab conquest of, far more advanced, settled, and wealthy populations of Christians, Jews, and pagans — and, with the attack on Sassanid Persia, Zoroastrians.

Within Islam, the supremacist ideology is expressed first, and perhaps most importantly, in linguistic and cultural imperialism. The Qur'an is written in Arabic, and was revealed first to the Arabs, the best of the Muslims who, as the Qur'an says, are "the best of peoples." That best of men, Muhammad, was an Arab, and so were the Companions. The Qur'an itself should ideally not be read in any language other than Arabic (the Arabic in which it was written, not in any simplified or updated version). Qur'anic recitation is in Arabic. The students in Pakistan or Indonesia or elsewhere outside the Arab lands pass their young lives in madrasas, memorizing Qur'anic passages in Arabic, a language that they hardly understand. Yet it is 7th century Arabs, real or imaginary, who must serve as a guide to existence. Was Muhammad against sculptures? Against music? Against painting of living creatures? Very well then. For all time, and in all places, good Muslims will emulate Muhammad. For he is central to Islam, far more significant than Jesus is in Christianity. Yes, it is true that "Allah knows best" but so too does

Muhammad — see Qur'an 33:21. They both know best.

Think of all the Pakistani and Indian Muslims, almost all of whom are the descendants of persecuted or terrified Hindus, who converted (or "reverted" as the Muslims say) to Islam in order to avoid either execution or the forced payment, as dhimmis, of the onerous jizyah. Many of these non-Arabs have taken Arab names, or appropriated the honorific Sayeed to indicate their connection to the Prophet. Think of how the Berbers and other non-Arab Muslims have had to struggle to save their own language. The Iranians supposedly managed to prevent linguistic arabization through the superior quality of their own poets — for after all, "Islamic literature" is mostly a product, not of Arabs, but of Persians. High Islamic civilization was very much a product both of non-Muslims and Muslims, and in the latter category, the Arabs played a much smaller role than the Persians.

The riots in Tizi-Ouzou a few years ago — unreported in the Western world except in France — reflect the unhappiness of the Berbers with this cultural and linguistic imperialism. So does the greater participation of Berbers in such organizations as "Maghrebins laiques" in France. The Kurds, the black Africans with their marabouts and syncretism, and even those described as Malaysian "intellectuals" and Indonesian "intellectuals," have realized that the Arab supremacist view, which encourages all Muslims to ignore their own pre-Islamic or non-Islamic history and heritage, leaves a lot to be desired. This is similar to the phenomenon in Brazil, where what prevails is not always orthodox Christianity, but some blend of Catholicism with pagan African beliefs and traditions that gave rise to Candomblé.

And then there are so many examples of Arabs riding roughshod, and worse, over non-Arab Muslims. Think of the treatment of the Berbers, especially, but not only, in Algeria. Or of the black African Muslims in Darfur, or in Chad, or elsewhere where Arabs and blacks, even if all of them are Muslims, collide. There is also a religious dimension. Though there are non-Arab Sunnis (Turks, Kurds, Pakistnis, Indonesians) and Arab Shi'a (see southern Lebanon, Yemen, the Hasa province of Saudi Arabia, Bahrain, Kuwait), Sunni Islam is identified with the Arabs, Shi'a Islam with Iran.

In Saudi Arabia there is apartheid: the signs "Muslim" and "Non-Muslim" are everywhere, both physically and in the minds of men. But "Muslims" are further divided into Arab (first class) and non-Arab (second class). This has not escaped the attention of the many Muslim non-Arabs who live and work in Saudi Arabia — or at least not the attention of all of them.

As Infidels seek out ways to divide and weaken Islam, surely the exploitation of this linguistic, cultural, and political imperialism of the Arabs should be high on the list. Remember how the "Arabs" were hated even by some of their "Afghan" allies whom they treated with such cannon-fodder contempt — at least according to all the reports that have come out of Afghanistan. The resentment of non-Arabs, of Kurds, Berbers, blacks, Persians, Malays and so on, is perfectly understandable. The use of Islam as a vehicle for Arab supremacism is not a Western invention. It has not in any way been fanned by the West. It need not be. It need only be pointed out. And even then, the Arabs themselves help this cause by continuing to show their contempt and indifference for non-Arabs, though they wish those non-Arabs to adopt whatever causes they, the Arabs, deem important.

Part of weakening Islam is to show many Muslims that Islam was simply an Arab invention and export, a poisoned chalice that has lain low higher and superior civilizations. This is likely to resonate especially in Iran among those who have had their fill of the Islamic Republic of Iran — that is, every thinking and morally aware person in Iran.

The treatment by the Arabs of non-Arabs has been at least high-handed, and as the glinting daggers of Arab aggression tell us, often of a more horrid hent.

Yet at the same time, the pride in Uruba — Arabness, Arabdom — that affects so many Arabs, has also convinced many non-Arab people who speak Arabic that they too are, or must be, or should be "Arabs." The scholar Franck Salameh has written a brilliant analysis of linguistic imperialism, of how the Arabic-user (even the Maronites) comes to believe that he therefore must be an "Arab" — even if his ancestors clearly were living in, say, the Lebanon long before the Arabs arrived on the scene. It is quite a trick.

Almost all of those — overwhelmingly Christian— who left Lebanon and Syria between 1880 and even as late as about 1930, even if their passports identified them in some cases as "Turks" (they were still in the Ottoman Empire), knew that they were something else, and that the best way to describe themselves was as "Lebanese" or as "Christians." Only later did some of them begin to think that they were "Arabs." Muslims in the United States have tried to create a false sense of an identity of interest, using that meretricious term "Arab-American." This is meant to enroll in the Muslim Arab campaign for acceptance the descendants of people who not only were not part of the Muslim Arab world, but were the main victims of that very world — people who left the Middle East precisely because of their growing insecurity among the Muslims. From 1860 on there were massacres of Maronites and Assyrians and other Middle-Eastern Christians in present-day Turkey, Syria, Lebanon, and Iraq.

The Christian Arabs, or those who have considered themselves Arabs, needed to find a place in the sun. They knew they had to appeal to something, anything, other than Islam straight up. What was Ba'athism, which a Christian from Damacus, Michel Aflaq, co-founded (he made a deathbed conversion to Islam), but an attempt to find a way for the Christians of the area to be enrolled in something that, in its philosophy, would be aggressive, totalitarian, but more pan-Arab than pan-Islamic? So it was that the political movement known as Ba'athism was born and found its greatest appeal in the two countries where, for various and complex reasons, the religious minorities that would ultimately rule found Ba'athism a way to overcome their minority status. The Alawites, though only 12% of the Syrian population, held the country in thrall for fifty years, while disguising the Alawite rule, instead promoting the idea that the government was conducted by Ba'athists whose political party was supposedly open to all. In Iraq, the Sunni Arabs were only 20% of the population, but Saddam Hussein presented his rule, just as did Hafez al-Assad in Syria, as being Ba'aathist in nature, and again, theoretically open to all, though few Kurds or Shi'a Arabs, and only one Christian (Tariq Aziz) were in the ruling elite. Had Baathism not existed to disguise their rule, the minority Alawites in Syria would long ago have been crushed by the Sunni Muslims, and the minority Sunnis in Iraq would have been kept from power by the Shi'a.

Note that the phenomenon of "Islamochristians" is particularly pronounced among the "Palestinian" Arabs, despite the obvious and steady pressure on Christians and Christianity wherever the "Palestinians" have extended their sway. Naim Ateek and Hanan Ashrawi, both of them Christians and both stout defenders of Islam and even of Muslim terrorism, are perfect examples of the cunning propagandistic use to which Islamochristians can be put. Naim Ateek is the go-to guy for the Christian churches' Middle-Eastern policy, judging by all the divestment measures he has skillfully managed to promote and to convince Christian churchmen to adopt And we all know of the requited affection between the late Peter Jennings, the ABC News anchor, and Hanan Ashrawi, whom he had as a special guest on September 13, 2001, to discuss you-know-what.

Compare, among those Christians who live in or have left predominantly Muslim lands, the non-Arab and the Arab Christians. It is fascinating to see the difference. Christian Pakistanis have nothing to do with Islam. They do not defend it in the slightest. Look at Christian Iranians. They do not defend Islam. They have nothing to do with it. Look at Christian blacks in Nigeria or the Sudan. They have nothing to do with Islam. Look at Christians in Indonesia. They feel no need to defend Islam.

But many (although by no means all) Christian Arabs do defend Islam. This is prompted by pride in being an Arab — or thinking one is an Arab because everyone tells you that if you speak Arabic you must be an Arab. Islam is the great gift of "the Arabs," Islam and the Arabs go way back, and it's hard for some Arab Christians not to end up as Defenders, not so much of the Faith (that Faith being Islam), but of the political attitudes and atmospherics that arise so naturally from Islam, including deep antipathy to Israel.

CHAPTER FIFTEEN

Western "Reverts" to Islam

THE WHOLE QUESTION of who in the Western world "reverts" to Islam — or to borrow a phrase from Jim Jarmusch, reverts to "His Own Private Islam" — is worth investigating. There are the clearly marginal characters, at the bottom of society, such as the Shoe-Bomber, Richard Reid. Then there are the former gang members, such as José Padilla, wishing to find another kind of community for solace, and choose the community of the umma al-islamiyya, the Muslim Believers. There are also the spoiled brats whose minds are packed with YouTube videos rather than with books, and whose parents, themselves comically adrift, offer little guidance, and produce such horrors as John Walker Lindh. (It should be noted that there are wonderful parents who do everything right, yet their children unaccountably fail to appreciate this and become a constant heartache for parents who did absolutely nothing to deserve it.) There are those who, having married a Muslim, "revert" to please him, or her, and may come to realize that there is a bit more to this belief-system than had at first been apparent, and then are forced to cope as best they can.

Some native speakers of English, including those who seldom read books in their own immediately accessible literature, will spend years learning another language, in their search for the picturesque or unusual. Not Dickens, but Gottfried Benn or Raymond Roussel, is what their souls seem to require. A taste for the new and the exotic drives so much in this world. One wants to be different, to display unusual tastes. And in becoming a Muslim in the West, one is also making a statement not only that fortunately is still one that is unusual, but also contains elements of defiance and alienation.

Too many people are Serial Seekers After the Truth. They try on now this, and now that Way to Happiness and Explanation of Everything. Make up your own list: Rolfing, crystal therapy, Hare Krishna, Tantric yoga, Scientology, Marxism, Trotskyism, Sokka Gakkai, Liberation Theology, not to mention controlled substances, sex of every conceivable and inconceivable sort, and compulsive shopping by sad hearts at the supermarket.

Those who, in their Journey In Search of a Final Truth, pull the cord and get off at the stop marked "Islam," may not only cause the remaining passengers to exchange looks of wariness and suspicion, but also slight smiles, because there is also something comical about these Western "reverters" as well.

One suspects that such a person must be just a bit off — just as 20 or 30 years ago one regarded those who joined what were then easily dismissed as cults, and had to be de-programmed, with a mingling of sympathy and contempt. Muslims, however, understandably regard Western "reverters" as objects of great interest, especially if they appear outwardly to be respectable and not the dregs-of-society sort. They carefully toss out the same well-known names of such "reverters:" the French doctor Maurice Bucaille, the Jewish convert Leopold As'ad, the Qur'an translator Mohammed Marmaduke Pickthall, and a few others. For such an aggressive belief-system there seems to be a touching need to be validated by the "reversion" of non-Muslim Westerners — not Africans, not Indians, but Westerners. And the more famous these "reverts" are, like Cat Stevens (born Steven Demetre Georgiou), the better. The Reid-Padilla-Lindh variety of sad sacks fails to impress, but a Hollywood star, a famous guitarist, even Tony Blair's sister-in-law Lauren Booth— well, now you're talking.

But apart from those who marry Muslims and tepidly "revert" to Islam, in an updated domestic version of All-for-Love-or-the-world-well-lost, there are few such "reverters." What motivates those few? A need for the solace of certainty, and of complete regulation of what is haram and what halal, a need to be special, when one is otherwise so un-special? Students of the psyche, get your smartphones ready to record. Islam can trump everything else. Islamic texts carefully instruct "reverts" to Islam in how to treat their non-Muslim relatives, and make clear where their loyalties must lie. No doubt, when the lands of non-Muslims were first conquered, and the conquering Muslim Arabs were dwarfed in numbers by the settled, wealthy, stable, and far more advanced peoples — Christians, Jews, and Zoroastrians, chiefly, and then later Hindus and Buddhists — such instruction was essential.

But of course not everyone dislikes, or cannot cope with, the messiness of existence. And as for the "meaning of life" — well, one may invoke the answer that J.P. Morgan gave when someone asked how much his yacht had cost. "If you have to ask," he said, "you can't afford it." My sentiments exactly.

CHAPTER SIXTEEN

Exiting the Dream Palace

THE WORLD OF ISLAM is a world of nonsense and lies and denial and deception and filial piety that refuses to face up to facts. It could be called, too sweetly in my view, the "Dream Palace of the Arabs." Come to think of it, it has been called that by the late Fouad Ajami, who was too intelligent not to know the truth about Islam, but too afraid that he would be cutting his ties, and his career prospects, and his usefulness, if he were to engage with the real subject that underlies his "we were all Nasserites in those days, sitting in Beirut cafes and drinking endless cups of thick muddy coffee..." (or words, and shtick, to that effect).

The Arab Mind by Raphael Patai is said to be read earnestly at the Pentagon. Fine. But it continually fails to relate the behavior of Arabs, as uber-Muslims, to Islam itself. A better book for those purposes is André Servier's *The Psychology of the Musulman*, last published in 1923.

The sheer craziness that Islam induces is abetted by Western journalists who quickly — too quickly — adapt to it, and silently make allowances for it. Why do they apply the lowest of standards to Muslims and to Arabs, and even at times participate in the farce — as when the most absurd statements about so-called "atrocities" of Americans or Israelis are bruited about? How lazy, how weak, how incurious can these journalists be? How monstrously they have covered Islam: never has the American, or the European consumer of news, in the press, on radio, on television, on the Internet, been given more than a dim glimpse of the thick miasma of lies that one immediately encounters throughout the Muslim world, in minds that find reality too painful. Whenever Muslims can find solace by blaming Infidels, by lying about them, they will.

And they will continue to do so until things everywhere in the Muslim lands become as they now are in the Islamic Republic of Iran — where Islam itself has been on trial in the mental courts of all who can think, and has been found guilty as charged.

This craziness goes on virtually unnoticed while Western authorities occupy themselves only with the most suave, well-spoken, decent people who were born into Islam, such as the late Fouad Ajami. In Iraq, the Americans were partly snookered, and partly wanted to believe, that the "good" Shi'a exiles truly represented Iraq and were an earnest of the belief that Iraq could be transformed into a democracy and a "Light-Unto-the-Muslim-Nations." These smooth men — Ahmed Chalabi and Ayad Allawi and Rend al-Rahim and Kanan Makiya (who remained at Brandeis instead of returning to Iraq after Saddam's fall) — did not represent more than a handful of Iraq's population. Similarly, some Americans believed that Fouad Ajami's example was evidence of the sweet reasonableness of the Lebanese, when it was evidence only of the sweet reasonableness of Fouad Ajami, or that Azar Nafisi's *Reading Lolita In Teheran* was somehow evidence that we should not attack Iran, lest it cause a rally-round-the-flag response that would harm the anti-regime forces in the Islamic republic, or that in Syria we should make common cause with Fawaz Ghadri, or in Egypt with Salah Eddin Ibrahim. But we can't put our trust in princes, or politicians, no matter how plausible, if they remain Muslims. No more being led astray by those whose interests, in the end, are not those of Infidels. It's a different story if they have well and truly abandoned Islam.

In Turkey, for example, the ostensible "secularists" still want Turkey to be admitted to the E.U. And it is understandable why. Yet Turkish "secularists" at every turn have shown that they took Kemalism, secularism, for granted, and did not continue ruthlessly to constrain and contain Islam more and more and more. Instead, they let the Islamists, Erbakan and then Erdogan and their supporters, to cleverly out-maneuver them at every step. Now the "secularists" are feeling worried. In order somehow to make their own positions more secure, they would like to dilute the power of Islam in Turkey by making the problem not that of the Turkish secularists alone, but of all the non-Muslims in the E.U.

The policy for survival of Infidels should not be based on the siren-songs or the unrepresentative nature of those perfectly presentable, highly articulate, deeply self-interested "Muslim-for-identification-purposes" Muslims. It should instead be based only on what will give the greatest security to the Infidels. That means keeping Turkey out of the

E.U. That means not hesitating a minute to attack the Islamic Republic of Iran, even if some in the Iranian opposition believe that "if only" the West stays its hand, finally some internal revolt will solve the problem. But of course, Iran, as a Muslim state, cannot ever be permitted to acquire nuclear weaponry — not unless there is a mass apostasy, a return to Zoroastrianism, or an embrace of Christianity, and a willingness to tolerate free-thinking disbelief. And that sea-change in the minds of Iranians will not come quickly. Meanwhile, Iran is just weeks away from being able to manufacture six nuclear weapons.

PART II

The Truth About Islam

CHAPTER SEVENTEEN

Ten Things to Think When Thinking of Muslim "Moderates"

M ANY STILL BELIEVE, even at this late hour, that "moderate" Muslims will be the salvation of Europe, and the world.

1. Not only Muslims, but "Islamochristians" objectively promote and push the propagandistic line that disguises the jihad imperative (evidence of which can be found in the behavior of Muslims worldwide, where they have committed close to 48,000 acts of terrorism since 9/11) and misleads as to what prompts that jihad —not "poverty" nor territorial disputes, but the anti-Infidel precepts of the belief-system that is Islam. Muslims will not be satisfied if the Indian army leaves Kashmir, if Chechnya becomes an Islamic republic, if Israel is squeezed back within the 1949 armistice lines as part of an absurd "two-state solution," or better still, disappears altogether, or if Muslims by the millions continue to be admitted into Europe. For the True Believers, the jihad does not end until the entire world has submitted to Islam.

2. Islamochristians such as Fawaz Gerges and Rami Khoury, and the late Edward Said, exhibit a loyalty to the community of the Arab people, whose centuries of history are so intertwined with the faith of Islam. This causes many of them to be as loyal to the Islamic view of things as if they had been born Muslim. They stoutly defend Islam-prompted behavior — such as the attacks by Hamas on Israel — and constantly assert, in defiance of all the evidence of terrorism, from Bali to Beslan to Madrid to Paris to London to Washington, that the "problem of Israel/Palestine" — the latest, and most sinister formulation of the jihad

against Israel — is the *fons et origo* of Muslim hostility to the West, and the cause of the murderous aggression by Muslims against non-Muslims throughout the world. That, of course, isn't true: that hostility toward the West predates the existence of the state of Israel by 1350 years.

Save for the Copts and Maronites, who regard themselves not as Arabs, but as "users" of the "Arabic language" (and reject the idea that such "users" therefore become "Arabs"), many Arab Christians have embraced the Islamic worldview, that is, the worldview of those who have made the lives of Christians in the Middle East so uncertain, difficult, and perilous. The attempt to be *"plus islamiste que les islamistes"* — more Muslim than the Muslims — which is the approach of such Islamochristians as Rami Khoury and Hanan Ashrawi, has not lessened the hostility of Muslim Arabs to Christian Arabs. Habib Malik, son of the Lebanese statesman Charles Malik, and other Maronites in Lebanon who have seen themselves not as Arabs but as the direct descendants of the non-Arab Phoenicians, have most lucidly described the Islamic persecution of Christian pseudo-Arabs in a clear-eyed fashion. Indeed, the best book on the legal status of non-Muslims under Islam is that of the Lebanese (Maronite) scholar Antoine Fattal: *Le Statut légal des non-Musulmans en pays d'Islam.*

Any "Islamochristian" Arab who promotes the Islamic agenda, by participating in a campaign that can only mislead Infidels and put off their understanding of jihad and its various instruments, is objectively as much a part of the problem of Islam in the West as the Muslim who knowingly practices taqiyya in order to turn aside the suspicions of non-Muslims. Whoever acts so as to keep the Infidels unwary is helping the Islamic enemy.

Those Christian Arabs who lie on behalf of Islam — some out of fear, some out of an ethnocentric identification so strong that they end up defending Islam, and some out of venality (if Western diplomats and journalists can be on the Muslim Arab take, why not Christian Arabs?), some out of careerism. If you want to rise in the academic ranks, and your field is the Islamic Middle East, unless you are a scholar with an international reputation, such as the late Bernard Lewis or Michael Cook or the late Patricia Crone — it makes sense to parrot the party line of your Muslim colleagues, which costs you nothing and gains you friends in tenure-awarding, grant-giving, reference-writing circles.

3. The word "moderate" cannot be reasonably applied to any Muslim who continues to deny the contents of Qur'an, hadith, and sira. Whether that denial is based on ignorance, or embarrassment, or filial

piety (and an unwillingness to wash dirty ideological laundry before the Infidels) is irrelevant. Any Muslim who, while seeming to deplore Muslim aggression, aggression based on clear textual sources in the Qur'an and hadith, that offers the example of Muhammad as depicted in the most reliable ("sahih") hadith and in the canonical biography (sira) — still defends Muhammad as an exemplary "model of conduct" (*uswa hasana*) and the "perfect man" (*al-insan al-kamil*) — is objectively helping to mislead the Infidels. And any Muslim who helps to mislead Infidels about the true nature of Islam cannot be called a "moderate."

4. What should we make of a Muslim who says that there are unpleasant things in the sira and hadith, and we must find a way to cancel or dismiss them, so that this belief-system can focus on the rituals of individual worship, and offer some spiritual sustenance as a simple faith for simple people. This would require admitting that a great many of Muhammad's reported acts must either be denied, or given a figurative interpretation, as a way to remove them as part of his "model" life. As for the hadith, one would have to argue that Bukhari, and Muslim, the two most respected scholars of hadith, had not examined those isnad-chains (where A reported to B on what Muhammad said or did, and B reported to C, and so on down through the centuries) with the necessary rigor, and that many of the hadith regarded as "authentic" must be reduced to the status of "inauthentic." And, following the 19th century Hungarian Jewish scholar Ignaz Goldziher, some modern scholars might even wish to cast doubt on all of the hadith, regarding them as imaginative elaborations from the Qur'an, without any necessarily independent existence.

5. This leaves the Qur'an. Any "moderate" who wishes to prevent inquiry into the origins of the Qur'an, whether it may be the product of a Christian sect, or a Jewish sect, or of pagan Arabs who decided to construct a book, made up partly of Christian and Jewish material mixed with bits and pieces of pagan Arab lore from the time of the jahiliyya, or to prevent philological study of, for example, Aramaic loan-words in the text (the kind of study that we associate with Christoph Luxenberg) and thereby impedes the enterprise of subjecting the Qur'an to the kind of historical study that the Christian and Jewish Bibles have undergone in the past 200 years of inquiry, is not a "moderate" but a fervent Defender of the Faith.

6. The conclusion one must reach is that there are, in truth, very few true moderates in Islam. For if one grasps the full meaning of Qur'an, hadith, and sira, and sees how these texts have affected the behavior of Muslims during over 1400 years of conquest and subjugation

of non-Muslims, and in stunting the development — political, economic, moral, and intellectual — of Muslims everywhere, it is impossible
not to conclude that Islam is not in any sense susceptible to moderation.

What must an intelligent Muslim, living through the hell of the
Islamic Republic of Iran, start to think of Islam? Or what must he think,
that Kuwaiti billionaire whom I know, with houses in St. James Place
and Avenue Foch and Vevey, as well as the family's palace in Kuwait
City, who sends his children to the American School in Kuwait, and
boasts that they know English better than they know Arabic, and used
to host the late Fouad Ajami when he visited Kuwait, and is truly heart-
sick to see Kuwait's increasing Islamization? Would he allow himself
to say what he thinks of Islam in public, or in front of his half-brothers,
or Arab friends, knowing that at any moment, they may be scandalized
by his free-thinking views, and his candor runs him the risk of losing
his place in the family business? Better to keep quiet, except when in
the company solely of non-Muslims. He has unburdened himself to me.
Secretly, he is no longer a Believer.

The mere fact that Muslim numbers will inexorably grow in the
Western world— unless the peoples of the West wake up and close their
borders to Muslim immigrants — represents a permanent threat to Infidels. This is true even if some of those Muslims are "moderates" —
i.e., do not believe that Islam has some kind of divine right, and need,
to expand until it swallows up dar al-harb and covers the globe. For
if they are still to be numbered as belonging to the Army of Islam, not
as Deserters (Apostates) from that Army, their very existence in the bilad al-kufr (the Lands of Unbelief) helps to swell Muslim numbers, and
therefore perceived Muslim power.

And even the "moderate" father may sire immoderate children or
grandchildren — that was the theme of the Hanif Kureishi film, qua-
si-comic but politically profound, *My Son the Fanatic*. Whether through
campaigns of da'wa (the Call to Islam), that have been especially successful in prisons, or because Muslims have large families, any growth in
the Muslim population will threaten free expression (see the murders of
Pim Fortuyn, Theo van Gogh, the eleven murdered French cartoonists
at *Charlie Hebdo*, and the attempts made to kill Geert Wilders, Ayaan
Hirsi Ali, Lars Vilks, and others). With more Muslim voters, politicians
eager to win the Muslim vote will minimize their baneful effect on society, and strive to have the state yield to Muslim demands, including
the admission of ever-increasing numbers of Muslim migrants, And
more Muslims increases the number of Muslim missionaries — for ev-

ery Muslim is a missionary — whether conducting "Sharing Ramadan" Outreach in the schools (where a soft-voiced Pakistani woman is usually the soothing propagandist of choice), or conducting da'wa in the prisons.

And this brings up a most important problem: the impermanence of "moderate" attitudes. What makes anyone doubt that someone who appears to have definitely turned his back on jihad, and will have nothing to do with those he calls the "fanatics," if he does not make a clean break with Islam and become an apostate, will at some point "revert" to a more devout, and thus more dangerous, version of Islam?

Individual Muslims may have started out as mild-mannered and largely indifferent to the violent verses in the Qur'an, and have then undergone some kind of crisis and reverted to a much more fanatical brand of Islam. That was the case with urban planner Mohamed Atta, following his disorienting encounter with modern Western ways in Hamburg, Germany — Reeperbahn decadence and all. That was also the case with Mohammad "Mike" Hawash, the Internet engineer earning $360,000 a year, who seemed completely integrated (American wife, Little League for the children, friends among fellow executives at Intel who would swear up and down that he was innocent) — until one fine day, after the World Trade Center attacks, he made out his will, signed the house over to his wife, and set off to fight alongside the Taliban and Al Qaeda in Afghanistan (he never made it to Afghanistan) against his fellow Americans. In other words, he started out as a moderate Muslim but then "self-radicalized." Whatever emotional crisis he underwent, "Mike" Hawash found his answer, not surprisingly, in … more Islam.

7. Much the same lesson can be drawn from the experience of whole societies. In passing, one can note that the position of non-Muslims under the Pahlavi regime in Iran was better than it had been for centuries — and under the regime that followed, that of the Islamic Republic of Iran, that position of Infidels became worse than it had been for centuries. "Secularism" in Islamic countries is never permanent; the threat of a return to full-throated Islam never disappears.

The best example of this is Turkey since 1924, when Ataturk began his reforms. He tried in every way he could — through the Hat Act (banishing the salat-friendly fez); commissioning a Turkish translation of the Qur'an and an accompanying *tafsir* (commentary) in Turkish; ending the use of Arabic script for Turkish; establishing government control of the mosques (even attacking recalcitrant imams and destroying their mosques); giving women the right to vote; establishing a system that discouraged the wearing of the hijab; encouraged Western dress; and in the army prevented preferment of any soldier who showed too great an interest in religion. This attempt to constrain Islam was successful, and was reinforced by the national cult of Ataturk as "Father of the Turks."

But the past few decades have shown that Islam cannot be permanently constrained; like Rasputin, it keeps coming back. In Turkey, despite the creation of a secular stratum of society that perhaps amounts to 25% of the population, with another 25% wavering in their support for secularism, and 50% continuing to be traditional Muslims, Recep Tayyip Erdogan has been relentlessly re-Islamizing Turkey. He has built tens of thousands of mosques, expanded the network of Islamic Iman Hatip schools that prepare students to be imams while also undergoing vocational training, and promoted army officers who are devout Muslims, the very opposite of what was done before Erdogan came to power, when those officers deemed to be "too religious" were not promoted. Meanwhile, the second-generation of Turks in Germany have become not less, but more fervent in their faith than their parents. And Turks who follow Erdogan have re-emerged to support his systematic assault on Kemalism. Under Erdogan, a majority of Turks have supported his systematic undoing of the handiwork of Ataturk. Kemalism was temporary; Islam is forever.

8. That is why even the designation of some Muslims as "moderates" in the end means almost nothing. They swell Muslim numbers and thus add to the perception of increased Muslim power; those who claim to be "moderates" may help to mislead, to be in fact even more effective practitioners of taqiyya/kitman. Their motive may simply be filial piety, or embarrassment, not a malign desire to fool Infidels in order to disarm and then ultimately to destroy them.

9. For this reason, one has to keep one's eye always on the objective situation. What will make Infidels safer from a belief-system that is inimical to art, science, and all free inquiry, that stunts mental growth, and that is based on a Manichaean division of the world between Infidel and Believer? And the answer is: limiting the power — military, political, diplomatic, and economic power — of all Muslim polities, and Muslim peoples, and diminishing, as much as possible, the Muslim presence, however amiable and plausible and accepting of non-Muslims a part of that presence may appear to be, in all the Lands of the Infidels. This should be done not out of any spirit of enmity, but simply as an act of minimal self-protection — and out of loyalty and gratitude to those who

produced the civilization which, however it has been recently debased by its own inheritors, would disappear altogether were Muslims to succeed in Islamizing Europe — and then, possibly, other parts of the world as well.

10. "There are Muslim moderates. Islam itself is not moderate" is Ibn Warraq's lapidary formulation. To this one must add: we Infidels have no sure way to distinguish the real from the feigning "moderate" Muslim. We cannot spend our time trying to perfect methods to make such distinctions. Furthermore, in the end such distinctions may be meaningless if even the "real" moderates hide from us what Islam is all about, not out of any deeply felt sinister motive, but out of filial piety, or ignorance (especially among some second or third-generation Muslims in the West). And finally, yesterday's "moderate" can overnight be transformed into today's fanatic — or tomorrow's.

Shall we entrust our own safety to the dreamy consolations of the phrase "moderate Muslim" and the shapeshifting concept behind it that can be transformed into something else in a minute?

CHAPTER EIGHTEEN

The State of Islamic Reform

WHAT WE EXPECT NOW of Muslims is so little that we are in danger of exaggeratedly praising that which is not a forthright condemnation either of jihad, or of the entire Believer-Infidel division that runs through all of Islam. We applaud the Muslim condemnation of Muslim attacks on fellow Muslims, as Sunnis on Shi'a and vice versa, without noticing that no similar outrage has ever been displayed when the victims are non-Muslims. Muslim reformers are seldom if ever asked if they would object to attacks on Jews in or out of Israel, or if they would agree that the entire division of the universe between Believer and Infidel, dar al-Islam and dar al-harb, between whom there must be endless enmity, is illegitimate.

The imperative to wage jihad, whether conducted through terrorism or other means, cannot be eliminated through appeals to Qur'an, hadith, and sira, and any would-be Muslim reformer must know it. The only way forward is to jettison altogether the Sunnah (i.e., hadith and sira), and perform some interpretive prestidigitation that will permit the elimination of, or at least the complete spiritualization of, the many passages in the Qur'an that counsel violence against the Infidels. Unlikely in the extreme.

There is now a good deal of support being provided in the West to those who have been perceived, or often described themselves, as "Brave Young Muslim Reformers." Fellowships, academic appointments, even radio and television shows, can follow. But almost all of them — Ed Husain, and Mustafa Akyol come immediately to mind — just like Professor Khaled Abou el Fadl of UCLA, they are nothing of the sort, but simply thrusting careerists, apologists for Islam of the most transparent taqiyya-and-tu quoque defensive kind — and given to bouts of hysteria as well. When Abou El Fadl saw the apologist (that is, pro-Muslim) movie on the Crusades, he predicted there would be attacks on Muslims. "I stake my professional reputation" on this prediction, said the hysterical self-promoter. There was not a single attack.

A particular offender is the Carnegie Foundation that under the late Vartan Gregorian began spreading its bounty to every Scholar of the House who claimed to be busily engaged in "Reforming Islam." How are they reforming Islam? In what way? Are they changing the texts? Or not changing the texts, but changing how those texts will necessarily be received by 1.9 billion people, not all of whom are quite so impressed with Khaled Abou El Fadl and the other so-called Reformers as they are with themselves? Are these "reformers of Islam" imitating Rashid Rida, or any of the others who failed completely, in the last century and a half, to "reform" Islam as they thought it should be reformed? How could the Carnegie Endowment for International Peace conceivably suspect that there might be something amiss in supporting the "reformers" of Islam who may not successfully "reform" anything, but are quite successful at grant-getting, a skill that is increasingly unrelated, and sometimes in inverse proportion, to merit? They can't conceive of such a thing. Why? Because such reform simply has to be possible, because if Islam can't be reformed, then what?

Self-professed Islamic reformers, or those who see that something is wrong with the world of Islam but do not claim to be able to reform it, of whom there may be some tens of thousands out of a total Muslim population of 1.9 billion, are a thin reed on which Infidels can rely. And only a few hundred Muslims have dared, and always in the safety of the Western world, to write openly about what they think must be done to Islam to make permanent coexistence between Muslims and non-Muslims possible. That figure does not impress.

Even these "reform-minded" Muslims can never bring themselves to write openly of the long history of mistreatment and, in the case of India, the mass murder, of non-Muslim peoples, the destruction of their houses of worship, their artifacts, their histories. They cannot write about what is in the hadith and sira, for to even adumbrate the subject of Muhammad's behavior is too dangerous. Some of these would-be "reformers" present themselves as latter-day Calvins and Zwinglis, in their use of that phrase "sola scriptura." The Turkish "reformer" currently presenting the Acceptable Face of Islam in certain American publications, one Mustafa Akyol, is particularly fond of invoking "sola scriptura," in his case meaning "let's stick to the 'inoffensive' Qur'an, and forget about the hadith and the sira"— as if such could ever be accepted by 1.9 billion Muslims. It is the Qur'an's very opaqueness that allows it to be discussed — for what is opaque there is crystal-clear in hadith and sira. That is why some Muslims even say the Qur'an cannot truly be understood without the Sunnah, but the reverse is not true.

If certain Muslim organizations eagerly distribute the Qur'an, it is because they know just how much of it is incomprehensible even to native speakers of Arabic, and therefore how inoffensive and unalarming that Qur'an may appear to be to Infidel readers, who in any case will not know about the doctrine of "abrogation" and will be eager to focus on the half-dozen Qur'anic passages constantly repeated by apologists including, "There is no compulsion in religion" (imposition of the jizyah on non-Muslims certainly constitutes "compulsion") and "He who kills a man…it is as if he has killed the whole world" (5:32, that leaves out the modifying phrase in 5:33 that provides the circumstances that justify killing). These are misunderstood, quoted out of their proper context, and in no way are representative of the full message of the Qur'an. The same is not true of the hadith or the sira, which are quite direct and easy to understand. Hence Infidels will not be receiving the same free copies of hadith and sira any time soon.

One notices that the most advanced of these outwardly westernized, and therefore rational beings, who publish their criticism of their own countries and regimes, often in *Al-Asharq Al-Awsat* or other London-based papers (which represent the summit, and also the limit, of their mental freedom) they never list, among the matters needing attention and reform, the terrorist attacks on Israelis and Jews, of which there have been many thousands, and in the annals of Islamic terrorism, certainly deserve pride of place.

For that is the real test of a Muslim reformer: does he want to call a halt to the jihad being waged against the tiny Jewish state? For Israel is an Infidel state situated smack in the middle of the Muslim Arab world, dividing Maghreb in the west from Mashriq in the east. Israel puts advanced Muslims on the spot. The Jewish state is not out to dominate the Middle East or to expand its borders "from the Nile to the Euphrates." Such ideas are preposterous. Instead, it has repeatedly offered again and again to collaborate on economic and security matters with its Arab neighbors, and continues to hope, once the war in Gaza is over, to renew its efforts to deepen its ties to the UAE, Bahrain, and Morocco, and to normalize ties with Saudi Arabia. Does Mustafa Akyol concede that Israel has a right to exist with defensible borders? Does Ed Husain? Does Khaled Abou El Fadl?

One key test of Islamic Reformers is their ability to admit that Infidels, including the Israelis, even within the limits of dar al-Islam (a concept that sums up the Manichean division of the world between the Infidels and the Believers) are entitled to a sovereign state of their own. Perhaps they can approach the issue, by first admitting that non-Arab Muslims — the Kurds, say, or the Berbers — have a perfect right to sovereign states of their own in the Middle East and North Africa. It is a hard thing for Muslim Arabs to admit. Can an Egyptian Muslim "reformer" not merely protest the mistreatment of the Copts in Egypt, but also dare to publicly relate that mistreatment to the teachings of Islam, and note that what the Copts endure is what all other indigenous Christians and Jews in the Middle East and North Africa, have endured for 1400 years? And then would he be willing to discuss the 60-70 million Hindus killed by Muslims during 250 years of Mughal rule, or to mention that the Indian and Pakistani Muslims of today are the descendants of Hindus who, forced by immediate threats of death, or by the slower unendurable anguish of the dhimmi status, converted to Islam — is that something any Muslim "reformer" can recognize and admit?

When it comes to the jihad against Israel, how many Arab "reformers of Islam" are able to reexamine Arab propaganda, and to admit to themselves, much less to others, that that propaganda has been based on a rewriting of the demographic history of two Ottoman vilayets— and a separate sanjak for Jerusalem — that made up the territories of Mandatory Palestine. Can they continue to overlook the land ownership under the Ottomans (with 90% of the land in Israel/Palestine owned by the state)? How many are prepared to admit that Jews had lived continuously, albeit in small numbers, in what is now Israel, for the last 3500 years, two millennia before there were any Muslim Arabs to be found anywhere? How many of those "moderate" reformers will accept that while in a few places, where the European powers had been particularly influential (Baghdad in the 1920s and 1930s, Cairo and Alexandria from roughly 1880 to World War II), Jews were allowed to live and obtain a certain amount of prosperity in some Arab capitals, elsewhere, as in Yemen, their condition amounted to chattel slavery? How many might admit that everywhere in Arab lands the Jews lived in a state of permanent insecurity, and even the prosperous Jews of Baghdad could become victims of the "Farhud" (violent dispossession) of June 1-2, 1941, when hundreds of them were murdered?

The sympathetic understanding of the rights of non-Muslims, not just of the Jews of Israel to a state of their own, but also of such Christian minorities as the Maronites, who once dominated Lebanon, which was their refuge from Islam, but have seen their numbers, and power, steadily diminish, is a litmus test for those who present themselves as Islamic "reformers." They should be put to the test: do non-Muslims, even non-Muslims in possession of this or that territory within dar al-Islam, have rights that are independent of whatever Muslims may deign to accord them? Or is the very idea one that is impossible for Muslims, even "reforming" Muslims, to ever accept? Decades of ARAMCO and Arab League propaganda have convinced too many that the Middle East and North Africa belong exclusively to Islam and to Arabs — this is what the phrase "the Arab world" means. But there are many others, both non-Arab Muslims, and non-Muslims, present within that so-called "Arab world." They should not be forgotten.

In Israel, with its Zionist idealists from Russia and Eastern Europe, its refugees from Hitler, its concentration-camp survivors, and its continued flow of Jewish immigrants, both those who necessarily sought a refuge and those who left lives of comfort in the Western world for an ideal, are now outnumbered by those Jews, and their progeny, who arrived in Israel after 1948 from the Arab lands of the Middle East and North Africa. Similarly, the Kurds and Berbers, the Maronites and the Copts, are not foreign to this "Arab world." They predate the arrival of the Arab Muslim conquerors, and should be recognized as indigenous to the countries — Iraq, Algeria and Morocco, Lebanon, Egypt — they now live in. Their claims to be free of mistreatment, and to be able to practice their religion (the Maronites and the Copts), or to maintain their non-Arab identities (the Kurds and the Berbers) without fear should not be ignored or begrudgingly discussed, but openly so, by those Arab Muslims who wish to convince us that they do indeed bear the mantle of "reform" within Arab Islam.

These non-Muslim and non-Arab Muslim peoples are not fossils, their ethnic and religious identities are not to be trifled with, nor should they be regarded as insufficiently "Arabized," meaning that they have not yet submitted to the linguistic and cultural imperialism of the Arabs, which is furthered by the fact that the Qur'an must be read in Arabic, and Muslims must turn toward Mecca, in Arabia, five times a day, when they say their canonical prayers. That acceptance of that part of Arab identity, and the forgetting of one's own non-Arab past, becomes a way to enroll Christians in Arab lands in Muslim causes. They come to see the world through the prism of Islam, and identify, as so many "Palestinian" Islamochristians do, with the jihad against Israel. Even in the West, these continue to identify with Islam — through that meretriciously imposed "Arab" identity that makes some of the descendants of Lebanese Christians, for example, forget that their own ancestors did not see themselves as "Arabs" but as "Maronites" or "Christians," and that many of them left the Middle East for Europe and America in the first place because of the massacres of Maronites by Muslims that began in the mid-19th century, and because of the constant pressure, and hostility, and insecurity, that they endured even in the absence of pogroms.

All of these people, in the view even of "reforming" Arab Muslims of the most advanced kind, appear to have only such rights as are to be granted by the Arab Muslims. This is the wrong way to look at the matter.

It will be hard, but necessary, for those "reforming" Arab Muslims, if they want to avoid a permanent war between Islam and the West, to do much more than they have so far been willing to do. They should be willing to admit, for example, that the recent, deliberate, tendentious invention, after the Arab-Israeli war of 1967, of the "Palestinian people" has been a useful way to reframe the jihad against Israel as merely a matter of "competing nationalisms" — though one would have difficulty finding anything unique to distinguish "Western Palestinian" Arabs from "Eastern Palestinian" Arabs (i.e., Jordanians), or for that matter, from those people who are called "Israeli Arabs."

These "reformers" should themselves point out that nowhere in the writings and speeches of such figures as the Mufti of Jerusalem, or George Antonius of "The Arab Awakening," indeed, nowhere at all in the pre-1967 speeches and writings of any Arab diplomat or leader, does the phrase "Palestinian people" occur. So many of these "Palestinians" arrived from outside "Palestine," with the defeated army of Abd el-Kader in Algeria, with the veterans of Mehmet Ali in Egypt, with the European Muslims transferred by the Ottoman government from the former Muslim-ruled lands in the Balkans in the 1880s. Others arrived from Iraq and Egypt and the Emirate of Trans-Jordan in the period 1920-1940, attracted by the thriving economy that the Zionists had created.

If a small Infidel state cannot be permitted to exist, cannot be permanently accepted within borders that reflect the legal, moral, and historic claims that made sense to the League of Nations when it created the Mandate for Palestine, and, if anything, make even more sense today, then the whole notion of ending the jihad is shown to be nonsense.

You cannot end it only "in part" because here or there, the enemy has proven too resilient. And while violent jihad can be put on the back burner, should Infidels prove too strong, the imperative to wage jihad cannot disappear. Not even if a hundred thousand Brave Young Reformers claim to have done so, with American foundation money backing them up.

The morally and intellectually most advanced people born within the world of Islam, the ones who have been given the freedom, by living in the West, to see the farthest into the problem of Islam, have concluded (and it is much harder for Arabs to do this than for those who do not have their ethnic identity so entirely wrapped up in Islam, such as Iranians and Indonesians) that Islam itself cannot be reformed and must be abandoned. That is the conclusion of Ibn Warraq and others who have left Islam with no regrets. As John Locke and Pierre Bayle noted centuries ago, freedom of individual conscience is the freedom that matters most. This is something that Islam must permit to those born into Islam through no fault of their own — the complete freedom to leave Islam.

Only then will something like progress be made. Neither Ibn Warraq, nor Ali Sina, nor Azam Kamguian, nor Irfan Khawaja, nor a thousand or ten thousand other articulate ex-Muslims, get anything like the attention — much less the financial support of foundations — for their lucid articulation of what Islam is, and why Muslims need to reject so much of it, leaving only the rituals of worship. Why is this? Why are ex-Muslims, the bravest and clearest sighted of all those born into Islam, forced to fend for themselves, while only those who stoutly cling to Islam despite the mental and moral compromises they must make and the apologetics and falsities they must necessarily proffer to non-Muslims, are feted and financed and hailed?

We are grateful for any truth-telling at this point. But only the full truth, nothing but the truth, about Islam will do. And there are standards by which to judge: the lucid written words of Ibn Warraq, the piercing spoken words of Ayaan Hirsi Ali, the relentless debater's energy of Ali Sina.

CHAPTER NINETEEN

How to Discuss Islam Properly

FOR PEOPLE TO discuss Islam properly, they would need to do a number of things. The first thing would be to recognize that the Qur'an itself is only the most important but hardly the sole text, and that the other great source of Islamic beliefs and acts come from the Sunna, which means "Custom" or "Tradition," and which itself is comprised of the hadith, records of the sayings and doings of Muhammad, and the sira, which is Muhammad's actual biography. (Obviously there is a great deal of overlap between these two.)

Once all that has been clearly understood, one would have to undertake the following:

1. Read, and reread, together with the most authoritative Muslim commentaries, or at least some of them (as well as *Umdat al-Salik, The Reliance of the Traveller*, which is a most enlightening and helpful compendium of Islamic law put together for the use of Muslims), the three canonical texts of Islam: the Qur'an (available online in various English translations set out synoptically), the hadith (available online in the recensions of Bukhari, Muslim, Malik, and, partially, Abu Dawud), and the sira (chiefly the earliest, that of Ibn Ishaq in the recension of Ibn Hisham). For the sira, in addition to the Muslim version, see also the many biographies of Muhammad by Western scholars of Islam: Sir William Muir, Professors Arthur Jeffery, and Tor Andrae, Maxime Rodinson, and Robert Spencer. All are readily available.

2. Study not only the texts, but how they are received. Are they taken literally? Figuratively? Are there different guides available by which Muslims reconcile seemingly contradictory elements, as for example the doctrine of abrogation, or "naskh," where later verses cancel earlier vers-

es when the latter contradicts the former? And is that doctrine of abrogation helpful in smoothing out the harshness and hostility in many passages, or does that doctrine, on the contrary, make the Qur'an far harsher in its impact than a cursory reading, and a misunderstanding, might suggest?

3. Study the role of Islam in the lives of Muslims. How potent is that religion, how much does it pervade and suffuse everyday life, down to the slightest conversational allusion? For that one would need to read, and not quickly, both in the historical sources (Muslim and non-Muslim) and in the reports of European travelers, diplomats, visitors, and in modern times, the sociologists who live for several years or more in Muslim lands, or like Fr. J. L. Menezes, who lived among Muslims in India, and tended to them over many decades, and left a record of their observations. One would also have to consult the testimony of both those who were born into Islam, and remained Muslims, and those who became "defectors" from Islam, though intimately familiar with it — such people as Ibn Warraq and Ali Sina and Azam Kamguian and Irfan Khawaja and Ayaan Hirsi Ali and other articulate writers on the subject. Many of these people are presently in this country, and the rest, of course, are in other non-Muslim countries where they are safe from the penalty for apostasy — for now.

4. Study the psychology of Muslims. What does belief in Islam do to one's worldview, one's way of regarding the world, and one's understanding of facts about the workings of the natural world? How does it affect the way one regards the acts, and attitudes, of Infidels? Several books have been devoted to the analysis of *The Arab Mind* (the title of a well-known book by Raphael Patai), but more important is André Servier's study of *Islam and the Psychology of the Muslim*, — but it was last published in 1923, and is now out-of-print. Let us hope that some far-sighted publisher will rectify this.

The assumption, for example, that both Infidels and Muslims regard treaty-making in the same way is simply false. Infidels adhere to the principle of *Pacta Sunt Servanda* (treaties are to be obeyed), while for Muslims, the model of all subsequent treaties between Muslims and Infidels is the agreement made by Muhammad with the Meccans in 628 A.D., the Treaty of al-Hudaibiyya. Without understanding the significance of this treaty, one cannot begin to discuss the limited value of, for example, Israel's signing of solemn agreements (or what appear to Israel and the U.S. to be solemn agreements) with Egypt, Jordan, and, especially, the Palestinian Authority.

5. Attempt to comprehend how Islam promotes a Manichean view of the world, one of endless conflict between Believer and Infidel. This includes even urging Muslims never to take non-Muslims as friends (cf. Qur'an 5:51), never to wish them well on their own holidays, and never to accept even their seeming acts of benevolence as anything other than a sinister plot designed to soften up Muslims — the better to then have them heed the "whisperings of Shaytan" (Satan). That this seems incredible to Western man does not mean that Muslims find it so. The general lack of historical training in the West, and of training in the exercise of imaginative sympathy, among not only ordinary people but also among those who have a special duty to learn, and then to instruct, others (which includes academics, journalists, and government officials), now can be seen to have practical consequences.

6. Study and ponder— for it takes time to have this matter sink in — about what it means to be a "moderate" Muslim. Is it a question of simple nonobservance, nonchalance about the Faith? Is it based on ignorance, the ignorance of an illiterate Bedouin, or Afghani villager, or someone deep in the Sumatran jungle, who knows he is a "Muslim" but has no idea what that may mean? To be a "moderate," is it enough not to be a believer or follower of "Wahhabi" Islam? If so, then must we class as moderates such notable non-Wahhabis as Ayatollah Khomeini, or Hassan Nasrallah of Hezbollah, or Hassan al-Banna, founder of the Muslim Brotherhood? Surely not.

Is a "moderate" someone who opposes the burka? Who opposes the full imposition of the Shari'a when it comes to the criminal law? Is it someone who accepts Western dress, Western ways of doing things, Western technology, and yet still believes that Islam has a divine right to spread across the globe — and that it must, as Muhammad said, come to "dominate and not to be dominated?"

Is a "moderate" someone who assures you that he is a "moderate," or do we need not assertions but proof, given the religiously sanctioned doctrines of dissimulation (taqiyya, kitman) and the existence of people who are well-versed in lying for the Faith and the wellbeing of Believers?

And is a "moderate" Muslim someone who assures you he fully accepts pluralism? What if you suspect that that is only because he is living in the West, where Muslims are still in the process of solidifying their position and the entrenchment of Islam? Could it be that for now he needs the protection of Western pluralism, tolerance, and a highly-developed system of individual rights, but that he has no intention of supporting pluralism in the West when he no longer needs it for his own purposes, and will make no move to ensure that pluralism is accepted in Muslim countries, with full rights for non-Muslim minorities, and the right of freedom of conscience for Muslims themselves (i.e., the right to become apostates without being killed)?

Is a "moderate" Muslim someone who is now "moderate" but who may, at some personal setback, some disappointment or depression or emotional *désarroi*, revert to the idea that Islam provides a Total Explanation of the Universe — and that Explanation includes regarding the Infidel, all Infidels, as the necessary objects of Muslim hatred and blame? Remember Mohammad "Mike" Hawash, the ideal Rotarian-turned-jihadist who seemed to fit into American life so perfectly, but felt a lack of meaning in his life, and then, one fine day, he chose to leave his American family and tried to join the Taliban in Afghanistan? Thus it is that we Infidels, when things go wrong in our own lives, can blame our parents, our siblings, our children, our spouses, Fate, the stars, our cholesterol level, our serotonin level, The System, The Man, Amerikkka, or even, at times, ourselves. Muslims, on the other hand, have it all so simple: they can blame the Infidels.

7. Study how changes in technology — such as the near-universal availability of audio and video recordings, satellite television channels, programs on the Internet — can affect the reception of Islam among those who are already convinced that they are "Muslims" and identify themselves as such, but are illiterate and living in rural communities, and are largely ignorant of a good deal of the contents of Qur'an, hadith, and sira. The Islam of such people will, until the jihadist recruiters arrive, consist of rather casual attendance at a small village makeshift mosque, recitation of the five canonical prayers, and observance of Ramadan. What does the existence of those Islamic tapes, satellite channels, and the Internet do to the practice of Islam? Does it make for more or less "moderation?"

8. Study how the unprecedented permission granted to millions of Muslims to live in the dar al-harb — from the Muslim point of view, behind enemy lines, within the Lands of the Infidels — has led to a situation that was not analyzed by the Western elites who permitted this extraordinary movement of hostile peoples into their lands. These tens of millions of Muslims now in Western Europe have create a situation with which few could disagree has made life for Infidels, in their own lands, far more difficult, unpleasant, expensive (the enormous cost of welfare benefits of every kind made available to those Muslim migrants, as well as the increased costs of security) and more physically dangerous, than

it would be without those millions of Muslim immigrants. Meanwhile, the numbers of the immigrants keep growing: the birthrates of Muslims in Western Europe are more than twice that of non-Muslims — so that if nothing is done, then Europe, well before the end of the century, will contain a sufficient Muslim population, determined and cohesive, that will effectively take possession of the historic birthplace of Western civilization, its art treasures, its museums, its wealth, its land, and its military capacity.

If, of course, we are fighting merely a "war on terrorism" and Islam itself is not a threat, then the Islamization of Europe, as long as it proceeds through peaceful demography and da'wa, should hold no terrors. But we now know better.

9. Study the history not only of jihad conquest, but of the consistency of the treatment of the much larger numbers of those conquered — people who were more advanced, wealthier, more settled, and more civilized than their primitive Muslim conquerors. Are there any similarities in the treatment, under Muslim rule, of the Christians and Jews in the Middle East, in North Africa, or in Spain, and the treatment meted out to the Zoroastrians of Sassanid Persia, or to the Hindus and Buddhists of Central Asia and of Hindustan? In other words, over 1400 years in time, and from Spain to the East Indies in space, are there differences in how Muslim overlords treated their subjugated non-Muslim populations, or do we find, upon close examination, that we are most struck by the astonishing similarity in the treatment meted out by Muslims to non-Muslims?

10. Study the nature of that treatment. What exactly did the ahl al-kitab, the People of the Book, the specially favored (so we are told) Christians and Jews, have to do in order to stay alive, and to avoid forced conversion to Islam, and to continue to practice their own religions? What were the disabilities — economic, political, legal, and social — under which those Christians and Jews, condemned to the status of dhimmis, labored? And what was the treatment meted out to Zoroastrians, as People of the Book? And why were Hindus, who under Muslim rule were at first offered only two possibilities — conversion to Islam or death — later on were allowed to live and practice Hinduism, as a special kind of dhimmi? And what was the financial reason that the Hindus, after the murders of 60-70 million of them (according to the Indian historian K. S. Lal), were finally granted a kind of honorary "People of the Book" status, and permitted to live, as long as they paid the onerous capitation tax known as the jizya, and endured the other indignities of

dhimmi status?

11. Study how the treatment of dhimmis changed, or failed to, under the pressure of Western powers on the Ottoman rulers, beginning with a study of how those Ottoman rulers actually executed the Tanzimat reforms of 1839, or any of the later reforms, in their treatment of non-Muslims that were supposedly undertaken in order to lessen Western (Christian) pressure on the Sublime Porte.

12. Study the persistence of the mistreatment of non-Muslims, including the massacres of Maronites in 1860, the massacres of Armenians in 1894-96 and then the full-scale genocide of 1915-1920, the massacre of Assyrians in Iraq in 1933, the various pogroms against Jews throughout the Muslim Arab lands, all through the nineteenth and twentieth centuries, until there were no more Jews left to enslave (as in the Yemen), or from whom to expropriate property (as in Iraq, Egypt, Syria, Algeria), or to murder (as in Egypt, Syria, Iraq, Algeria, Tunisia, Yemen, Morocco).

13. Study the persistence of jihad, as with the local jihads in West Africa (1804), North Africa (1830s), East Africa (1880s, in the Sudan), and the worldwide jihad declared by the Ottomans in Constantinople in 1915.

14. Study how OPEC oil money helped spread Islam, through the determined and relentless use of the of the "money weapon" in many ways:

* To acquire hundreds of billions of dollars' worth of the most advanced weaponry.

* To pay for infrastructure projects, some successful, some abandoned, some with an outcome still unknown, in Pakistan, Iran, Iraq, Egypt, Libya, Syria (with Egypt also receiving outside aid from the American government).

* To establish a network of academic centers, and posts for individual professors, dependent on Arab money and eager to do Arab bidding not only about the obviously most pressing topic (the Arab-Israeli conflict), but on the entire subject of the nature of Islam, its theory and practice — which is the Great Untaught and Unknown Subject on American campuses today.

* To establish a network of ex-diplomats and ex-intelligence officials, all Westerners, to act as defenders of Islam, helping to deflect criticism from Saudi Arabia in particular, and to keep insisting that it is Western (or American) policies, and not the tenets of Islam, that explain the obvious examples of jihad everywhere in the world — from

the southern Sudan and northern Nigeria (but at least they have not yet dared to blame Western foreign policy for Boko Haram, the Muslim terror group that last year killed tens of thousands of Christians), to Indonesia, where for 24 years the Muslim government of East Timor subjected the Christians of that territory to routine and systematic torture, sexual slavery, internment, forced disappearances, extrajudicial executions, massacres, and deliberate starvation. The persecution and murders of Hindus in Pakistan and Bangladesh were not part of some Pentagon conspiracy.

These diplomats-for-hire also served to muddy whatever clarity may ever have existed at the State Department about the proper definition of "terrorism" and to keep as many policymakers from understanding Islam as possible. These hirelings of the rich Arabs have included such retired diplomats as Raymond Close, James Akins, the late John C. West, and others. As "public relations advisers" or more commonly, as "international business consultants," or latterly, people specializing in "explaining Islam to the Western world in the hope that they may contribute to avoiding a clash of civilizations," as the retired British diplomat Alistair Crooke defined his role, these men expect and receive handsome payments from "concerned" Arab governments and individuals.

*To create large media companies with bottomless funds for its many platforms — social media, radio, television — that provide pro-Arab and pro-Islam propaganda worldwide. The leading example of this is Al Jazeera, that by now has a huge Western audience of tens of millions, who read it online, or watch Al Jazeera television. How much do you think Al Jazeera pays Google to ensure that its report on any event always comes up first?

There is much more. I could have listed ten points, or twelve, or a Baker's Dozen, or Thirty-Three, or Ninety-Nine Theses. I stopped at a Wilsonian Fourteen. That should be enough to jog a few people into beginning to study Muslims and Islam in depth instead of taking the word of those who keep repeating that Islam is a religion of "peace" and "tolerance," or who bleat that Western civilization owes "so much" to Islam, or who tell us that the bad old days of jihad are a thing of the past, and as for dhimmitude, pah! It doesn't exist, it's merely a figment of Bat Ye'or's imagination.

CHAPTER TWENTY

Islam is Permanent, Kemalism Transient

T HE TURKISH government's increasing hostility to Israel after the October 7 attacks, Erdogan's decrying of Netanyahu as "worse than Hitler," the acceptance of Arab propaganda about the "Palestinian people" which the Turks, who controlled the relevant territory for 400 years, know perfectly well is a convenient political fiction designed to disguise the relentless Arab jihad against Israel as a conflict between "two tiny peoples." each "struggling on what compromises to accept" and over the "adjustment of borders" (this is all nonsense, of course, for the Palestinians want all of Israel "from the river to the sea" for a 23rd Arab state) — this is all well known. Less well known is the inability of the Turkish secularists to properly defend secularism against the ruthlessness and guile employed by Erdogan, who has been busy building mosques and tens of thousands of Iman Hatip religious schools all over Turkey. Islamic clerics, encouraged by Erdogan, are busy throwing off the constraints on Islam that Ataturk had so carefully constructed and deployed. All of this should cause a few grim conclusions to be drawn in Washington.

To wit:

Islam is permanent, Kemalism transient. Islam will always be a threat, as long as it has not been so discredited, so weakened, so tied in knots, that it cannot again escape from its box.

The lesson of Turkey is that eternal vigilance on behalf of secularism is necessary, and those who have been the beneficiaries of such secularism are foolish not to recognize that it occasionally requires military force (that of the Turkish Army) and constant reinforcement of legal measures taken against the outward expression of Islam as a political and social force, to keep Islam in its place, since it cannot otherwise be dealt with or transmogrified into something less menacing.

The Cold War gave rise to some comforting assumptions about Islam which were false. The Americans did not know much about Islam. But they knew that Islam was incompatible with Communism, and that was good enough for them. They knew that the Turks they were likely to meet, the members of the Defense Ministry in Ankara, were stout fellows, secular, just the kind you could trust. And Turkey contributed troops to fight in Korea, which led to its being admitted into NATO. In the same way, the Americans "knew" that Iraq under "strongman" (that was his Homeric epithet, until his mutilated corpse was dragged through the streets of Baghdad following the 1958 coup) Nuri es-Said, or Nuri Pasha, would always be on "our" side, and was therefore a linchpin in that ill-conceived military pact known as CENTO (which died a natural death after that 1958 coup). The Americans also "knew" that the Shah was Our Man in Tehran, a "pillar of stability" (as Jimmy Carter called him, in making a toast to his regime on the eve of his overthrow). They "knew" that those Sandhurst-educated, ramrod-straight, Terry-Thomas mustachioed Pakistani generals were, like those Turkish generals, "our sort," and could be trusted to help us in the worldwide Campaign Against Communism, and so much more trustworthy than those Indian leftists, the anti-American Foreign Minister Krishna Menon, and the Left Book Club reader, Prime Minister Jawaharlal Nehru, still smelling of the bouquets of flowers that bedecked him at the Bandung Conference in 1955, where the nonaligned movement was born. The Indians were nonaligned, but the Pakistanis were squarely in the Western camp, as members of CENTO, a military alliance that in addition to the United States included Turkey, Iraq, Iran, Pakistan, and the United Kingdom.

When the Americans have made major investments in military bases in Muslim countries, they have sometimes been disappointed. The Nouasseur Air Base in Morocco and the Wheelus Air Base outside Tripoli, Libya, were closed down on the demands of Mohammed V and Muammar Qaddafi, respectively. There are now much smaller American bases in Bahrain, Qatar, Kuwait, and Saudi Arabia, but they are there not as part of some anti-Communist alliance but, rather, to keep the Arab regimes in power. Saudi Arabia and Bahrain worry about the threat from Iran and its proxies, including the Houthis in Yemen. Kuwait wants to make sure it never again will be threatened by an Iraqi regime claiming it to be, as Saddam Hussein did, the "19th province of Iraq." And Qatar, the odd man out in the Arab Gulf, houses an American base that the Qataris see as ensuring their security against threats to the regime from Saudi Arabia and the other Gulf Arabs, who are suspicious of Qatar's ties to Iran and of its support for Hamas.

It is too late to do what should and could have been done back in 1978 by the American government. It should then have demanded that Anwar Sadat allow America to stay in the Sinai, both to guarantee the peace between Egypt and Israel, and to take over those Israeli-built airbases in a region smack dab in the center of the Middle East, yet largely unpopulated by hostile locals (and with friendly Israelis nearby to provide R and R, medical care, and supplies to American airmen). In exchange for allowing the Americans to remain, Egypt could have been rewarded with more American economic and military aid. But Carter and Brzezinski were dead set on seeing the Sinai returned to Egypt. And an opportunity for creating a potent American military presence right in the Sinai was lost.

The American government, as part of its propaganda campaign against the clerics who hold Iran in thrall, should broadcast lessons about the history of Iran. Those lessons should describe high Persian civilization, beginning with the monuments still visible at Persepolis, a civilization which ended when the Muslim Arabs conquered Sassanian Persia between 632 and 654 A.D. The state religion of Iran, Zoroastrianism, was immediately subject to suppression by the Muslims. Zoroastrians were either executed, or forcibly converted, or condemned to live as dhimmis, with a host of disabilities including, most notably, the imposition of a severe capitation tax know as the jizyah. In order to escape this status, over time many Persians converted; and the country that had been 99% Zoroastrian became a country where 99% of the population is Muslim. Iranians insist that the only reason they managed to maintain the use of Farsi, instead of replacing it with Arabic, was because of the writer Ferdowsi, who between 977 and 1010 wrote Iran's national epic, the *Shahnameh*. about the kings of pre-Islamic Iran, in Farsi. And the influence of that epic was so strong, that its beauty and verbal force helped keep Farsi not just alive but dominant when so many other Middle Eastern peoples, after being conquered by Muslims and subject to Islamization, accepted Arabic as their new mother tongue.

In other words, there cannot be any let up in what should be a relentless and imaginative campaign to exploit all fissures, all internecine warfare, all resentments, within dar al-Islam. Berbers in Algeria and Morocco resent the linguistic and cultural imperialism of the Arabs. In Egypt, Copts resent mistreatment by their Muslim fellow citizens, in Lebanon both Christians and Sunni Muslims fear the power of the Shi'a Hezbollah, in Yemen Sunnis and Shia continue to fight one another, in Saudi Arabia the Shi'a in the Eastern Province, some 10% of the population, have rioted in protest at the oppression they endure from the Wahhabi (Sunni) government. In Syria the Alawites — adherents of a Shi'a sect — for half-a-century controlled the government and the officer corps, and even though they constituted only 12% of the Syrian population, were able to mercilessly crush the Sunni opposition to Bashar Assad's rule until his overthrow in 2025, which unleashed a Sunni massacre of the Alawites. The de facto president of Syria, Ahmed Al-Sharaa, has tried to reassure the minorities — the Alawites, the Kurds, the Druze, the Christians — that they will be treated as equals to the majority Sunnis, but given the massacre in March 2025 of more than a thousand Alawites in Latakia by Sunnis, including members of the security services, and the attacks in April and May by Sunnis on Druze villages, those minorities are not assuaged, but rather, in a permanent state of alarm.

The Western powers should be working to widen these fissures, both ethnic and religious, in the Muslim lands, and thereby to demoralize and weaken the camp of Islam.

CHAPTER TWENTY-ONE

Persecution and Discrimination against non-Muslims in the Islamic World

THOSE WHO NOW are not paying attention to the steadily increasing Islamization of Europe need to be jolted out of their complacency. They should consider the future facing Europe by examining the plight of non-Muslims in the Islamic world. The kidnapping of Christian girls by Muslim Arabs and Kurds in Iraq in the last few years — and the suicide of at least one Assyrian girl following rape by her Kurdish master — is a subject that can be found discussed at Assyrian websites, but not elsewhere. Christian girls have been raped, murdered, and kidnapped by Muslims in northern Nigeria. Since 2000, 64,000 Nigerian Christians have been murdered by Boko Haram.

Hindu and Sikh girls have been raped and then forced into marriage with their Muslim rapists in Pakistan and Bangladesh. Hindus in Pakistan and Bangladesh, and even in India itself have had their shops destroyed, their homes burned down, and in some cases, they have been murdered for "blasphemy" by Muslims. Even Pakistani officials who have tried to defend the Christians have been killed by Muslim fanatics. One such Muslim politician, Salman Taseer, had spoken out against a law punishing people for "insulting Islam." For his pains he was gunned down. Shahbaz Bhatti, the first Christian Federal Minister for Minorities Affairs and the highest-ranking Christian in the Pakistani government, publicly defended Asia Bibi, a Christian woman who had been sentenced to death for "blasphemy." He, too, was murdered.

Asia Bibi's case is a representative one, revealing the full horror of life for Christians in Pakistan, for Muslims "the Land of the Pure." She had been out berry picking with other women, all of whom were Muslims and had tried repeatedly to convert her to Islam. At one point she was asked to fetch them some water from a nearby well. When she went to get the water, she also found an old metal cup lying next to the well and stopped to take a drink. A neighbor of Asia, who had been involved in a running feud with Asia's family about some property damage, saw her drinking and said it was forbidden for a Christian to drink water from the same cup from which Muslims drink. The workers believed Asia to be unclean because she was a Christian. She was accused, falsely, of then making remarks critical of Islam, and was arrested for "blasphemy."

This led to her being sentenced to death. For many years she remained on death row until, in a new trial, she was exonerated of all charges. She continued to be held in jail for her own safety, until her secure exit out of the country could be arranged. Finally, after this incredible ordeal, she went to Canada where she now lives Her story is not unique. Many Christians in Pakistan have been murdered in extra-judicial killings by their neighbors, some after being charged with "blasphemy" or "insulting Islam," and others simply for being Christian. Christian employees have also been beaten to death by their Muslim employers merely for trying to quit their jobs that paid slave wages.

Reporters for the Western media simply have not taken the trouble to study Islam; so that they are unable to provide their audience with an understanding of this faith, and how its texts and teachings over 1400 years have prompted so much murderous hatred for non-Muslims. As a consequence, those reporters usually end up offering "mere" reportage of Muslim outrages but fail to explain, because they do not comprehend, the link between Islam's teachings and the behavior of its adherents toward non-Muslims.

Take, for example, the coverage of the "Palestinian" conflict with Israel – that is to say, the Arab jihad against Israel, where the local Arabs renamed themselves after the Six-Day War in 1967 as the "Palestinian people," and with help from Edward Said, Rashid Khalidi, and others made everyone forget the following:

1. Many of the Jews now in Israel came from Yemen, Iraq, Syria, Egypt, Morocco, Iran, and elsewhere in the Muslim world, where for 1400 years they were cruelly mistreated as dhimmis (and in some places, such as Yemen, as chattel slaves) — and not from Europe.

2. More than 90% of the land of what became Mandatory Palestine had been owned by the Ottoman state, and then passed to the successor

authorities, first to the government of Mandatory Palestine, and then to the state of Israel. The small amount that was privately owned was bought and paid for by the Jewish National Fund, and other Samaritan organizations, often at exceedingly high costs, from absentee Arab landlords — not a single dunam of land was appropriated until the 1948 attack on the nascent Jewish state by five Arab armies.

3. The ruin and desolation in the territory that became Mandatory Palestine was testified to by European and American travelers to the Holy Land, from Lamartine and Chateaubriand to Melville and Mark Twain. Lamartine, reporting on his visit to the Holy Land in 1835, in *A Journey to the Holy Land,* wrote that "outside the gates of Jerusalem, we saw indeed no living object, heard no living sound. We found the same void, the same silence … as we should have expected before the entombed gates of Pompeii … a complete, eternal silence reigns in the town, on the highways, in the country … the tomb of an entire people."

Mark Twain visited Palestine in 1867. He described his visit in *Innocents Abroad*: "There was hardly a tree or a shrub anywhere. Even the olive and the cactus, those fast friends of a worthless soil, had almost deserted the country.

"A desolation is here that not even imagination can grace with the pomp of life and action. We reached Tabor safely. We never saw a human being on the whole route."

Palestine sits in sackcloth and ashes. Over it broods the spell of a curse that has withered its fields and fettered its energies. Palestine is desolate and unlovely.

4. The Treaty of al-Hudaibiyya in 628 A.D. remains the model for all subsequent treaty-making by Muslims with non-Muslims. In that year Muhammad made a "truce" treaty with the Meccans, recognizing the rights of the growing community of Muslims in Medina, and their right, too, to make a pilgrimage — not the hajj — to Mecca. The treaty was to last 10 years, but after only 18 months, sensing that his forces had grown stronger than the Meccans, Muhammad broke the truce treaty, attacked the Meccans, and defeated them. That treaty is held up by Muslims as an example of Muhammad's cleverness in lulling the Meccans into complacency, and then launching his surprise attack. In Western lands, the ruling principle for treaty-making is *Pacta sunt servanda* — treaties are to be obeyed. In Muslim jurisprudence, treaties with non-Muslims can be broken by the Muslim side whenever it is advantageous for them to do so. This treaty-breaking is discussed at length in the exhaustive study

by the Iraqi scholar, Majid Khadduri, *War and Peace in the Law of Islam*.

Now we come to the recent discussion in the West of Christians in Arab lands. In Lebanon, for example, during the Civil War that lasted from 1975 to 1990, it was quite something to observe the evident want not only of sympathy, but of any understanding, of what the Maronites and other Christians were facing in Lebanon. They were consistently described as "right-wing" Christians, though that epithet was meaningless. What made Christian farmers and peasants in Damour, with hundreds massacred by the PLO, into "right-wingers?" Nothing at all, except that the Homeric epithet is used as an all-purpose damning device by a credulous media that took the Muslim side in the Lebanese civil war.

As for the Copts in Egypt, who bothered, under the reign of Saint Sadat, either to report on, or to note the significance of, the self-imposed internal exile of the late Coptic Pope Shenouda, who with this dramatic move was trying to draw international attention to the persecution of the Copts. His attempt failed. The Copts never made common cause with Egyptian Jews, nor did the Assyrians in Iraq do so with Iraqi Jews. That pioneering scholar of dhimmitude, Bat Ye'or, has noted a consistent pattern among the various dhimmi communities that, instead of identifying with and helping each other, tried to strike their separate deals with the Muslim overlords who terrorized them.

And if the treatment of the Maronites in the world press was unsympathetic, and that of the Copts nearly as unfeeling, so have been the handful of reports on the Assyrian and Chaldean Christians in Iraq. They are the true indigenes, the descendants of those who were in Mesopotamia long before the Muslim Arabs arrived and relentlessly managed to Islamize and then to Arabize, most of the non-Muslim and non-Arab peoples. The remnant that managed to survive both as Christians and non-Arabs — the Assyrians and Chaldeans — were marginalized again after their American protectors left Iraq, the victims of executions, forced displacement campaigns, torture, violence, the target of Sunni Islamist groups like ISIS and Al Qaeda, and sometimes, too, the subjects of attacks from ordinary Iraqis. In 2003, there were 1.3 million Christians in Iraq; today there are fewer than 250,000. How many will there be in 2030?

The Kurds, themselves victims of Arab Muslims, have been painted in the American press as worthy of our sympathy and support. Syrian Kurds have been our most effective allies against ISIS. If the Americans were to decide to help Kurdish separatists attain a state of their own — they are now spread out between Turkey, Iran, Iraq, and Syria — it will

be less out of sentimental reasons, and more out of the cold calculation that a free Kurdistan will weaken those states (Iraq, Iran, Syria, and
Turkey), not one of which can now be considered a friend of the West.
There are 40 million Kurds in the Middle East; they deserve a state of
their own. Far better to work for a free Kurdistan whose existence would
weaken our enemies, than spend time on aiding the Arabs to squeeze
the Jewish state back within the 1949 armistice lines, as a waystation
on the road to expelling the Jews "from the river to the sea" in order to
create a 23rd Arab state.

It should also get the American public thinking about all the
minorities in the Middle East and North Africa, either non-Muslim
or non-Arab Muslim, that deserve our diplomatic support. Lebanese
Christians are hanging on; they need to be armed to be able to defend
their villages against Muslim enemies, including Hezbollah. Perhaps
Christians from Iraq and Syria could, instead of leaving the Middle East,
move to the Christian parts of Lebanon, and be supplied with American
weapons to keep the Muslim wolf at the door. An independent Kurdistan might also inspire Berber separatists in Algeria. An independent
Berber state in the Kabyle region of Algeria was discussed by the celebrated Berber writer Kateb Yacine (1929-1989), who hated the forced
Arabization and cultural oppression of the Berbers by the Arabs, and
since his death, Berbers both in France and in Algeria have made his
work the focus of their attention.

As is well known, the European powers attempted to force the Ottoman government to begin treating its non-Muslim populations with
decency. That government proved most reluctant to do so, and again
and again European pressure had to be brought to bear long after the famous Tanzimat "reforms" were initially declared in 1839 and continued
through the 1870s. In the end as part of the government's modernizing
of the army and civilian institutions, non-Muslims were declared to be
equal citizens with Muslims, and the dhimmi status they had endured
for so long was ended.

The 1869 massacre of Armenians and of other Christians (chiefly
Maronites, who were not then limited to Lebanon) by Kurds, was followed in 1894-96 by the massacres of Armenians by Turks that served
as a kind of prelude to the 1915-1922 genocide. Eyewitness accounts by
American missionaries testify to the role of the Kurds in this massacre
as well, and there were a number of books brimful of such collections of
American outrage in the 1890s. In the later genocide, Kurds took part
enthusiastically. And why not? This was a war not just of Turks against

Armenians, but of Muslims against the "giavour" (Christians).

As is well known, many of the Jews in the Middle East endured the status of virtual slavery, chattel slaves who could be killed at will. This practice was especially common in Yemen. The scholar R. S. Serjeant's articles on Yemeni Jews reveal a horrifying practice: If a Jew. belonging to Arab Tribe A, was killed by a member of Arab Tribe B, then an Arab of Tribe A could, in revenge, kill a Jew belonging to Tribe B.

In Kurdistan, too, the Jews lived as virtual slaves, the result of centuries of Islam. But how many are aware that the so-called "Kurdish Jews" were, in fact, simply Jews who were owned as slaves by Kurdish masters, and whose lives, and property, could be disposed of at will?

American soldiers and officials who served in Iraq may be aware that the Iraqi Christians, Chaldeans and Assyrians and Armenians, had to be extremely careful about what they said and what they did, always aware that the Muslims were observing them. They were in a peculiar position. While Saddam Hussein was in power, his household staff, including his food-tasters, chauffeurs, and maids, were largely comprised of Christians who, after his toppling, fulfilled the same function for American officials in the Green Zone. Saddam had employed them not because he was a wise and tolerant man, but because he was cunning, and knew that of all the groups in Iraq, it was the Christians who were the most vulnerable to persecution, and would be no threat to his regime, unlike his Muslim enemies, both Sunni and Shi'a. The Christians needed his protection, and he needed them because they were the one group that could be trusted not to betray him.

PART III

Islam for Infidels

CHAPTER TWENTY-TWO

Taqiyya and Tu Quoque

THE RETICENCE about what Islam actually teaches and what its adherents intend, has been largely responsible for the plight of Europe today, with tens of millions of Muslims already living throughout Europe and more arriving every day. What did Angela Merkel know about Islam when in 2015 she welcomed more than a million Muslims into Germany with her foolish insistence that "Wir schaffen das!" — "We Can Do This!" No, it turns out that the Germans can't.

Consider what NPR was telling its audience about Islam two decades ago. From NPR's *All Things Considered*, January 7, 2005: "Jihad" is one of the few Arabic words used in English. It means "spiritual struggle," but many Muslims have pointed out that "jihad" is almost always used in English in the context of terrorism, even though the actual meaning is broader. Commentator Anisa Mehdi would like to propose a word that could be used instead of "jihad." From NPR:

> Anisa Mehdi, a guest on NPR's All Things Considered, suggested that for the word "Jihad" — possibly the word of greatest significance in the texts, and history, of Islam — another word could be used. For Muslims, she insisted, were made uneasy by the continued use of this word "in the context of terrorism" when its "actual meaning is broader." And so, to prevent unnecessary harm to Islam's image, she asks if it might not be possible to avoid the word "Jihad" altogether.[1]

---

1 "Muslims," *Frontline* Program #2020, May 9, 2002
https://www.pbs.org/wgbh/pages/frontline/shows/muslims/etc/script.html.

Mehdi had a point. And we will sharpen her point, with a pen-cil-sharpener of our own choosing. But first it would be useful to de-scribe the current state of Infidel knowledge about Islam, and of Mus-lim attempts to shape or limit that knowledge. An army of apologists for Islam, both Muslim and non-Muslim, is abroad in the land today, yet some Infidels, thankfully, by now are no longer willing to follow the apologists' script. Some appear determined to educate themselves, rather than rely on the Interfaith Outreach Programs of local imams in local mosques or, for that matter, of suave Muslims on National Pub-lic Radio. Not everyone seems quite as willing, as they once were, to swallow the pabulum of Islam-embracing Karen Armstrong or the as-surances that "Islam has been misunderstood" from John Esposito, the Saudi-supported former director of what since 2006 has been known as the "Prince Alwaleed Center for Muslim-Christian Understanding."

Infidels have discovered websites where four or even five Qur'anic translations are laid out for comparative reading, a horizontal pentapla. At the same site, or at many others, Infidels can now read for themselves hundreds of the most important hadith (the sayings and acts of Muham-mad), as collected and catalogued according to their relative authentic-ity by such trusted hadith-compilers, or muhaddithin, as Bukhari and Muslim. In addition to reading Qur'an and hadith, Infidels can read the sira, or life of Muhammad. As the Model of Conduct (uswa hasana) and the Perfect Man (al-insan al-kamil), the figure of Muhammad is at the center of Islam, and everything he is reported to have done or said, or even remained silent about, in 7th century Arabia, remains as vivid, compelling, and emulous for Muslims today as it has for Muslims over the past 1400 years.

And finally, not content with reading Qur'an and hadith and sira, those Infidels have embarked on learning about the history of jihad-con-quest of those vast lands where, far more numerous, settled, wealthy, and advanced populations of Christians, Jews, Zoroastrians, Hindus, and Buddhists all lived, and upon conquest, when not killed or forci-bly converted at once to Islam, were permitted to live as "dhimmis," as non-Muslims under Muslim rule were called, subject to carefully elab-orated financial, legal, political, and social disabilities that made life for them one of humiliation, degradation, and physical insecurity.

It has been quite an effort to prevent Infidels from getting the wrong (that is to say, the right) impression of Islam, at least until such time as Muslims in the West currently singing the praises of "pluralism" no longer have any need for Infidel good will and tolerance. To date, the twin techniques of taqiyya and tu quoque have been relied on. "Taqiyya" is the religiously sanctioned doctrine, with its origins in Shi'a Islam but now practiced by non-Shi'a as well, of deliberate dissimulation about religious matters that may be undertaken to protect both Islam, and the Believers. A related term, of broader application, is "kitman," which is defined as "mental reservation." An example of "taqiyya" would be the insistence of a Muslim apologist that "of course" there is freedom of conscience in Islam, and then quoting that Qur'anic verse — "There shall be no compulsion in religion."

But the impression given will be false, for there has been no mention of the Muslim doctrine of abrogation, or naskh, whereby such an early verse as that about "no compulsion in religion" has been cancelled out by later, far more intolerant and malevolent verses. In any case, history shows that within Islam there is, and always has been, "compulsion in religion" for Muslims, and for non-Muslims. The "compulsion" for Muslims comes from the treatment of apostasy as an act punishable by death. And though "dhimmis" are allowed to practice their religion, they do so under conditions of such burdens and restrictions that many, not as an act of conscience but rather as a response to inexorable Muslim pressure, have converted (or "reverted") to Islam.

"Kitman" is close to "taqiyya," but rather than outright dissimulation, it consists in telling only a part of the truth, with "mental reservation" justifying the omission of the rest. One example may suffice. When a Muslim maintains that "jihad" really means "a spiritual struggle," and fails to add that this definition is a recent one in Islam (little more than a century old), he misleads by holding back that information and is practicing "kitman." When he adduces, in support of this doubtful proposition, the hadith in which Muhammad, returning home from one of his many battles, is reported to have said (as known from a chain of transmitters, or *isnad*), that he had returned from "the Lesser Jihad to the Greater Jihad" and does not add what he also knows to be true, that this is a "weak" hadith, regarded by the most-respected muhaddithin as of doubtful authenticity, he is further practicing "kitman."

The use of the word in Qur'an and hadith, and constantly through 1400 years of Muslim history, has certainly endowed the word "jihad" with a meaning of struggle, usually through military means, to expand the domain of Islam. Almost all Muslims understand that "warfare" (qital, qatala) is the essential meaning of the word. But Infidels, who prefer to think otherwise, have eagerly snapped up little guides such as that put out a few years ago by Karen Armstrong, a compleat apologist and no scholar of Islam, who made sure to quote that hadith in support of her proposition that jihad is a "spiritual struggle." The meaning of words comes from their common and accepted usage, not from what someone wishes to convince us should, for the purpose of a temporarily comforting harmony, be believed to be the meaning.

Jihad as military conquest is of course discussed in the Qur'an and hadith, and in the commentaries on the Qur'an. And while "qital" or combat is mentioned 27 times in the Qur'an, other instruments of jihad are also commonly discussed; any Islamic website will provide examples. One is the use of "wealth" to create the conditions that will help to spread Islam. Another is the use of "pen, speech" — persuasion, propaganda — to spread Islam. Still another instrument of jihad discussed, for example, in the pages of Muslim newspapers, is the use of demography as a weapon of jihad. Muslim populations within the *bilad al-kufr*, or Lands of the Infidels, are seen as helping to spread the faith through da'wa, the Call to Islam, and in their own increasing presence within Infidel lands, both contributing to the inexorable spread of Islam.

The situation in the world today borders on the fantastic. Never before in history has one civilization allowed large numbers of those who come from an alien, and immutably hostile civilization, to settle deep within that first civilization's borders. Never before have the members of one civilization failed to investigate, and even willfully refused to investigate, or to listen to those who warn about, the consequences for all non-Muslims of the belief-system of Islam.

In history, the phenomenon of the Barbarians at the Gates is hardly new. Those barbarians laid siege to the lands of more advanced civilizations; if they won, they entered in triumph. Should they lose, the advanced civilization survives. But never before have the gates of cities been opened by the civilized voluntarily, inviting in an entering force of the uncivilized who have not even been identified or understood. Never before have the inhabitants of the by-now vulnerable West made such efforts not to recognize, or to realize, what they have done, and what they have failed to do.

That demographic intrusion shows no signs of diminishing. The systematic building of mosques and madrasas in Western Europe, and the payments to their imams, paid first by Saudi Arabia and now by Turkey as well, everywhere in the Western world, helps to make the conduct of Muslim life easier in that West. Western populations have been trained to make much of "celebrating diversity" and "promoting difference" and constructing, on a base of militant but unexamined pluralism, an edifice of legal rights and entitlements. These rights, these entitlements, this militant pluralism, are exploited by Muslims who do not believe in pluralism. Nor do they accept the individual rights of conscience and free speech, the legal equality of men and women, and of religious and racial minorities, recognized, for example, in the Universal Declaration of Human Rights.

Their current claim to support pluralism is based on the need to protect, and increase the power of, the Muslim umma, or Community, within the West, until such time as that umma no longer needs to pretend to have any interest in Western pluralism and Western values.

"Taqiyya" and "kitman" are no longer needed for Muslims addressing purely Muslim audiences. While in the early days, the Shi'a were afraid of Sunni persecution, and therefore needed to practice taqiyya, today both Sunni and Shi'a, by and large, do not find that they need dissimulate about the nature of Islam for other Muslims. It is only when non-Muslims may overhear, and begin to understand, an intra-Muslim discussion, that the need to dissimulate is emphasized. Yassir Arafat could, with impunity, refer to the Treaty of al-Hudaibiyya in speeches to fellow Muslims. He was fortunate; no Westerners, or even Israelis, seemed to think that the significance of his repeated allusion to Muhammad's treaty with the Meccans in 628 A.D. needed to be examined. He was signaling to his Muslim audience not to worry; he had no intention of respecting the solemn commitments he had made to uphold the Oslo Accords.

Among those who saw no need to practice taqiyya when rousing fellow Muslims, but instead saw the need to remind their listeners of the central tenets and teachings of Islam, were Osama Bin Laden, Ayman al-Zawahiri, and Abu Musab Al-Zarqawi. The canonical texts supported their view of the need for violent jihad. And they received a good deal of support, and admiration, all over the Muslim world. For they were not renegades, not unorthodox, not the promoters of a wild misinterpretation of Islam. Their view of Islam was exactly what Muhammad, Ibn Taymiyya, Al-Ghazali, Ibn Khaldun, and all the greatest Qur'anic commentators, muhaddithin, and theologians in the history of Islam, would have understood and shared.

Some Muslims believe that at the moment, Islam is too weak, and therefore, for the sake of Islam itself, the truth of its teachings should not be so clearly expressed and acted upon. It may be that the successors of Bin Laden and al-Zawahiri themselves will reach the same conclusion. That would not constitute an abandonment of jihad, but rather a prudent relinquishing of terrorism as a weapon of jihad, and greater emphasis on other, tactically more effective, weapons of jihad, such as da'wa and demographic increase. The idea that "jihad" is primarily a "spiritual struggle" would cause laughter everywhere in the world's mosques and madrasas, for Muslims know that this definition is flatly contradicted by their texts and their entire history. Yet, the same imam who gives a fiery speech about jihad can show up at an Interfaith Rally and, with seemingly complete conviction, assure his Infidel audience that, of course, "jihad" refers only to "a spiritual struggle." This kind of thing is second nature.

Infidels need to understand that however wary they may pride themselves on being, they are still not prepared for the world of the Muslim East. After many decades of work in Egypt, Lord Edward Cecil affixed, as the epigraph to his once-famous *Memoirs of an Egyptian Official,* the following: "Here lies one who tried to hustle the East." Many Englishmen regarded that epigraph as the perfect summary of their own encounters with the Muslim world. "War is deceit," Muhammad said, and those who regard him as *al-insan al-kamil,* the Most Perfect of Men, have themselves become past masters at the art of deceit. It is nearly impossible to find a Muslim who will admit to the full truth of what Islam teaches about Infidels, though occasionally it happens. Ex-Muslims are just as well-versed in the teachings of Islam as those who remain Muslims, for they do not suddenly cease to understand Islam when they leave the faith. They remain the best sources of knowledge about what it means to grow up as a Muslim, in a Muslim society, enveloped in the hostile attitudes toward Infidels that Islam engenders and promotes.

Sometimes taqiyya is not enough. Muslim spokesmen often attempt to convince an audience of Infidels that Islam is a religion of "peace" and "tolerance." This, nowadays, works less well than it used to, and if an audience shows signs of not being completely convinced, another tack — that of tu quoque — is attempted. Now these same spokesmen, who a minute before were all sweetness-and-light, begin to attack Christianity and Judaism for their own lack of "peace" and "tolerance." They support this attack with bloodcurdling passages from Leviticus or some obscure text, possibly attributed to a rabbi from 2500 years ago.

The Crusades are presented by Muslim apologists as a defining moment in Muslim-Christian relations, a moment in which the peaceful and inoffensive Muslims were attacked without cause. In this version, not a word is uttered about the centuries of Muslim jihad-conquest that preceded the Crusades — nearly 400 years of seizing lands formerly occupied by Christians in Mesopotamia, Syria, Egypt, North Africa (where, among other Fathers of the Church, Tertullian and St. Augustine were born and lived).

Nor is what prompted the Crusades ever mentioned. For in 1009 A.D. the Fatimid Caliph Hakim had ordered the destruction of the Church of the Holy Sepulcher in Jerusalem, and for almost a century the Muslims steadily made encroachments on the Christian presence in, and access to, what was for Western Christendom the Holy Land. The Crusades were not wars of aggression, but wars of self-defense against the aggression of Muslims who had prevented Christians from visiting the Holy Land. That Muslim aggression was also to be observed in the Mediterranean.

There were, for a thousand years, until the 19th century, a constant series of Muslim raiding-parties that attacked Christian shipping, plundering their contents and enslaving Christian seamen. Muslim raiders also attacked coastal villages throughout Western Europe, as far as Ireland and even, in one instance, Iceland. Villages were razed, and many villagers killed, and a million European Christians were kidnapped (see *White Gold* by Giles Milton), brought back to dar al-Islam, enslaved, and often forcibly converted. The Crusades have to be understood in their full context, that of Muslim aggression in the Holy Land, on shipping in the Mediterranean, and in murderous raids of plunder and kidnapping along the coasts of Western Europe.

In Islam the world is uncompromisingly divided between dar al-Islam, the House of Islam, and dar al-harb, the House of War, where Infidels have not yet been subjugated to Islam. "Islam is to dominate and not to be dominated" said Muhammad, and eventually, all of the world, which belongs to Allah, will become part of dar al-Islam. The jihad is the "struggle" to expand Islam, to create the conditions where Muslims may rule, and Islam may prevail. This jihad to spread Islam has lasted nearly 1400 years. It has no end, until its goal is reached, whatever periods of quiescence must be observed because of lack of effective instruments or power. Not every Muslim heart beats with passion for this idea, but around the world, a great many do. Furthermore, Infidels can never know when a Muslim who seemed so Westernized, so removed from such matters, may undergo a transformation, and become a much more menacing True Believer.

The Christian Crusades were quite different from the Islamic jihad. They were limited in both time and space. There was no interest in re-conquering, for Christianity, any territories held by Muslims beyond the Holy Land itself. The Crusades lasted a mere 200 years. The jihad lasts forever, and its goal is to make Islam dominate the world. Yet this difference is never noted by Muslims intent on blaming "the Crusades" on Infidel aggression, and not on the underlying history of jihad-conquest of Christian lands, including the Holy Land, and of the subjugation of Christian populations to Muslim rule and to Muslim oppression of the non-Muslims it conquered. The "dhimmi" was not so much a member of a "protected people" (that is, "protected" from attack by Muslims themselves) as of an "oppressed" – because deliberately humiliated and degraded — "people."

Tu quoque, the rhetorical claim, thrown back at non-Muslims by Muslims, that "you do it too" has led to real absurdities. At one gathering with a Muslim panel and an audience of Infidels, a Muslim professor recently assured his listeners that "Ku Klux Klan members used to sing Christian hymns as they crucified Afro-Americans." No one bothered to point out that the Ku Klux Klan did not "crucify," but lynched, its victims; that the Grand Kleagle did not lead his followers in song, much less Christian hymns, during these lynchings, and that the stoutest enemies of slavery, and then of the Ku Klux Klan, were to be found in the churches themselves, beginning with such celebrated abolitionist ministers as the Reverends Theodore Parker and Henry Ward Beecher.

Though NPR has had hosts and guests who allude to Islam, those hosts, and those guests, almost without exception, are well-versed graduates of the taqiyya and tu quoque schools or, as the taxonomically-minded rhetoricians would say, *suppressio veri* and *suggestio falsi*. Those well-versed in taqiyya insist on focusing on that "handful of extremists," and "radical Islamists" who, the taqiyya-artists assure us, have nothing to do with "the real Islam," the "peaceful, tolerant Islam" practiced by "the vast majority of moderate Muslims." Graduates of the tu quoque academy like to refer airily to "fundamentalists on all sides" who pose an equal threat to one another, and how important it is to "rein in the crazies" that "every society" and "every religion" throws up. But now, at least one invited guest commentator on NPR has suggested that things need to be taken one step further, and the word "jihad" be dispensed with altogether. And should that absurd step be taken, all the king's horses and all the king's men will not be able to put NPR's coverage of Islam together again.

CHAPTER TWENTY-THREE

A Lesson From Humpty-Dumpty

TAQIYYA AND TU QUOQUE are handy defenses to deploy should Infidels show some interest in a critical scrutiny of Islam.

But, strangely, the major press, radio, and television, have not shown such an interest in almost 24 years since the attacks of September 11, 2001. There have not been any programs on what is taught in madrasas, or spoken in the khutbas (sermons) at Friday Prayers. There are allusions to "fundamentalist Muslims" and, of course, to "moderate Muslims," but no discussions of what these terms could possibly mean. Commentators have stayed well away from any discussion of what is actually contained in the Qur'an, the hadith, and the sira, the latter two of which, together, constitute the "Sunnah" or the customs and ways of 7th century Arabia that are held, by most Muslims, to be models for behavior today.

The jihad that promoted and justified the conquest of vast territories in early Islam subsequently led to the subjugation, by the Muslim Arab conquerors, of far more numerous, settled, and advanced populations of non-Muslims. In turn, these conquests led to the institution now known as "dhimmitude," under which those non-Muslims, those who were not killed or forcibly converted by their Muslim masters, were treated as "dhimmis" (from "ahl al-dhimma" or "People of the Pact"). Their condition did not vary much either in time (over 1400 years), or in space (from Spain to East Asia). Yet, when historians of the Middle East manage to spare only a sentence or two, even in large books, for the dhimmis by reference just to the "jizya" or head-tax, or at most, by adding the phrase "and other disabilities," one has reason to question the

135

value of the entire work. The dhimmi is one of the most misunderstood and superficially treated of subjects, not just by Muslims themselves, but also by a certain kind of Western sentimentalist who refers to the wonders of the Abbasid court of Haroun al-Rashid, or to Cordoba as the "ornament of the world" where, as in the rest of Islamic Spain, a supposed "convivencia" among Christians, Jews, and Muslims is said to have flourished, or to the supposedly benign "pluralism" of the Ottoman Empire. What needs to be studied is the treatment of those once-vast non-Muslim populations that, over time, were largely converted as their own cultures and civilizations were subject to slow asphyxiation. Given the increasing Islamization of Western Europe, if forceful and systematic measures are not put in place, this history has direct relevance for Europeans today.

Islam is based on immutable texts. Muslims regard the Qur'an as the Word of God. The hadith, those stories which purport to record the sayings, and deeds, and even silences, of Muhammad, are of great significance. For many Muslims, they serve as a kind of gloss on, and supplement to, the Qur'an, with almost equal significance. The hadith number in the tens of thousands. To winnow the "strong" or most authentic hadith, from the "weak" hadith regarded as of less authoritative, or even doubtful authenticity, occupied many muhaddithin, or hadith-scholars, in early Islam. They worked by studying the narration-chain, or *isnad*, by which these stories were related: A told to B told to C told to D. If A was one of the Prophet's companions, and B and C and D were all known to be trustworthy, then the hadith in question would be regarded as "strong."

If there were some problem along the way, some doubt about the veracity or memory of someone on the "isnad-chain" of a certain hadith, that hadith would be regarded as "weak," and the size of the problem would determine the amount of the "weakness." The collections of several of the muhaddithin, especially Bukhari and Muslim, are believed to observe the greatest fidelity to the truth. Hadith are assigned different levels of authenticity by the muhaddithin: based on the study of their isnad-chains. Now those "authentic hadith" have been fixed in amber, as have the hundreds of thousands of hadith that have been dismissed as lacking convincing isnad-chains.

The sira, or life of Muhammad, the man regarded by Muslims as the Model of Conduct and the Perfect Man, cannot be rewritten to omit those unpleasant parts, in which he, as a successful military leader leading his troops against non-Muslims, behaved in a manner that would cause modern Infidels concern. Muhammad participated in 78 battles; he approved and took part himself in the beheading of the 600-900 prisoners taken among the Banu Qurayza; he ordered an attack on inoffensive Jewish farmers of the Khaybar Oasis in order to seize booty, including women to serve as sex slaves. He called for his followers to "rid him of" — i.e., assassinate — those who mocked him, including a poetess, Asma bint Marwan, a Jewish poet, Ka'b bin al-Ashraf, and still another Jewish poet, the 120-year-old Abu 'Afak. All three were murdered by those hoping to win Muhammad's favor.

Muahmmad married Aisha when she was six years old, and consummated that marriage when she became nine. Yet he remains for Muslims the Model of Conduct, and for fourteen hundred years, they have married girls as young as nine. Muhammad's behavior inspired the Ayatollah Khomeini to reduce the marriageable age of girls to nine in the Islamic Republic of Iran. Khomeini himself had married his wife when she was fifteen.

When such contemporary would-be "reformers within Islam" as Irshad Manji (a flamboyant Canadian who, though born into Islam, does not by birthright possess a thorough grasp of Islamic tenets, or the history of previous attempts at reform) are given attention, and the admiring interviewer does not bother to raise the awkward question — just how does one "reform" a religion when all of its canonical texts, Qur'an, hadith, and sira, are immutable — then the listener is left in the dark, or misled as to the likelihood, or even possibility, of "reform" within Islam. In the modern history of Islam, the heyday of supposed "reformers" was the period 1900-1930.

This corresponded with the revelation, to the most advanced people in the Muslim world, of the weakness of Islamic countries and societies, and the understanding, not always expressed, that this weakness, these political and economic and intellectual and social failures, were attributable to the tenets of Islam itself, and the attitudes and atmospherics they engendered. But there is no such recognition today. Islam is cushioned from its failures by the accident of geology that provides fantastic oil wealth to some Muslim states, by the solicitousness with which Infidel countries hasten to supply foreign aid, including military aid, to oil-poor Arab states (think of the vast amounts of American aid that have gone to Egypt and Jordan), and by the attitude of extreme deference in the West toward Muslim sensibilities. If this deference is continued toward Muslims living in the Western lands where millions of them now live, it will have catastrophic consequences for the Infidels themselves, who will not be able to summon the will to deal effectively with what should be understood as an enemy invasion, by halting further immigration by Muslims, and using both carrots and sticks to convince Muslims in the West to return to their countries of origin.

If there is no grounding in Islam itself, all discussion, argufying, opinion-making, about Islam and everything related to it (such as the Arab-Israeli conflict, or the question of the Islamization of Europe, or the wisdom of the "Light-Unto-the-Muslim-Nations" Project that some in the American government once presented as a plausible, worthwhile, eminently doable undertaking in Iraq) becomes pointless. If commentators, news broadcasters, columnists persist in presenting their views on Islam, full of soothing clichés and slogans about "moderate Muslims" and a "handful of extremists," and cannot be bothered to study either the tenets of the faith, or the history of Islam conquest and savage mistreatment, including forced conversions, of tens of millions of non-Muslims, then Western publics, and their governments as well, will persist in wallowing in soothing ignorance about the most serious of matters — whether Europe can resist being transformed by the inexorably-increasing numbers of Muslims in its midst.

The media have a duty to discuss the attitudes toward Infidels that Islam encourages, by offering the real contents of Qur'an, hadith, and sira, not sanitized or expurgated versions (such as Michael Sells' *Approaching the Qur'an*) or carefully crafted handouts of Qur'anic verses where, for example, Sura 9, full of its commands to attack the Infidels, is omitted entirely. Its audience should not be kept in the dark about the doctrine of "abrogation" (naskh), which will enable them to understand that Muslims do not receive all Qur'anic verses as equally binding. That doctrine of "abrogation" justifies replacing the earlier, and milder verses of the Qur'an by later, harsher verses treating the same subject.

The Arab-Israeli conflict, a matter obsessively discussed on every conceivable news program and guaranteed to receive hypertrophied attention around the world, is raised by every Arab or Muslim spokesman, whatever the ostensible matter at hand, and always discussed as if it had nothing to do with the texts, or teachings, of Islam. But surely, in the Middle East, among Arabs who are almost entirely Muslims, the main subject to be analyzed is Islam. What does it teach? What are Muslims taught to think? Would it not be useful for listeners and readers to come to understand that in Islam, no Infidel state, whatever its dimensions, can be permitted to remain on land that was once Islamic, for that would violate the essence of Islam. Islam, said Muhammad, is "to dominate and not to be dominated."

No land once part of dar al-Islam can ever be allowed to fall under Infidel control again. The whole world belongs to Allah, and to his people, the Believers, but pride of place must go to the territories once conquered by the forces of Islam. The land on which Israel now sits, and other lands, including the Balkans, much of south-central Europe, much of southern Russia, most of India, and of course Spain, were once all part of dar al-Islam, and must again be returned to it. But Israel, an Infidel sovereign state run by the Jews, and sitting smack in the middle of dar al-Islam, is particularly disturbing to Muslim sensibilities. If it remains a sovereign state, not only is land once Muslim not yet regained (as the whole world will eventually be either regained, or gained, for Islam), but the non-Muslims in it will not be living as dhimmis, subject to Muslim rule, and owing whatever rights they possess to Muslims. To make matters worse, Israel is now the state of the despised Jews, who are described in the Qur'an as "the strongest in enmity to the Muslims." And the Jewish state now divides the Maghreb (Western Arabdom) from the Mashriq (Eastern Arabdom).

If the Islamic basis for Arab opposition to Israel were understood, then the naïve belief in that "two-state solution" would dissipate. There is no territorial compromise that would permanently satisfy Muslim Arab appetites. If the Jewish state were reduced to one square dunam, it would still be too much for the Arabs. The pro-Hamas mobs who scream "from the river to the sea" are telling the truth: they want nothing less than the complete disappearance of the Jewish state, and its replacement by a 23rd Arab one. The hostility felt by Muslim Arabs for Jews has existed for 1400 years, long before the state of Israel was declared, and it has no end.

The five Arab armies that unleashed their 1948 war on the Jewish state, which had a mere 600,000 inhabitants at the time — many of them Holocaust survivors, who had then been kept in D.P. camps until they were finally allowed to set sail for Israel — call their failure to destroy Israel the Nakba, or Catastrophe. It was an almost unbelievable victory by the Jews. Israel in 1948 was under an arms embargo, though Zionist sympathizers did manage to smuggle in small arms and to buy some rickety planes from Czechoslovakia that proved critical in preventing the Egyptian army from moving on Tel Aviv. The Arab armies, on the other hand, were well-stocked with weapons. The Arab Legion of Jordan was British-officered, and led by General John Bagot Glubb, "Glubb Pasha." The Arab Legion was the most formidable of the Arab forces, and indeed, it was the only Arab army in that war that managed to hold onto territory — that part of Judea and Samaria which the Jordanians in 1950 renamed as "the West Bank." Everywhere else, the Jews were triumphant. That was the humiliating "Nakba" — the failure of the circumjacent Arab States to wipe out the Jews of Israel, and the flight of 600,000 Arabs from Mandatory Palestine beginning in late 1947, and continuing through the 1948-1949 war, from a new state called Israel.

It was bad enough that the Christians of Lebanon in the post-Ottoman period did not always behave as dhimmis, for they were at least kept constantly on edge, especially when their traditional protector, France, showed in the late 20th century that it had thrown in its lot with the forces of Islam to curry petrodollar favor. But the Jews declaring the state of Israel represented an even worse affront — for by inheriting the Ottoman state-owned domains, Israel possessed land that had once been and was supposed to remain Muslim land. Between dar al-Islam and dar al-harb, a state of war exists until the final spread of Islam across the globe. In Israel's case, it is irrelevant what its borders are; if it exists, it remains an affront, an outrage, a catastrophe, the greatest injustice in the history of the world (as Arab spokesmen routinely say).

The very phrase a "final peace settlement" rings hollow to anyone familiar with the tenets of Islam. For there can be no "final peace settlement" between Muslims and non-Muslims, anywhere. The model for treaties between them is the agreement made between Muhammad and the Meccans in 628 A.D., the Treaty of al-Hudaibiyya. It was supposed to be a "truce" treaty that would last 10 years. It lasted scarcely 18 months, when Muhammad, feeling that his forces had grown sufficiently, breached the agreement on a pretext, and attacked the Meccans. As Majid Khadduri notes in his *War and Peace in the Law of Islam*, this Treaty of al-Hudaibiyya became the model, and basis, for all future "treaties" with Infidel peoples and polities.

Public discussions about Arab-Israeli negotiations and assorted peace-processes never devote attention to the long and disheartening history of agreements and treaties between Israel and the Arab states. The Arabs were not originally interested in any agreements with that Infidel state for, despite the Israeli victory in 1949, they thought they could, within a reasonable period, again attack the Jewish state, and go in for the kill, this time with success. And so there were no "peace treaties" but, at Arab insistence, only agreements that did not recognize any final borders, just armistice lines. Despite the fact that those armistice agreements included a promise by Egypt of the cessation of hostile acts,

more than 19,000 separate acts of terrorism against Israel took place
between 1949 and 1956, from Egyptian-held Sinai.

The Sinai Campaign was launched to end that terrorism; Israel
won the entire Sinai. In the mid-1950s, the heyday of John Foster Dulles, the American Secretary of State, Islam was seen not as a threat to
the West, but only as a much-touted "bulwark" against Communism.
At the same time, it was believed that certain Arab Muslim states had to
be bribed to keep from falling into the Communist camp. Both beliefs,
though contradictory, led to American pressure on Israel to withdraw,
for some flimsy guarantees, from the Sinai. It would have been perfectly
appropriate for Israel not to have done so, for the aggression launched
by the Egyptian fedayeen over six years certainly would have entitled
any state to seize, and to keep, territory from which such aggression was
launched.

Despite Egyptian propaganda, the Sinai was never historically part
of Egypt. Even in the 19th century, the titles that Europeans gave to their
books testify to the clear distinction between Egypt and the Sinai. The
celebrated photographer Francis Frith produced a famous work of early
photographs. It appeared, in 1862, significantly titled *Egypt, Sinai, and
Palestine*. (Modern reprints of his book, just as significantly, bear the
inaccurate title *Egypt and Palestine* — with the Sinai, apparently, now
seen as part of Egypt). An Anglican cleric, Arthur Penrhyn Stanley, published in 1881 his famous *Sinai and Palestine*. The conjunction in both
cases is telling. In the time of the Ottoman Empire (as for thousands of
years before) the Sinai had always been regarded as a corpus separatum,
as desolate deserts so often were, and not as part of Egypt. When, after
World War I, the British managed to arrange for the Sinai to be assigned
to Egypt, at least one well-schooled British officer on Allenby's staff,
Colonel Richard Meinertzhagen, argued that, given its tenuous connec-
tions to Egypt, a good deal of the Sinai should have been assigned to
Mandatory Palestine.

Gamal Abdel Nasser's "good will" needed to be earned if he was to
be kept out of the Soviet camp, and the Israelis were pressured by Washington to give back the Sinai, when it should have urged the Israelis to
keep the Sinai as a permanent buffer — for if it had done so, subsequent
Arab-Israeli wars would have been far less likely. And had Islam been
understood in 1956, the Sinai might even have been a place where permanent American bases might have been established, rather than where
they had then been positioned in the Muslim world, only to be closed
down by local rulers. That's what happened to the Nouasseur Air Base

in Morocco (1951-1963), closed by King Hassan, and to the Wheelus Air Base in Libya (1943-1970), closed down by Muammar Qaddafi after King Idris was overthrown.

There was another chance in 1978-79, during the Sadat-Begin negotiations brokered by the Americans, for America to take over the Sinai. Had Carter and Brzezinski any geopolitical sense, the United States might have persuaded Israel in 1979 to turn the Sinai over, not to Egypt, but to the United States for its use as a military base. The Egyptians might have protested, but only weakly, because they were desperate for American aid. American control of Israeli-built airbases in the Sinai, far from any population centers, and ideally located between the Middle East and North Africa, would have given the United States a permanent base for operations throughout the area.

When he was President of Egypt, Nasser eventually broke every commitment he made to President Eisenhower in 1957 about freedom of shipping in the Straits of Tiran, about allowing Israeli ships to pass through the Suez Canal, about halting the terrorist attacks by fedayeen launched from Egypt. But this was not because Nasser was particularly untrustworthy. No one who had bothered to study the model of treaty-making, and treaty-breaking, by Muslims with Infidels — Muhammad's Treaty of Al-Hudaibiyya — should have been surprised.

So Israel, after the Camp David Accords, gave back to Egypt for the second time the vast territory of the Sinai, along with oilfields that the Israelis had discovered and developed, and several airbases it had built, and other infrastructure, including the resort at Sharm el Sheikh. That the Israelis later on were surprised that the agreements they made with the Palestinian Authority were eventually breached by the Arab side, testifies to their own remarkable incuriosity, in failing to investigate what Majid Khadduri's *War and Peace in the Law of Islam* lays out in such crystalline fashion. It should not have been a surprise that the Palestinian Authority, under Arafat, and then under his successor Mahmoud Abbas, would fail to keep its commitments in various agreements with Israel.

And today Israel is still being told by much of the world to prepare to make "peace," after the horror of Oct. 7, a peace that will be based on that "two-state solution" that is constantly invoked. Mahmoud Abbas, President of the Palestinian Authority, is a more plausible, milder-mannered "Palestinian" leader than the late Yassir Arafat. Yet the doctrines of Islam remain immutable. A Jewish state smack in the middle of Arabdom, splitting the Maghreb from the Mashriq? Not to be tolerated. Abbas differs from Hamas only in tactics, relying on diplomacy rather than terrorism, and in timing. Abbas is prepared to wait longer than Hamas, relying on salami-tactics to first squeeze Israel within the now-indefensible 1949 armistice lines, and once that is achieved, only then should the Arab armies try again to attack Israel Whatever Abbas or any other Palestinian leader claims or feigns, and whatever any war-weary Israeli hopes, or whatever any useful Western tools or fools Muslims may exploit or manipulate against the interests of other non-Muslims in order to buy time, or a temporary peace, no real and durable peace can be made by Muslims with any Infidel sovereign state. It is the duty of Muslims, mandated by Islam and the example of Muhammad, to renew conflict, whatever agreement has been signed, as soon as the Muslim side is stronger.

This means that deterrence, and only deterrence, can keep the peace. The doctrine of necessity, or "darura" — i.e., the fact that an Infidel enemy possesses, or seems to possess, overwhelming military power — is the only thing that Arab leaders, or at least those reluctant to make war, can invoke as an excuse not to attack Israel. This is why, if one were genuinely interested in preserving peace between Israel and the Arabs, one would be looking at every possible way to preserve, and strengthen, the perception of Israel as impregnable — and to do nothing which, to Muslims looking at a map, might make them gain a different impression.

The position of non-Muslims in Muslim lands, which derives from the Qur'an, hadith, and sira, has been studied in detail by many scholars, with its fullest expression the book-length compendium by the Lebanese scholar Antoine Fattal, *Le Statut légal des non-Musulmans en pays d'Islam.*

The history of dhimmitude is laid out by Bat Ye'or in a succession of studies, a history which, in turn, has relied on a great many other students of the subject whose work lay, unrecognized, uncollected, and underused, until she came along, made memorable use of those studies and, with her comprehensive grasp of detail, and of the psychology both of dhimmitude and of dhimmis, created her own memorable body of scholarship.

After World War II, it became harder to subject Islam to critical scrutiny. The Cold War demanded that the Western world find allies among certain Muslim countries; they were even praised for their Islamic beliefs, for those beliefs were seen as stoutly anti-Communist. And so they were. But unstated, because not understood, was that Islam is just as strongly anti-Western, opposed to the ideas of freedom of thought and religion for its citizens, and of liberal democracy that depends for its legitimacy on the support of those citizens. Islam was against Communism not because it was Communism, but because it was not Islam. The enmity and rivalry between the United States and the Soviet Union led to a bidding war for the affections of many, including Muslim states and peoples. If there ever was a connection between the policy objectives of Western countries, and the study of Islam by Western scholars, it was not, as Edward Said charged, during the period of Western colonialism. It was, rather, during the Cold War, when candid analysis of Islam became impossible, for reasons of unrealistic realpolitik.

A second reason for the silencing of critical study of Islam, has been the "anti-colonial" movement — as opposed to anticolonialism itself, that allowed certain Arab states to pose as victims of the same colonialism that so much of sub-Saharan Africa, and Asia, had endured. It was not noted that, except for North Africa (and there, mainly in Algeria), the Arabs had suffered hardly at all from classic colonialism. In the Arabian Peninsula, save for the entrepot of Aden, the small British garrisons along the coast were established for three reasons: to suppress the Arab slave trade with Africa; to prevent inter-tribal warfare (hence the "Trucial" states); and to guard the sea-route to India. There was no European colonialism in the entire Arabian peninsula; it was the British who freed the Arabs from the domination of the Ottoman Turks, in Arabia, in Mesopotamia, and throughout the Middle East. With the exception of the intrepid Captain Shakespear crossing the Rub al-Khali, or Empty Quarter, hardly an Englishman even set foot in the interior of Arabia before the 1930s.

Only in Algeria was there European colonialism, in the classic sense, for more than a few decades, with a settling of colonists from the French metropolis, beginning in 1830, and the exploitation of the land. But there was no wholesale removal of gold and diamonds as in parts of sub-Saharan Africa; rather, this "colonialism" consisted in the revival of agriculture by the French on land that the local Arabs and Berbers had allowed to go to ruin. The French also built the first hospitals and universities, and a system of roads, in Algeria. They spent more on Algeria than they took out. Some "colonialism."

Beginning with the Bandung Conference in 1955 (when it was still the "Undeveloped World" and had not yet become "The Third World"), at every Third World get-together since, various plutocrats of Arabia show up, pretending, despite their fabulous unearned riches, to be fellow "Third Worlders." The farce is permitted to go on, because no one wants to spoil the game of those who are so free with bribes. When one could be rewarded so handsomely for keeping silent, why bother to speak the truth?

As a result of the Cold War, and decolonization, the Arab and Muslim world entered a period when, as it happens, the Western world's scholars of Islam, one by one, were retiring or dying, and were not replaced. Who replaced C. Snouck Hurgronje, or Leone Caetani, or Charles-Emmanuel Dufourcq, or the Rev. W. St. Clair Tisdall, or Professors Arthur Jeffery and Joseph Schacht? The answer is: those who, less well-schooled in relevant languages, and lacking the kind of self-assurance that broad cultivation would bring, were more willing to dance to the tune of Western governments that wanted studies of the "Cold War and Islam" that ignored every aspect of Islam except that it was stoutly anti-Communist. And even that assertion proved, in the case of the less fervent Muslims, such as Nasser, insufficient to keep quite a few Arabs from playing off East against West.

The hatred of Infidels, especially of the Infidel West, throughout the Muslim world, is not a new phenomenon. If the Arabs supported one Infidel power, Nazi Germany, it was mainly because that power was the sworn enemy of the countries seen as the traditional leaders of Western Christendom in modern times, England and France (and besides, Nazi antisemitism in Arab eyes was an additional attractive feature). And if they supported the Soviet Union, it was because that country was seen as the chief enemy of the new head of Western Infidels, the United States. Hatred of Unbelievers, or Infidels, is not tangential but central to Islam, mentioned throughout the Qur'an, the hadith, and acted upon, by Muhammad, as told in the sira. Such Islam-inspired hatred is inculcated with special fervor among the Wahhabis of Saudi Arabia. What has changed is that the American propagandists of ARAMCO (the Arabian-American Oil Company, which enjoyed the Saudi oil concession for many years), who once hid from view the reality of Saudi Arabia, have been much less active since the Saudi government nationalized the company in 1980. The Saudis have suffered from two well-publicized events. The first was of course the terrorist attack on September 11, 2001 by Al Qaeda. Not only were 15 of the 19 hijackers Saudi citizens, but the leader of Al Qaeda was Osama bin Laden, a Saudi, the son of a billionaire contractor who was close to the ruling Al Saud family. Relatives of people who were killed on 9/11 have been trying to sue the Saudis, based on not just on the nationality of the terrorists, but on a belief that Saudi officials provided them with financial support. Another black eye for the Saudis resulted from the murder and dismemberment at the Saudi consulate in Istanbul of Jamal Khashoggi, a journalist and sharp critic of the Saudi ruling family. And there is now much more news in the West about the savage mistreatment of both construction workers and domestic workers in Saudi Arabia. Those rose-tinted sunglasses once distributed by the Saudi-employed propagandists to shade the burning fanaticism of the Wahhabi sun are no longer effective.

Furthermore, the events of the past few years have led to a brandnew awareness of what was always there, but that Westerners, and especially Cold Warriors, willfully refused to see. Some of those Cold Warriors, prematurely congratulating themselves on their victory over the Soviet Union, seem incapable of grasping that another even more dangerous enemy to Western civilization, its mental and political freedoms, its art and its science, now presents itself: Islam, and the carriers of Islam, of whom there are now fifty million in Europe. Communism, like Islam, emphasizes the collective. For Communists, it is — at least in Marxist theory — the proletariat whose interests must prevail. For Muslims, it is the umma al-islamiyya, the Community of Believers, that must "dominate and not be dominated" in the whole world. Though crude Marxist interpretations of art and science, as epiphenomena of underlying economic realities, was officially encouraged, the Soviet Union nonetheless managed at least to preserve the high art of the pre-Communist past. Islam, on the other hand, has no use for most art (sculpture, painting, instrumental music) nor for the enterprise of science (technology is a different matter), which fosters an attitude of skeptical inquiry that is dangerous to Islam, for you don't want Believers adopting such an attitude, that might then be used to evaluate the claims of Islam itself.

Only one Western achievement seems to interest the Muslim world, and that is weapons technology. Though Communism was a mortal threat to the Western world, it was still possible to engage in certain cultural activities, certain modes of expression, even to preserve the artifacts produced under what the Communists saw as a wicked *ancien regime*. Under Islam, there is, and has been, only Islam. Everything that is pre-Islamic is despised as coming from the jahiliyya, the "Time of Ignorance." Everything that is outside Islam today is dismissed as coming from the Infidels who are "the most vile of created beings."

When Arab Muslim intellectuals produced a report in 2012 for the U.N., deploring the state of culture in Arab countries, they noted the tiny number of translations into Arabic. What they did not add was an explanation of why this should be so, whether such lack of curiosity may have been prompted by Islam itself. That is a subject that Muslims are understandably reticent about, but it is no reason why Infidels should ignore the Muslim contempt for all things non-Muslim, except when they can be of direct benefit in the contest for dominance with the Infidel world. Mahathir Mohamed, the former head of Malaysia, speaking to Muslim heads-of-state at a meeting of the Organization of Islamic Cooperation in 2003, offered a view of Muslim "progress" that consisted almost entirely in calling for changes that would permit the acquisition of weapons sufficient to match, and then to surpass, the arsenals of Infidel enemies.

When it comes to free and skeptical inquiry, Islam does a much better job than Communism did in suppressing it — there are no Muslim dissidents equivalent to those in Soviet Russia. A Muslim Sakharov cannot exist, for he would, by definition, be someone who rejected Islam altogether, and he would be executed for apostasy, or forced to flee the Muslim world. And even then, he might not be safe. There is no mechanism, for real dissidents to remain unharmed within Islam, if they go so far as to criticize, as Sakharov and Russian dissidents did with Communism, the basic tenets of the belief. And there is one more difference.

Communism collapsed because too many of those who lived under it, including party members (some influenced by their liberal offspring) finally realized that it had failed, and in the very area where it had promised to succeed — providing a better standard of living for its people. The arms race with America succeeded in bankrupting the Soviet state.

But it is almost impossible to make Muslims see the political, economic, intellectual, and moral failures of Islam, for the system is one of thorough brainwashing that causes Muslims to dismiss almost everything that preceded the coming of Islam, and to fail to appreciate anything in the non-Muslim world beyond the goods it produces and that, with oil money, are so readily available for purchase by Muslims from the Infidels. Even for those who did not attend a madrasa, and who never or seldom attend a mosque as adults, Islam pervades the whole of society, fashions the attitudes, and the atmospherics, in which Muslims live. The cushion of unmerited oil wealth is so plump, that Muslims will be protected from recognizing the failures of their system until the Infidel world's trillions of petrodollars cease to prop it up.

Geopolitics makes strange bedfellows. During the Cold War, the world's leading liberal democracy found itself exchanging pillow talk with the primitive and fanatical Wahhabis of Saudi Arabia. They were not seen as either primitive or fanatical, but as fast friends, and stalwart anti-Communists, and what they did in mosque and madrasa was their own business. In the same way, the United States found itself offering all sorts of largesse to bribe Muslim states to permit the stationing of American troops at American bases in their lands. It happened in several states, and in several of them it came to naught.

There was Morocco, whose King Hassan ll, a relatively enlightened despot, allowed the Americans to continue to use the Nouasseur Airbase that his father, King Mohammed II, had allowed them to open in 1943. Rumor has it that the first nuclear weapons positioned abroad were at an American base in that country. The Moroccans not only received aid, but as happened so frequently, that American aid could be used to inveigle France into topping or at least matching the American offer. During the Six-Day War, when American bases all over the Muslim world were likely to become targets of attack (because Nasser concocted a story about American pilots being responsible for his losses rather than admit the Israelis had done it all by themselves), the King of Morocco announced with great sincerity to his own people that there were "no American bases" in his country, only "American instructors" training Moroccans at their own facilities. In the end, the American military were asked to leave.

In 1954, a year after Libya signed an agreement offering bases to Great Britain, it offered a similar deal to the Americans in return, of course, for economic aid. Wheelus Air Base just outside Tripoli became the most important American installation in Africa. But it was not to last. King Idris in 1968, on a trip to Europe for medical treatment, was deposed by Muammar Qaddafi, and the American bases were closed.

On the model of NATO, in 1955 a military alliance of Turkey, Iraq, Iran, Pakistan, and initially Great Britain (the United States came later) was formed. It was funded, and supplied by Great Britain and, with still deeper pockets, the United States. This Baghdad Pact did not last long. It came to an end in July 1958, when the government of Iraq was overturned in a coup, led by Major General Abdul Karim Kassem. The young king, Faisal II, was killed, and so was the Crown Prince Abd Al-lah (his body hung outside the Defense Ministry), and so was the famous "strong man" of Iraq, Nuri es-Said. A practiced plotter, Nuri es-Said ceased to be that "strong man" when he tried to escape from Baghdad in women's clothes, was caught, killed, and his mutilated body dragged through the city streets for the delight and edification of the populace. In Iraq the old order passed.

One man managed to have served both the *ancien regime* and the new one, and indeed to serve in every subsequent Iraqi regime save that of Saddam — that Baghdadian Vicar of Bray, the clever and unscrupulous Adnan Pachachi (he died in 2019) who was still in evidence, making sly trouble and looking, as always, after himself, during and well after the American war in, and occupation of, Iraq. At the beginning of the 1970s, Pachachi found himself in exile, working for Sheik Zayed bin Sultan Al Nahyan in Abu Dhabi, assigned to help the British scholar J. B. Kelly, the great expert on the Frontier Question in Arabia, prepare Abu Dhabi's case against the land-grabbing local bully, Saudi Arabia. Kelly told me that he once got into a taxi in Abu Dhabi, and was amazed to find on the taxi's floor some top-secret documents that were part of the case being prepared against the Saudis. He then discovered that the previous rider had been none other than Adnan Pachachi. What did that mean? Was Pachachi simply monumentally careless, or was he not only careless, but treasonously providing the Saudis with the case being prepared against them? Kelly never found out.

Iraq withdrew from the Baghdad Pact — also known as METO (Middle East Treaty Organization) in 1958, following the coup in Iraq during which both Prince Feisal and Nuri es-Said were killed. The pact was renamed CENTO (Central Treaty Organization) in 1959, and was composed of Turkey, Iran, Pakistan, and the United Kingdom, with the United States joining later. The organization shut down in 1979 after Khomeini withdrew Iran from the pact.

In Iran, the Americans never understood the permanence and significance of Islam. How could they? They judged a country by the elite westernized members of the ruling class whom they met, and believed the assurances they received. Jimmy Carter toasted the Shah as "a pillar of stability" in January 1979, the very year the Shah fell, to be replaced by the Ayatollah Khomeini. And he, with Brzezinski's help, then composed a letter to the Ayatollah, "from one man of faith to another." For all his delusions of grandeur, and his role in OPEC's quadrupling of oil prices, the Shah was the best Iran could manage, and certainly his attitude toward Infidels was benign. But he fell; Iran reverted to Muslim type, and the monstrous Islamic Republic of Iran was born. When that famous "pillar of stability" disappeared, other illusions went up in the smoke rising from the American Embassy, as secret files were being burned, in order to keep them out of the hands of the "students" who were in the process of plotting their infamous 444-day androlepsy at that same embassy in Tehran.

For decades, Pakistan was the favored child in South Asia of the Americans. The supercilious Indian prime minister, Jawaharlal Nehru, rumored to have been influenced, as a student in England, by all the wrong people (Beatrice and Sydney Webb, Bertrand Russell), and his left-leaning anti-American foreign minister, Krishna Menon, left Americans cold. How much more likable were those straight-backed, straight-talking Pakistani generals, with their fly-whisks and terry-thomas moustaches, some of whom had even gone to Sandhurst, and who could be counted on to stand with America against Communism because, as everyone knew, Islam is incompatible with Communism. The Americans neglected to recognize that Islam is incompatible with anything that is not Islam.

For a long time, in American eyes, Pakistan could do no wrong. It repeatedly abused American trust. In 1971, for example, it employed American military equipment to suppress the revolt in East Pakistan against the rule of West Pakistan. Pakistan has long supported terrorism, largely unreported in the West, against India. It did nothing to prevent the continued persecution of Hindus, Sikhs, and Christians throughout the country; Hindus fled and the Hindu population sank steadily from its 1947 level. Just before Partition in 1947, Hindus constituted 14.6% of the population of West Pakistan. Today they are a mere 1.6% of Pakistan's (formerly West Pakistan) population. In Bangladesh (formerly East Pakistan), Hindus were 30% of the population in 1947 and are 5% today. The Pakistanis helped create and give refuge to the Afghani Taliban, and through the Taliban, gave aid and comfort to Al Qaeda, two groups that brought death and so much woe to Afghanistan. Though everyone from Musharraf on down now rolls his eyes in mock-innocence, Pakistani generals knew about, and fully supported the amazing treachery of the Pakistani A. Q. Khan, the metallurgist who stole nuclear secrets while working in a lab in Western Europe, and made possible what Pakistan proudly describes as the "Islamic bomb."

After September 11, 2001, instead of reading Pakistan the riot act for its support of the Taliban and therefore, of Al Qaeda, which the Taliban had allowed to make its headquarters in Afghanistan, and threatening to cut off aid, to call a halt to Pakistani imports, and to arrange for the total collapse of Pakistan's economy, the American government chose to bribe Pakistan further. There was debt relief in the billions, more aid (also in the billions), more military supplies, in exchange for Pakistan's promise to do what it should have done anyway, which was to hunt down members of Al Qaeda. Even that seems to have resulted mainly in a lot of ostentatious rounding-up of just a few more of the usual suspects, while the Pakistani press and television continue to rant about Infidels, and Infidel Americans. Muslim Pakistan can never be relied on.

And in the end, Pakistanis are not our friend, no matter how much of our largesse they are happy to pocket, and then to ask for more. Pakistan, after all, failed to "find" Osama bin Laden —instead, some Pakistani generals obviously protected him, in his hiding place just outside Abbottabad, where Pakistan's Military Academy is located. Shakil Afridi, the Pakistani doctor who helped American intelligence locate Bin Laden, still languishes in a Pakistani prison; the Pakistani government clearly was unhappy that the Navy Seals managed to kill the arch-terrorist and fellow Muslim.

This leaves one last member of CENTO: Turkey. For the Americans assumed that Turkey was stable. Turkey was reliable. Turkey was permanently secular. Turkey could be counted on. The Turks had fought bravely in the Korean War (and even had time left over to conduct da'wa among the Koreans). Turkish officers were fine fellows, as far as the American military was concerned, and they got along swimmingly with their American counterparts. Kemalism was here to stay. True, in 1955 there had been attacks all over Istanbul on the Greek Orthodox, but that was regarded by the Americans as an aberration. True, the Turks have never admitted to the Armenian genocide — but perhaps they were just embarrassed, and needed time to come up with the right phrasing. After all, Turkey offered the U.S. the use of Incirlik Airbase and listening posts right on the border with the Soviet Union. Wasn't that more important?

But the Cold War is over, and Turkey is not as indispensable to the defense of the West as it once was. Kemalism, we have learned, is not as permanent a part of Turkey as we had allowed ourselves to believe. In his undermining of Kemalism, Erdogan has shown its hold on the majority of Turks is temporary, while Islam is forever. Though like all Muslim governments, that of Erdogan is happy to extract what it can from its American connection, it takes a much more malevolent view of Infidels than previous Turkish governments, and its threatening behavior with the E.U., as its candidacy for admission faced its first hurdle, was telling. Telling, too, was Erdogan's outrageous description of the American treatment of Iraqis as "worse than Hitler."

When the invasion of Iraq was being planned, those doing the planning confidently asked Turkey for permission to use the Incirlik base in Turkey in order to invade Iraq from the north. They were surprised to be turned down flat. They should not have been. Turkey will not cooperate militarily with the United States when the target is another Muslim state — unless that Muslim state is a sworn enemy of Turkey. Turkey wants to enter Europe — that is, to be accepted as a member of the E.U. — and has already shown how bullying it can be to obtain that goal. Under Erdogan, Islam has become unbound from the straitjacket placed on it by Ataturk, and the "reforms" demanded by the E.U. have only helped Erdogan weaken the power of the Turkish army, which is to say, to weaken the only institution that historically has shown itself prepared to defend Kemalism with force. If the United States is engaged only in a "war on terror," then of course it has no grounds for opposing Turkey's entry into Europe. Nor does it have any grounds for opposing the Islamization of Europe, through da'wa (the Call to Islam) and demography, as long as terrorism is not employed.

Now, yet again, the United States has been seeking bases in the Muslim countries. In the Middle East, it has had success with the small sheikdoms — Bahrain, Qatar — because those countries, given their size, want some protection from potential neighborhood bullies, including Iran, Iraq, and Saudi Arabia. But they are not exactly cutting down on anti-Infidel attitudes at home. Qatar, for example, is the owner, and the headquarters, of Al-Jazeera, a propaganda outlet for Arab Muslims that has been responsible, through its nonsense and lies, for the deaths of many American servicemen. But Qatar has not been told that it must shut down Al-Jazeera, even though without the United States base it now hosts and the protection it offers, Qatar could easily become the object of aggression from larger Muslim states in the Gulf. Qatar has for many years provided a refuge for the senior leaders of the terror group Hamas, including the late Ismael Haniyeh, and Khaled Meshaal. Qatar has long been recognized as Hamas' most important financial backer and foreign ally.

Islam continues to be misunderstood by many in the American government. Even American generals with immediate experience of the Middle East, whom one would think might have looked beneath the surface of the apologetics offered by local interlocutors, were fooled. The Americans in Iraq identified the problem in that country as "Salafist Jihadists," which is hardly the whole truth. Islam itself, and not the beliefs of a limited number of "Salafist Jihadists," explains the otherwise inexplicable hostility of most Iraqis to Infidel Americans who rescued them from a monstrous regime, and then asked only that they be allowed to spend more than a trillion dollars on building infrastructure devastated by war, and on providing goods and services to Iraqis. When it turned out that an American general in Iraq assigned books on Islam to his officers, and chose books by the most misleading and blatant of apologists, such as Karen Armstrong and John Esposito, one is alarmed. Apparently, the American government has still not decided to allow critical scrutiny of what Islam teaches, and what its adherents believe.

Now, however, the policy of winning the "hearts and minds" of the "moderate" Muslims has clearly come to naught. By failing to recognize that Islam itself, and not merely some misinterpretation of it, is a permanent problem for Infidels, false hopes are raised, and resources misallocated. Money has been poured into Muslim countries (including Egypt, Jordan, Pakistan, Iraq, Afghanistan) in the vain effort to win Muslim hearts and minds. The United States feels it must constantly demonstrate to Muslims that it is not "anti-Muslim," and that America is making war only on a particular means of warfare, terrorism, and says nothing about the other, non-violent, instruments of waging jihad, a word which the American government has been loath to use. But terrorism is neither the main, nor the most effective, instrument of jihad. Conventional warfare, economic warfare, propaganda, da'wa, and demography are all much more useful. In addition to the gigantic transfer of wealth to the mainly Muslim nations of OPEC, the Muslim states that do not have such oil wealth manage to extract a kind of foreign-aid "jizya," whether it is the states of the Maghreb being bribed by France (and latterly, Spain), to keep their populations at home, or American aid to Egypt and Jordan and Pakistan, to crack down on Islamists, including the Muslim Brotherhood.

The huge sums sent by the United States to Indonesia after the tsunami, for example, were often described as a "chance to show the Muslims we are not against them." But this is exactly the wrong rhetoric. It gives the Muslims precisely the wrong idea — that they can play on, appeal to, take constant advantage of, our misreading of the situation. The United States does not have any need to demonstrate its good will to Muslims. To express such a felt need is simply to signal our willingness to be further exploited. The American government has helped and rescued Muslims time and again. Think of how $80 billion in American aid to Egypt has kept that country afloat. Think of the trillions spent on the wars in Afghanistan and Iraq, in a vain attempt to make both countries into democratic states and improve the wellbeing of their peoples. Think of how the American army saved Kuwait by driving Iraqi forces out of the country. Yet the hostility against us, as Infidels, does not diminish.

And it is nonsense to depict American policy as "one-sidedly pro-Israel" (though, if the history of the area, and the nature of Islam, were sufficiently understood, it should have been). In 1948 the Americans put a total arms embargo on all sides; the armies of Egypt, Iraq, and Jordan, well-equipped, and even resupplied by the British, were the most effective against the Israelis, who had only small arms, and eventually acquired a mere handful of well-worn Messerschmitts from the Czechs. In 1956, John Foster Dulles put pressure on Israel to relinquish the Sinai for some flimsy promises by Nasser. Indeed, it was not until after 1967 that the Americans began to supply Israel with weaponry.

In May 1967, just like Britain and France, the United States could not locate the documents by which it had guaranteed to keep the Straits of Tiran open. In 1973, Henry Kissinger prevented Ariel Sharon from destroying Egypt's Third Army, which the Israeli general had surrounded. In 1979, Carter and Brzezinski, the former whining that he was "sick and tired of hearing about the Holocaust," pressed Menachem Begin mercilessly to make concession after concession to Sadat, who was treated by Carter's team, and the American media too, as a veritable Prince of Peace. The American government subsequently did nothing when Egypt, having pocketed the entire Sinai, failed to honor many of its solemn commitments under the Camp David Accords. The farce with Oslo, including Carter's frequent meetings with Arafat, whose measure ought to have been taken long before, continued — and continues still, with Arafat replaced by Mahmoud Abbas, in the proposed "two-state solution." Yet by dint of constant repetition that "America is unfair," the Arabs have managed to put some American policymakers in a position where they think they must do even more to "win Arab approval."

Furthermore, the American rescue of Muslims in Bosnia and Kosovo — and the general American indifference to Serbian fears of Alija Izetbegovic, whose stated intention as President of Bosnia and Herzegovina was to bring back Muslim rule, and impose the Shari'a, was completely ignored in the American press and television. The vast amounts of aid America has given to Muslim countries, including more than $80 billion to Egypt alone, a country where 98% percent of the population claims to dislike or hate America, has amounted to a kind of "jizyah" — the capitation tax imposed, historically, on Infidels in Muslim countries — that we provide in the hope of winning Muslim hearts and minds, so great is the fear of antagonizing people who, because of Islam, remain permanently hostile to us. Indeed, there is much evidence that when treated not gently, but roughly, by Infidels, Muslims have responded by becoming, if only temporarily, less violent themselves. The British phrase that was always used to describe the Muslim Arabs — "They are either at your feet, or at your throat" — was brutal. But it was not inaccurate.

Many of the American government experts on the Middle East, until recent years, were selected, as Robert Kaplan's *The Arabists* reveals, from among American missionary families. It was enough to know some Arabic and to have lived in Beirut. But what these Arabists did not possess, or did not think they needed to possess, was a knowledge of Islam — of Qur'an, hadith, sira. They did not know what was actually said in the khutbas —the sermons that accompanied Friday Prayers — and read in Muslim textbooks, and memorized in the madrasas. The dense web of Islamic allusion that thickens every conversation, every editorial, every satellite channel discussion, every turn of phrase and of thought, in Muslim countries, was beyond them. They met important Arabs who reassured them: "If only the Palestinian problem could be solved to the Arabs' satisfaction, all manner of things would be well." They were told certain things, even "confided in" by those Arabs. The Americans were, and many remain, naive beyond belief about the Arab capacity for taqiyya, that is, religiously sanctioned dissimulation. "War is deception," said Muhammad. Deception, in Arab lands, is a way of life.

When Madeline Albright told a television interviewer that the "Arab leaders" were "just as surprised as we were" about what had been going on in Iraq under Saddam Hussein — all that mass-murdering, for example, of the Kurds— one had to rub one's eyes in disbelief. Here was the former Secretary of State, confidently asserting that the Arab leaders, too, had been completely in the dark about Iraq. But of course, they never had been. Hundreds of thousands of Iraqi exiles all over the Arab countries conveyed in detail the nature of the regime of Saddam Hussein. Everyone knew what he did, including his massacre of the Kurds. Nobody cared. He was a strong man, an Arab hero, the man most likely to avenge the Arabs against Israel and the West. His murder of 182,000 Kurds in Operation Anfal did not matter; his victims were non-Arabs, after all. But Madeline Albright's innocence was not hers alone. It reflected an atmosphere of widespread misunderstanding of the nature of the Arab regimes and peoples, and of how Infidels, including Americans, are regarded by Muslims. Albright herself was the butt of many cruel and contemptuous jokes throughout the Arab world.

The perceived need for alliances with Muslim states thus limited, and continues to limit, the ability of the American government to see Islam steadily and whole, or to produce a cadre of people who, whether in the army, the security services, or the foreign service, will have studied Islam without the "help" of John Esposito and Karen Armstrong. Only such people are capable of understanding that the continued Islamization of Europe, not through terror but through da'wa and demography, is a mortal threat to the West, and hence to the United States.

One can see the consequences of such alliances even in the case of Turkey, the only Muslim state that, for a time, appeared to be genuinely on the road to a permanent secularism that might further reduce the political and social influence of Islam, though what has happened is the reverse. For the last fifty years, the Western world has participated in a whitewashing of Ottoman history. The treatment of non-Muslims — particularly Greeks and Armenians, but also of Jews under the Ottomans has, in the West, not been examined with sufficient disregard for the possibly ruffled feelings of pleasant, charming, thoroughly congenial Turkish officials and military men. The studies of Rumanian, Polish, Hungarian, Bulgarian, Serbian, and Greek scholars—all representatives of peoples hard done by under Ottoman rule, have not surprisingly been less friendly in tone. These scholars make wide use of sources in the relevant languages of the Ottoman Empire's European domains, and demonstrate the cruel treatment meted out to Christian subjects, and give the *devshirme* — the forcing of Christian and Jewish boys in the Balkans into the Turkish army — and Balkan dhimmitude, their full due. Celebrated historians of the Ottomans sometimes have had personal and professional ties to Turkey, and that may help explain their minimizing what dhimmis endured under Ottoman rule.

One such historian described the *devshirme* — the forced levy by the Ottomans of Christian (and sometimes Jewish) children, taken from their parents at a young age to serve as soldiers and bureaucrats for the Sultan — misleadingly as a "recruitment" of soldiers, and emphasized that, because these young victims were subsequently forcibly converted to Islam, and enrolled in the service of the Ottoman state, the *devshirme* could be described as a "means of social advancement" for Christian children that Muslim parents "envied." Such a view hides the horror felt by the Christians at the prospect of losing their children, as recorded by a number of Balkan historians. The victim's view of the *devshirme* seems to have escaped the notice entirely of at least one prominent historian — the late Professor Bernard Lewis — known for his studies of Turkish history, both Ottoman and modern, and for the range of his studies in the field of Islamic history.

During the Cold War period, a number of historical hells were passed over. The full story of large-scale German involvement — including regular units of the Wehrmacht — in the Nazi mass-murders were inconvenient, at a time when West Germany was an important ally, and even those who had served the Nazis as intelligence officers, for example Reinhard Gehlen, were now relied on, by the Americans, to provide intelligence from the Soviet bloc. In the same way, the Armenian genocide was downplayed, for it would have been impolitic to raise that atrocity during the very years that Turkey was being courted as an ally against the Soviet Union. Only recently have Western scholars rediscovered that genocide, and the American government still prefers to remain silent and not to press Turkey to recognize what was done, not only by the Turks, but by their fellow Muslims, the Kurds, in their genocidal attacks against Christian Armenians for being "giavours" or Infidels.

The Turks were Muslim, but our ally in NATO, just as King Saud was our sort because, as a devout Muslim, he would never tolerate Communism, and told Washington so. No one thought there might be another matter to worry about, which was that Saudi Arabia would never be a reliable ally for the American Infidels. Besides, the oil revenues were not yet in full flood, and even Saudi Arabia did not have money, in those days before 1973, to spend tens of billions of dollars on Wahhabi mosques and madrasas all over the Western world. Before the quadrupling of OPEC's oil prices in 1973, no one in Washington could have imagined the sudden bonanza for the Arab oil states, nor to what malign anti-Infidel uses that OPEC money would be put.

In the same way, the Shah of Iran was America's friend, a "pillar of stability," as Jimmy Carter called him, toasting him at the beginning of January 1979, the very year Khomeini would come to power. Oh, they were all splendid fellows, our Muslim friends. There was that nice Moroccan King Hassan II, and good King Idris who took such care of the Americans' Wheelus Air Base in Libya (until he was overthrown by Muammar Qaddafi), and good King Fahd bin Abdulaziz al-Saud of Saudi Arabia, who sold us oil and made it seem as if he was doing us a favor (but we paid the same price as everyone else), and the dashing King Hussein of Jordan, who drove racing cars and piloted planes and sent his son to Deerfield. And let's not forget the earlier Saudi ruler, King Abdulaziz, who we assumed would always be our stout ally. After all, didn't we have a photograph of him with President Roosevelt on that cruiser, the USS Quincy, in the Great Bitter Lake in the middle of the Suez Canal to prove it? Abdelaziz was fiercely anti-Communist; that was all we needed to know.

After the 1958 coup, Iraq withdrew from the Baghdad Pact. After the Shah fell, in 1979, Iran withdrew from the Central Treaty Organization (formerly the Baghdad Pact). Pakistan was later revealed to be, not our stout ally, but a supporter of the Taliban and hence of Al Qaeda. After Iran withdrew in 1979, the organization was disbanded. It had never been anything like the NATO it was expected to emulate; it had always been farcical and useless, but the West had failed to admit it. But by 1979, things were different. Now it was recognized to have been farcical and useless.

The Cold War has been over for nearly forty years. More than sixty years have passed since the French left Algeria, the only place, among all the Arab countries, where so-called "colonialism" lasted more than a few decades. (Everywhere else in the Arab Muslim countries, any "colonialism" that did exist cost the "colonial" power far more than it received in revenues from the colony.) But the study of Islam still has not recovered from either the pro-Islamic atmosphere created by those anti-Communist illusions about Islam, nor from the lament about "colonialism" that the Arabs managed to appropriate from the real victims of colonialism in Asia and in black Africa.

Arab states of the Gulf that had been failures in building modern economies, as they had been failures in everything else, suddenly were seen as success stories, not because there had been any burst of entrepreneurial activity or the emergence of a deep work ethic, as happened in Japan, and South Korea, and Taiwan, and Thailand, but because the OPEC countries managed to quadruple the price of oil. What happened to the Arab and Muslim countries was that, through an accident of geology, a half-dozen of them became the beneficiaries of the largest transfer of wealth in human history — some 7-8 trillion dollars since 1973. Not one of these states has yet managed to create a modern economy. Take away their oil and gas, and they have nothing else to sell to the world. But the oil money still gushes, year after year, and this prevents the full scale of the failure of Islamic states to create modern economies from being understood.

Still worse, that Arab oil money managed to stave off, for a few more decades, real scholarship on, and critical scrutiny of, Islam. For Arab oil money since 1973 has been carefully deployed to establish new "Centers" of Islamic or Middle Eastern studies, or to buy up pre-existing ones. This began at Bradford, Durham, and Exeter in England; it was extended to Georgetown, in the U.S., an obvious place to concentrate on, given its location and its role in training foreign service officers. Where centers were not established, well-upholstered chairs — The King Abdul Aziz II Chair of Islamic History, The Custodian of the Two Holy Mosques Professor of Islamic Law, and other academic thrones, with ornate arabesques, have also been positioned for maximum effect, hither and yon.

Overlapping with that careful deployment of Arab oil money was another phenomenon, this one coming not from the plutocrats of Arabia, but from the supposed anti-imperialist and therefore, of course, anti-Western school of thought. It originated with Edward Said, who was neither a student of Islam, nor even a Muslim. But as an Arab, he felt that his "Arabness" gave him special insight into Islam, and he, unlike Maronites and Copts, but like many "Palestinian" Arabs, was quick to identify with, and to promote, Islam and the Islamic worldview. For this worldview fit — indeed, explained — the Arab opposition to the Infidel state of Israel, though for the non-Muslim Western world, quite different justifications were plausibly offered. Said's polemical *Orientalism* was, as Ibn Warraq has described it, an act of "intellectual thuggery."

Said deployed personal invective, and an entirely specious use of evidence, to call into question the meticulous scholarship of generations of Western Orientalists. What prompted his charges was, no doubt, that the targets of his fury had understood the tenets and history of Islam too well, and had written their scholarly works too lucidly, as they elaborated upon the main features of Islamic jihad-conquest and treatment of non-Muslims. Said realized that this scholarship was dangerous, both for his own "Palestinian" cause, and for Arabs and Muslims generally. He was determined to stop it. He could not offer any scholarship of his own. He never was a student of Islam. He never demonstrated for readers in what way, for example, Ignaz Goldziher or Snouck Hurgronje or Leone Caetani or Arthur Jeffery or Joseph Schacht had been inaccurate, or prejudiced. Not a word, not a sentence, not a paragraph did he offer in evidence.

Said alluded, he attitudinized, he fulminated, but he never produced evidence that Western Orientalists were practically working for their respective colonial offices. Said further claimed that these scholars, most of them among the most learned, and dry, of authors, depicted the Arabs as "fanatical" and "sensual" and as exhibiting every conceivable vice. In so doing, he often dismissed such important works as Edward Lane's *An Account of the Customs and Manners of the Modern Egyptians*. Said was also highly selective; more than 95% of the most important

Western Orientalists were not merely never discussed in his "Oriental-ism," but never even received a passing mention.

In fact, while he insisted that the Western world had depicted the Arabs and Muslims most unfairly, it could be argued that the statement is true, but in a way opposite from that Said intended. In the last two centuries, where the Arab Muslims have been wrongly portrayed, it has been overwhelmingly to their benefit. One need think only of the allur-ing exoticism of the paintings of North Africa, and the Orientalizing verse of the Romantic period, from Leigh Hunt's "Abou Ben Adhem" (the humble Arab whose name, on God's list, "led all the rest"), and Tom Moore's passionate Persians in *Lalla Rookh*, and in the twentieth century, the glowering Sheik of Araby, Rudolph Valentino, and a host of popular songs and comic turns that treated the Muslim East not as fearsome, but as funny. The list of subject-matter for the Hasty Pudding Theatricals at Harvard, a useful guide to what tickled the fancy of the American upper classes, in the 1920s and 1930s was full of Arabian sub-jects, with camels, and date-palms, and amusing Arabs who are depicted often as comic, but never as hate-filled, hysterical, or homicidal, as Said would have one believe.

All through this period, from about 1940 to the late 1970s, AR-AMCO, as the chief Saudi hireling as well as the chief beneficiary of the oil concessions, kept Americans nicely misinformed about the nature of Saudi Arabia's regime and its people. All those recent excited discoveries about what horrible things are written in Saudi textbooks, memorized in Saudi madrasas, made the subject of sermons in Saudi mosques, could have been made ten years ago, or thirty, or fifty. That they were not, and that many Americans worked in Saudi Arabia for decades, living in their gated communities, without learning what Wahhabi Muslims believed, or if they did stumble upon some of the views Wahhabi imams incul-cated, never shared that knowledge with a wider public, says something about the incuriosity of American journalists, the role of the govern-ment in promoting certain views of foreign countries that may bear no relation to reality but that support a predetermined policy or belief — in this case, the belief that since Islam was a "bulwark" against Commu-nism, and a supplier of oil (at market prices — the Americans were not treated any differently from other customers), the fanatical Muslims of Saudi Arabia must be wonderful allies of America indeed.

Said did not refute the quite varied and unusual men whom he lumped together, for the purposes of jejune denunciation, as "Orien-talists," because he couldn't. What he could do was repeat his thesis:

that the entire history of Western study of the Muslim East was always merely a handmaiden to imperialism. Bernard Lewis has pointed out that the study of the languages and history of the Muslim East began, in the West, centuries before Western "imperialism," and that many of the greatest Orientalists were from countries, such as Germany and Hungary, that had no connection to Western "imperialist" ventures in North Africa and the Middle East, Lewis also noted a few of Said's representative howlers, both historical and philological. In the historical vein, there was Said's bizarre assertion that Byzantium succumbed to Islam before Spain, when Byzantium was Islamized seven centuries later. In the philological vein, there was Said's rage that, in Lewis's sober disquisition on the Arabic noun "thawra," a word which since the nineteenth century has been used in Arabic to mean "revolution," Lewis had begun "with a brief look at the basic meanings of the Arabic root from which it was derived" and included the following: "The root th-w-r in classical Arabic meant to rise up (e.g. of a camel), to be stirred or excited, and hence, especially in Maghribi usage, to rebel."

Said found this mention of a camel to be, as Lewis notes, an "elaborate, hostile, and wholly absurd interpretation" which was being wantonly thrust – sexual overtones aplenty — "into a lexical definition of an Arabic root" quoted "from the classical Arab dictionaries." The full reply to Said's hysterical vituperation offers a memorable example of Lewis at his suaviter-in-modo best, and one particularly admires Footnote 6 in his *The Question of "Orientalism."*

Serious historians of the East and of Islam must have agreed with the distinguished British historian of India, Clive Dewey, when a few years ago he described the quiddity of Said's *Orientalism*:

> When Edward Said's "Orientalism" first appeared in 1978, historian after historian must have put it down without finishing it — without imagining, for a moment, the influence it would exert. It was, technically, so bad; in every respect, in its use of sources, in its deductions, it lacked rigour and balance. The outcome was a caricature of Western knowledge of the Orient, driven by an overtly political agenda. Yet it clearly touched a deep vein of vulgar prejudice running through American academe.[1]

That "vein of vulgar prejudice" is now the main artery of Western

1 Clive Dewey, "How the Raj Played Kim's Game," *Times Literary Supplement*, April 1998, 10.

academic life, pumping not blood but the poison of ressentiment, made permanent by that world-without-end of "postcolonialism" (but time, even "post-colonial" time, must have a stop), inflicted on unwary students who are brainwashed early. Some never manage to learn to consider the evidence of history, never manage to think for themselves.

Said also offered a Jobs Program, for the implication of what he said meant that one could trust only those who were themselves the "victims" of (Choose One): colonialism, post-colonialism, imperialism, Zionism, the American Empire. A Muslim Arab native of Baghdad would, for example, by dint of that fact, possess an insight into and understanding of the 3000-year-old artifacts of ancient Mesopotamia that, of course, had been denied such Western non-native scholars as Sabatino Moscati, Leo Oppenheim, and Henri Frankfort, though neither Italy, nor Germany, nor France had been colonial powers in Iraq. A Baghdadi native's meager scholarship on Mesopotamian civilization of 3000 B.C. was entitled, in the crazed but fashionable logic of the age, to be given greater weight than that of those three eminences, because it lacked the Original Sin of being tied to "colonialism, post-colonialism, imperialism, Zionism, the American Empire." (Again, choose one.)

Book after book is churned out by members of the Middle Eastern Studies Association of North America, but when it comes to the politics of Arab Islam, very few are not quickly obsolete. How many books, on the "creation of Palestinian identity" or *Agriculture in Tunisia, 1870-1913*, or *Portable Seclusion: the Veil and New Muslim Feminism* now sit on groaning shelves, books that neither their own authors, nor anyone else, would wish to read. Meanwhile, the Islamic studies of Schacht and Margoliouth and Jeffery and Goldziher and Lammens are not dated, but were written beautifully and lucidly about significant subjects in the history of Islam; they retain their value and transcend their time. Bookshelves groan with decades of "studies," now quaint and utterly démodé, on The Development of Arab Nationalism in Libya, Tunisia, Egypt, Morocco, Lebanon, Iraq, the U.A.E., Kuwait, Syria, Lebanon, Algeria, etc., all of them studies which never connect "Arab nationalism" to Islam, never interpret the former as simply a more modest subset of the latter, emphasizing the Arab supremacist idea in Arab-ruled countries (where the non-Arabs, such as the Copts and the Maronites and the Assyrians, steadily lose population, influence and significance). Several decades of books have been churned out that manage to overlook entirely, or to obscure, the permanent and overwhelming role of Islam in the lives and mental outlook of Arab Muslims, and even in those of Arab "Islamochristians" whose own sense of Arabness is indelibly linked to Islam.

But now "Arab Nationalism" can be seen as both transient, and as a subset of, rather than in opposition to, the traditional promptings of pan-Islamism. For "pan-Arabism" was the earlier, pre-OPEC version, of that "pan-Islamism" about which few Muslim Arabs, except of the most fervent Muslim Brotherhood school, dared, in the 1940s and 1950s and even 1960s, to dream. Now that those studies on "Arab nationalism" have run their course, the latest variant on ways to avoid talking about Islam have been modish "cultural studies," with film festivals, and young faculty living with the Bedouin in Egypt or on the Libyan desert, or with tribesmen in Yemen.

This tends to produce works which are a cross between the purely anthropological, Middle Eastern equivalents of such studies as Margaret Mead's *Coming of Age in Samoa*, and the appreciation of an "outsider" who tries to sink below the surface of things as did Lawrence Wylie with French rural life in *Village in the Vaucluse*, but with an Arabic cast, with an updated version of Laurentian adoration of the leathered, weathered faces of the desert dwellers, and the ceremony of the zarf-enclosed coffee cup, part of a drinking ritual, and the comfort of a Cairene café's proffered nargilah, or hubble-bubble pipe, and of course the Arabian desert, and the Arab steeds, and the camel's milk, and the eternal verities evoked by the vast night sky of Araby. But those picturesque illiterate Bedouin do not give one an understanding of what those in Fallujah, or Baghdad, or Riyadh, or Cairo, or Algiers, or Gaza, take in, read about, discuss, when they read and talk about Islam. And unless one can exercise one's imaginative faculties or even sympathies beyond what has been possible heretofore, one is likely to miss that most important subject of all — Islam, and the view of Infidels that it promotes.

Unlike the European "customs-and-manners" histories of yore, with such exemplars as Edward Lane, with his *An Account of the Customs and Manners of the Modern Egyptians*, where Islam was always in view, for Lane realized just how important Islam was even to the "Modern Egyptians" of the early 1800s, academics today who write about the Middle East go out of their way, it seems, to avoid discussing, analyzing, understanding, reporting on, Islam There is everything else under the sun: the "Construction of Palestinian Identity" (good), and "the Construction of Israeli Identity" (bad), and Iranian cinema, and the Arab political novel, "Israeli archeology as a colonial project" and "why non-Muslims cannot possibly understand Mesopotamian civilization of 3000 years ago" But it is likely, and indeed almost certain, that undergraduates and graduates who have taken courses on the Middle East will not come away with a thorough grasp of what is contained in Qur'an, hadith, and sira.

Islam itself — the subject without which nothing else in the Muslim world makes sense, is omitted, or willfully ignored, or de-emphasized, in what so often passes for scholarship on the Middle East. It may reflect the fact that many current students and teachers of Middle Eastern matters in the Western world are now either Muslims themselves, or connected, by close professional and personal ties (including, in some cases, marriage) to Muslims, and naturally are keen not to offend Muslim colleagues who can help, or hinder, their professional advancement in a hundred sundry ways.

Those few scholars of Islam who, over decades, have come to understand the innate defensiveness with which Muslims, even those whose own faith is tepid, present Islam to non-Muslims, would do well to realize that the luxury they have permitted themselves, a luxury of reticence, of taciturnity, of oblique hints, does not meet the present case, where Europe itself has been threatened with possibly unstoppable Islamization.

Many in the Western world have adopted an adversarial stance toward their own, messy, silly, and obviously imperfect civilization. There is much to deplore in the Western world, and in the United States. But Islam is now the preferred vehicle of protest against that civilization, and hence, while Islam tends to be defended by Muslims out of belief or out of filial piety or out of a sense, on the part of Arab "Islamochristians" (Christians who minimize the malevolence of Islam), that Arab ethnic identity, and Islam, are one, some non-Muslims may defend it not out of real sympathy, but only because Islam is seen as the best current vehicle for fighting "the System, Amerika, Capitalism, the West" — you name it. It is not surprising that the campus brownshirts at Columbia did not call only for the obliteration of Israel, but also called for "the eradication of Western civilization."

It has been a difficult task, to depict Islam as a benign force for greater human freedom, but many have proven equal to that task.

They must ignore Islam itself, a system in which the rights of women are severely restricted, where homosexuals can be murdered and sexual freedom does not exist, where all non-Muslims can be offered, by those who long for a state that is fully Sharia-compliant, only three possibilities — death, conversion to Islam, or a life of permanent humiliation, degradation, and physical insecurity as dhimmis under Muslim rule. Islam emphasizes the collective and discourages, even punishes, individual freedom of conscience and other aspects of mental freedom, including many forms of artistic expression (sculpture, most painting, and instrumental music) that are prohibited in orthodox Islam.

Free and skeptical inquiry about anything is something to be prevented and punished, for otherwise Islam itself might become the subject of such inquiry. Muslims are not fighters for "social justice" or paladins of progress on the march to earthly paradise. Muslims still practice slavery, in Niger, Mali, Mauritania, and Sudan. They are fighters against all Infidels, and their instruments are various, depending on what proves most effective. They are far less concerned with justice here below (and "justice" means, in any case, the triumph of Islam) than were Marxists. The Muslim Paradise is purely sensual, and the 72 promised houris are Paradise enow. It is quite something, the spectacle of disappointed Marxists, as a sort of consolation prize, now rushing to the barricades to defend Islam — that smacks so much of traditional Fascism — from its liberal democratic detractors.

But the study of Islam in the West, where unfettered intellectual freedom can be found, is again looking up. There are signs here and there, first with John Wansbrough, then with the late Patricia Crone and Michael Cook, and now with Christoph Luxenberg and others engaged in philological analysis of the early Qur'an and contemporaneous works, that important studies of early Islam is being done. Such work, of course, can take place only if the Qur'an and hadith and sira are regarded as permissible objects of study, and not just of veneration or adoration. New work on the condition of "dhimmitude," based for the first time on testimony from the dhimmis, and from non-Muslim travelers, visitors, and diplomats, has changed much about the understanding of how vast lands, formerly peopled entirely by non-Muslims, were conquered by Muslims and then, over time, turned into lands that are now peopled almost entirely by Muslims. It was a complicated and lengthy process; think of Zoroastrian Iran becoming 99% Muslim, or of Turkey, once Christian Byzantium, becoming 99% Muslim. One can see it happening today in Iraq, where the Christian population has gone from 1.1 million in 2003 to 300,000 today, in Egypt (a country where the Christian Copts have been reduced to a mere 10% of the population), and in Lebanon, where the Christian share of the population has steadily declined over the last century.

Little of this important new work from Cook, Crone, Luxenberg, is ever mentioned in the American mass media, though Luxenberg, whose philological research led him to conclude that the Qur'an is based on a Christian lectionary, did receive a single paragraph years ago in *Newsweek*; the mere appearance of that paragraph caused the magazine to be banned in Pakistan and in other Muslim countries.

Most exciting has been the work of scholars at the Institute for Early Islamic History and the Koran, known as Inara, a research institute devoted to the scientific. historical-critical, philological investigation into the Qur'an, the origins of Islam and its early history. Not a word about Inara has appeared in the American media. Why?

The same scrupulous media that would never permit a doctor in the pay of Merck or Pfizer to shamelessly tout that drug company's latest pill, without identifying who pays him, apparently thinks it has no duty to report on Middle East "experts" in the same way. But most of this media, unlike many academic departments, has not been infiltrated by Muslims or apologists who carefully keep out all those who would wish to study Islam without inhibitions or a desire to please Muslims. This failure may simply reflect the dreamy belief that reporting — mere reporting — on the Muslim world in the Western media is sufficient, and that there is no need for any detailed study of Islam by members of that media, because Islam is a "religion" and we are expected not to question the baseless view that "all religions want the same thing" — as President George W. Bush, like so many others since, insisted in his public assurances after 9/11. Of course it isn't true.

Consider with what alacrity the phrase "Dialogue of Civilizations" has been taken up by the mainstream media. This is a feelgood way for Muslims to encourage continued Infidel inattention to the tenets of Islam, to the history of Islamic conquest, and to treatment of non-Muslims. These "Dialogues" are for everyone. At the Grand Panjandrum Level, Jimmy Carter was able to learn about the Middle East, and especially the Arab-Israeli dispute, from his old friend and sometime host, Prince Bandar of Saudi Arabia. British diplomat Chris Patten, formerly of the E.U., was able to exchange warm bon-mots with Egyptian diplomat Amr al-Moussa of the Arab League. As for French politicians, some have been "subsidized" with generous financial expressions of esteem from rich Arabs. These include former Prime Minister Nicolas Sarkozy, convicted of having received many millions — some say as much as $52 million — from Libyan dictator Muammar Qaddafy. Some believe that the deeply-corrupt former Prime Minister Jacques Chirac was also the object of Arab gratitude, expressed in French francs The French politicians who were "deux-rivistes" viewed France, on the northern bank of the Mediterranean, as indissolubly linked to the Muslim Maghreb on the southern bank, and promoted the view that Islam has been a much misunderstood, much undervalued, indeed practically indispensable contributor to Western Civilization.

At a slightly less luxurious level, high-powered bureaucrats in Christian and Jewish organizations have been invited by Arab governments and organizations to participate in interfaith "dialogues," often involving an all-expenses-paid week at a luxurious hotel in Marrakesh or Cairo or Abu Dhabi. Here the promised discussion quickly metamorphoses into a presentation, by Muslim hosts, about the House of Wisdom in Abbasid Baghdad, or about the Convivencia of Muslims, Christians and Jews in Islamic Spain. It is de rigueur to mention Maimonides in Islamic Spain, but the fact that he fled Cordoba, and religious persecution in Spain as a teenager, will not be mentioned. And finally, the latest entry in the Muslim-Tolerance-and-Pluralism *son-et-lumière*, the Ottoman Empire, where the habit of the sultans, the padishahin, of employing Jewish doctors, will be mentioned to calculated effect. But the *devshirme*, or forced levy of Christian children in the Ottoman lands in Europe to supply the Sultan's army, will not.

As Morocco is a favored site for the "Dialogues of Civilisations" perhaps the palace of Mulay Ismail will be shown to those taking part. But the Infidel visitors will not learn what they could have picked up from a short review of *White Gold* by Giles Milton in *The Times Literary Supplement*:

> Between 1609 and 1616, 466 English trading ships were seized and their crews forced into slavery. The corsairs of Barbary also launched hit and run raids around the coast of England. By the end of 1625, the mayor of Plymouth believed that at least a thousand of his townspeople had been kidnapped. The men were most often put to work from dawn to dusk, toiling away under the blistering heat on the Moroccan Sultan Mulay Ismail's new palace – the largest construction project in history.

At the lowest level, at local Mosque Outreach Programs, Christian and Jewish participants arrive, take off their shoes, and settle down for an evening of "Interfaith Dialogue" during which a handful of plausible and smiling Muslim spokesmen (with the few congregants who deigned to come; most stayed away, rather than endure the spectacle of Infidels defiling the mosque with their presence, even if it was all for a good, taqiyya-and-tu-quoque cause) explain everything, and then take a handful of questions that seldom present any real difficulty, and afterwards, the Infidels get to enjoy curried chicken, pita, and even baklava. And yes, of course, Mrs. Levine, please take some home for your husband; so sorry he could not be with us tonight.

Nothing could be more fitting for this Alice-In-Wonderland period than what Humpty Dumpty said to Alice in *Through the Looking-Glass*: "When I use a word, it means just what I choose it to mean, neither more nor less." As we have seen, that Muslim spokesperson on National Public Radio suggested that the word "jihad" was being used incorrectly, and gave Infidels the wrong idea. If, she suggested, it is simply impossible to convince Infidels that the word, in its primary meaning, is entirely devoid of any menace and threat, then she thought that it should be taken out of circulation altogether. This kind of linguistic defensiveness is supported by many non-Muslim commentators, news-hosts, and columnists. They are quick to hew to the mantra, "war on terrorism" but never come close to the subject of Islam. As another NPR news-show host insists, with self-assured illogic, that negative comments about Islam or Muslims amount to "racism," even though Muslims are of every race.

That guest speaker on *All Things Considered* showed that she, and Islam's large supporting cast, have not only learned something from Humpty Dumpty, but they have gone him one better in suggesting that his phrase be Islamically expanded: "When I use a word, it means what I want you to think it means, neither more nor less."

CHAPTER TWENTY-FOUR

Friends with Benefits

EARLY IN THE 20th century, the Islamic world was not only weak, and in disarray, but its weakness and disarray could not be hidden from the view of the most educated and thoughtful Muslims. They had contact with Europeans; some of them had traveled, and could compare for themselves the political, economic, intellectual and social progress in Europe, with what they saw in the Ottoman Empire, or in other lands where Muslims lived. Some of these people concluded that Islam needed to be "reformed."

Indeed, the highwater mark of Islamic "reformation" — such as it was — was that period 1900-1930, when Islamic societies did not possess the accident of oil wealth to hide their own failures, and to buy the services of Western diplomats, government officials, business men, journalists, and academics to churn out a steady stream of apologetics that confused the vast non-Muslim public, and managed to play to the resentments, and sense of victimization — a victimization that was keenly felt by Muslims for, in their mental makeup, they had been taught that it was proper and necessary for Islam, and for Muslims, to dominate and to rule, and so any deviation from that well-merited position seemed not merely wrong, but against the right ordering of the universe.

A handful of soi-disant Muslim "reformers" arose, and they sensed, as do some of those who claim nowadays to be on the cusp of reform, that the word "jihad" was a problem. When those "reformers" were addressing powerful non-Muslims, whose goodwill they needed, they denied that "jihad" meant anything like aggressive warfare.

Despite more than 1400 years of textual evidence, and Muslim behavior prompted by and based on, that textual evidence, these "reformers" offered the argument that the primary meaning of "jihad" was a "spiritual struggle." Indeed, the "reformer" Sheikh Muhammad Rashid Rida maintained that it was non-Muslims who were responsible for the aggressive, militant definition of the word. Self-assuredly defining "jihad" as a "spiritual struggle," Rida argued that others, the Infidels, had given Muslims a mistaken understanding of their own word. Exactly how could it have happened, that in all the centuries of jihad-conquest, and calls for jihad, and discussions of jihad, it had somehow all been a colossal misunderstanding based on things presumably bruited about by those non-Muslims living in Mesopotamia and Syria and Judea?

The same bizarre definition of "jihad" as making war on the Infidels, the reformers insisted, should be replaced by understanding "jihad" as a "spiritual struggle." The definition of "jihad" as violence against Infidels in order to ensure that Islam everywhere will triumph and Muslims will rule everywhere, was apparently whispered in innocent Muslim ears, leading those missionaries astray, by those to whom they had come to peacefully spread the faith across Christian North Africa, and then in Spain to the north, and then to the Zoroastrians in Sassanian Persia to the east.

In other words, the jihad-conquest of Christian, Jewish, Zoroastrian, Buddhist and Hindu lands and peoples was all based, we are being asked to believe, on a misunderstanding of what "jihad" was all about — a misunderstanding caused, unbelievably, by the victims of that "jihad" themselves. If only they had told the truth to Muslims about what "jihad" meant, everyone could have saved themselves a great deal of trouble. Rida knew that "jihad" meant "spiritual struggle," but many other poor Muslims had been led astray into a mistaken understanding by non-Muslims. Exactly why non-Muslims would have wished to have done this remained, in the writings of Rida and other "reformers," a mystery.

In an article on "jihad" in *Moslem World* (Vol, 2, 1912, pp. 348-349) the scholar W. R. W. Gardner described the tortuous logic-chopping of such early 20th-century "reformers" as Muhammad Rida and Chiragh Ali:

> There is undoubtedly a feeling, if not a belief among many Westerners that a Moslem regards it as a duty binding on him in accordance with the literal command of the Koran, to kill any and every unbeliever whom he may meet once jihad has been proclaimed. Sheikh Rida acknowledges that this conception of the duty of a

Moslem during jihad may have been in the past, and may even now be common among the ignorant or less educated Moslems, but he says that much of this feeling has been the result of mixing with foreigners (non-Moslems), who have had the mistaken idea of what Moslems mean by jihad, and that this mistaken idea of these non-Moslems has crept into Moslem minds, and has thus given apparent support to the belief that this is really a Mohammedan conception of one's duty in jihad.

Gardner points out that while a very few Muslims — precisely the kind of educated, westernized, plausible Muslims among whom both real, and feigning, "reformers" were to be found — may have believed, or allowed themselves to believe, or pretended to believe, that "jihad" meant something other than violence directed at Infidels, almost all Muslims had acted, in time and space, as if they did not agree:

Let us note here that it is because this conception of the duty of a 'believer' in time of jihad is, as a matter of fact, the common belief of the ignorant Moslems (as the Sheikh admits, and for practical purposes it matters not how it arose), and because the ignorant Moslems form the greater part of the population in any Moham-medan land, that the non-Moslem subjects and residents in any land under Moslem rule have come to fear the word 'jihad', and to appeal to the more enlightened to be careful in their use of it. For they know that however it may be used by educated writers, the common people understand it to mean attack on non-Moslems, and believe that it is their duty to destroy as many as possible of these unbelievers. Further, they know well how easy it is for an ig-norant mob to get out of hand, especially when, rightly or wrong-ly, it believes that any action which has as its object the glory of God and the better establishment of the true religion, would be looked upon by those in authority with a lenient eye, if not with actual sympathy. For the question of what jihad is cannot be settled by reference alone to the etymology of the word jihad. The Koran plainly teaches in many passages, notwithstanding claims put for-ward by Chiragh Ali, the duty of fighting for the faith or 'in the way of God', by using the word qatala, and El Zamakhshary says, 'Fighting in the way of God is jihad for the glorifying of his word and the strengthening of the Religion'. And whatever may be the etymological meaning of the word jihad, there can be no gainsay-ing the fact that it is sometimes used in the Koran in the sense of warlike actions, a warfare for the sake of the Faith — Is war for the extension of Islamic rule also jihad?

In considering this point, not much light is to be got from the writings of the more recent Moslem authors, such as those we have
quoted. They simply deny that it is a principle of Islam that jihad
may include wars of aggression. By denying this, they do not prove
anything. For what we are considering is, what Mohammedanism
is and has been - that is, what orthodox Mohammedanism teaches
concerning jihad, founding its doctrine on a certain definite interpretation of those passages in the Koran which speak of jihad.
Until the newer conceptions, as to what the Koran teaches as to the
duty of the believer towards non-believers, have spread further and
have more generally leavened the mass of Moslem belief and opinion, it is the older and orthodox standpoint on this question which
must be regarded by non-Moslems as representing Mohammedan
teaching and as guiding Mohammedan action. We may sympathize
strongly with the newer ideas; we may hope that those who ad-
vance these ideas may succeed in having them generally accepted
by Mohammedans; but it is the older and narrower orthodox conception of Muhammad's teaching alone, which we can as yet regard
as representing the views and practice of Islam with regard to jihad
on this question of aggressive war. And the words of Chiragh Ali
are such that we need not spend any time in trying to prove that
orthodox Mohammedanism believes and teaches that, according
to the Koran, it is the nature of jihad to be aggressive. Let us quote
his words again: 'The Mohammedan Common Law is wrong on
this point when it allows unbelievers to be attacked without provocation.' We take then as proved, the statement that Mohammedan
Common Law allows unbelievers to be attacked without provocation.[1]

One can understand the difficulty of these "reformers" in dealing with immutable texts. They did not want to draw the obvious conclusion that Islam could not be reformed. In the case of Muhammad
Rida, he attempted to convince his Muslim, and non-Muslim audience,
that non-Muslims, intent on believing that "jihad" is aggressive and
threatening, are actually responsible for convincing peace-loving, spir-
itual-struggling, Muslims that "jihad" means something militant and
dangerous. It is the non-Muslims, in Rida's version of Islam, who are
responsible for giving Muslims all those bad ideas. Gardner, who knew
Islam, and was writing at a time when truths now seldom told were then
obvious to all serious non-Muslim students of Islam, pointed out the
absurdity of Rida's position.

---

1 *Moslem World* (Vol, 2, 1912, pp. 348-349).

As for Chiragh Ali, who dismisses what he calls, in charmingly misleading fashion, "the Mohammedan Common Law" (i.e., the Shari'a), which, he says, "is wrong on this point when it allows unbelievers to be attacked without provocation." This statement is breathtaking; he, Chiragh Ali, appears to admit that the Shari'a "allows unbelievers to be attacked without provocation." He follows up this bold admission by something even more startling for a Muslim; he claims that in doing this the Shari'a — the Holy Law of Islam — is flatly "wrong." In fact, he permits himself a boldness here no contemporary reformer would ever permit himself.

Yet Chiragh Ali does not tell us how the Shari'a, the product of many scholars, who constructed it out of the principles derived ineluctably from Qur'an and Sunnah (the latter, in turn, drawn from the hadith and the sira), could possibly be wrong, or if it is wrong, then those jurisconsults, those Qur'anic commentators, were also wrong — and even more unacceptably, what Muhammad did was wrong when he "attacked without provocation" non-Muslims.

But what non-Muslims do not realize is that Chiragh Ali allows for his own escape clause. For "attacked without provocation" may have a much narrower meaning in Islam than non-Muslims would suspect. Just as "defensive" action can include, for example, attacks on Infidels who put up the slightest resistance to the spread of Islam — for example, a Muslim might well regard bombs in the Paris metro as "defensive" acts because the French government has banned hijabs in schools, which can be easily interpreted as "resistance" to the spread of Islam — so at times simply being a non-Muslim might constitute a kind of "provocation."

How else can one interpret the attack on the inoffensive Jewish farmers of the Khaybar Oasis, who had done nothing to oppose Muhammad and his followers, but simply presented the promise of booty? Their primal sin was that they were Jews, and other Jews had, according to the sira, opposed Muhammad's message. The attack on the Khaybar Oasis marked a new step in the history of Muhammad, and therefore in the history of Islam. It became clear that "jihad" could now be waged on non-Muslims simply because they were non-Muslims, and as non-Muslims who had the opportunity, but did not take it, to become Muslims, they could be depicted as an "obstacle" to the spread of Islam. And if they were such, then jihad could be declared, and they be attacked, and their wealth and women seized.

CHAPTER TWENTY-FIVE

On the Commanded and Prohibited in Islam

T O UNDERSTAND BETTER what is not only past in Islam, but also passing and, most importantly, to come, members of the security services in the Western world should learn what Islam teaches its adherents, whether they ignore most of those teachings and in fact dissent (and do not do so merely for the sake of infidel good will) from them (the so-called "moderates") or whether they choose to follow those teachings in a more observant fashion (what we may call the "rigorist" or "immoderate" Muslims, of whom there are a great many).

Islam is based on divisions, or perhaps one should say polarities. And these polarities explain the widespread bipolar disorder of Muslim peoples, swinging from gloom (as in June 1967) to elation (as on the afternoon of September 11, 2001). For Infidels, the main polarity to be aware of in Islam is the absolute divide between the Believer and the Unbeliever. Fellow Believers must be supported, must never have war made upon them in the service of Unbelievers (or Infidels). Unbelievers, on the other hand, must not be taken as friends ("Christians and Jews are friends only with each other"), not be treated as equals but subject to all sorts of disabilities, and while they may be exploited in every possible way, that exploitation should not lead to any felt gratitude toward the Infidels.

The division between Believer and Infidel in the world is mirrored in how the world itself is divided, between dar al-Islam, the lands where Islam rules and Muslims dominate (though they need not be a majority of the population), and dar al-harb, the House of War, where Infidels, for now, have not yet been conquered, nor subjugated to Islam.

174

The divisions of the great world are mirrored in the divisions that rule all of life. Everything one does is either halal (permitted, licit) or haram (prohibited, illicit). It is all laid down, or if not laid down in some book, then a fatwa or opinion may serve as the final guide of how a Muslim should act. Muslims living in the Lands of the Infidels face new questions. May they, for example, obey Infidel laws? (Answer: Only to the extent that those laws do not contravene Islam.) Now a good guide to what is halal and what is haram is *Al-Halal wal Haram fil Islam* by the well-known Sheikh Yusuf al-Qaradawi, who was toward the end of his life the most renowned and beloved Islamic authority in the world. He made everything clear. Hairdos in the shape of a camel's hump? Haram. Statues that have not been vandalized or defaced? Haram. A nice glass of fruit juice? Halal. A leg of lamb, from a lamb that has been killed in the Halal manner (oops, this is a trick question). Halal.

Some years ago, Michael Cook wrote a much-praised study entitled *Commanding Right and Prohibiting Wrong in Islam.* In Christianity, one is expected only to promote what is "right," and to discourage people from doing "wrong." The Christian version of Cook's book would be "Commending Right and Discouraging Wrong." Christianity commends; Islam commands. Christianity discourages. Islam insists; Islam demands of Believers absolute slavish submissiveness to the Rules of Islam. And Unbelievers, too, must obey the rules of the game, for if they are allowed to live, they owe their very lives to Muslims who have generously permitted that result, in return for those non-Muslims' willing acceptance of their painful status as dhimmis, and for not putting up resistance to the spread of Islam.

Those who do not do this are liable to be attacked, and this is increasingly a real risk in the West, particularly for ex-Muslims. By all the laws of civilization and of the United States of America, to kill such people would be strictly wrong, forbidden, prohibited, haram. According, however, to the fanatical views of the "immoderate" Muslims (as opposed to the other kind about whom we hear so much, but from whom we hear so little), if such dissidents were to be killed, they deserved what they got (as part of "an intense Islamic revolution all across America that holds the right and bring down [sic] the falsehood that they've created," as someone says at an Islamic website). For in the eyes of their killers, they should behave in America just as they know they must do in Islamic lands. That rule applies as well to Christians who have left the Middle East for the West. To many Muslims, those Christians are supposed to carry their dhimmitude with them wherever they go.

CHAPTER TWENTY-SIX

MESA Nostra

YET, NONE OF THIS is taught in American colleges and universities. This is due to the work of MESA.

"MESA" is the acronym of the Middle East Studies Association, the professional group of those who at American universities and colleges are charged with the responsibility of teaching the American young, those trusting, innocent, infinitely malleable young, with learning about the Middle East — which is to say, about Islam.

As an organization, MESA has over the past two decades slowly but surely been taken over by apologists for Islam. Many of these are Muslims, and many are non-Muslims. The latter includes quite a few people who are married to Muslims, or who, to get along with their colleagues (and remember, the most political place in the entire universe is a university faculty, and that institution which Randall Jarrell immortalized in his satirical novel of academe, *Pictures From An Institution* — the Departmental Meeting. Junior faculty owe everything to, and therefore must curry favor with, senior faculty. If that means signing a BDS petition that denounces the mighty empire of Israel, *fons et origo* of everything that has ever gone wrong with the Muslim and Arab states and peoples, then so be it. Funny thing about being a trimmer, however, is that the mere act of signing something you really don't believe helps to convince you that you really do believe it, otherwise you would have to come to terms with your own cravenness, your own pusillanimity. And no one wants to do that.

The method of apologetics is simple: concentrate on Israel, or the more tendentious reification of an alternative future state, "Israel/Palestine," keep clear of such topics as land ownership under the Ottoman

Empire, the actual demographics of the Ottoman vilayets and sanjak of Jerusalem that made up what became Mandatory Palestine, don't even whisper that more than half of the Jews in Israel had never left the Middle East but lived as dhimmis in Iraq, in North Africa, in Syria, Egypt, and as chattel slaves in Yemen — because officially, all Israeli Jews are "European colonialists."

Finally, do not under any conditions mention that a goodly number of the ancient "Palestinian people" (invented post-1967) are the descendants of Arabs and Berbers who were veterans of Abd el-Kader's failed campaign against the French in Algeria, Egyptians who arrived with Mehmet Ali, Muslims from the Balkans and Bulgaria and other Ottoman territories in Europe who were transferred, en masse, by the Turkish government as the high tide of Islam receded — for that area (a/k/a in the West as "Palestine") was by far the most desolate and under-populated in the Ottoman Empire, always excepting the Empty Quarter of Arabia).

The apologetics consists in hardly ever discussing jihad, dhimmitude, or indeed even introducing the students to the full text of the Qur'an. Sometimes an expurgated version — such as the Michael Sells' book-length horror, *Approaching the Qur'an*, or his compilation of ten suras, *The Generous Qur'an* — is assigned to students. The hadith and sira are seldom mentioned. Books by well-known apologists for Islam, such as Karen Armstrong and John Esposito, are assigned, as well as feel-good interfaith nonsense such as Maria Rosa Menocal's *The Ornament of the World* that celebrates the supposed "convivencia" among believers in the three monotheistic faiths living in "tolerant" Islamic Spain.

But not everyone who is a member of MESA should be consigned to the outer darkness. There are respectable Ottomanists, scholars of the history of science in Muslim lands, students of agricultural practices in Muslim lands, and so on and so innocuously forth. MESA is a little like the Soviet Union of Writers, which had thousands of members but hardly a single real writer. When one considers Michael Cook, Patricia Crone, Bernard Lewis, on one side of the balance, and the assorted Khalidis and Dabashis and Massads and El Fadls on the other, you can guess which side kicks the beam.

No member of MESA has done as much to make available to a wide public important new work on Muhammad, on the origins of the Qur'an, and on the history of early Islam, as that lone wolf, and apostate, Ibn Warraq. No one has done such work on the institution of the dhimmi as that lone louve, Bat Ye'or. It is an astounding situation, where much of the most important work is being done not in universities, because many university centers have been seized by a kind of Islamintern International. Willy Munzenberg could have learned a lot from Edward Said, who was the only begetter, with his *Orientalism*, for a good deal of this "post-colonial hegemonic discourse" stuff that permanently stunts the mental growth of students and teachers alike.

Presidents of MESA have included Lisa Anderson, the well-versed and compleat academic operator — what with her membership on Councils on this and Committees on that, all very impressive if you are impressed with that sort of thing, as well as the former Dean of Columbia's School of International and Public Affairs, the chair of the political science department, and the director of the Middle East Institute; Joel Beinin, an anti-Israel Jewish professor and political radical; Laurie Brand, about whom you may google; former PLO propagandist in Beirut, and now professor emeritus at Columbia, Rashid Khalidi; and Juan Cole, the leather-jacketed author of antisemitic blogs and a professor, alas, at the University of Michigan.

In any case, even MESA has its constraints. For example, a few years ago it had to award, it could not avoid awarding, a prize for the best scholarly book of the year on Islam to Michael Cook for his 720-page *Commanding Right and Prohibiting Wrong in Islam*, even though Cook is suspiciously learned and has cowritten another book with the late Patricia Crone, which treats respectfully the studies of Christoph Luxenberg, studies that suggest there is an Aramaic substratum to the Qur'an, and therefore Cook and Crone are anathema to Muslims.

Why do I refer to MESA as "Mesa Nostra"? Because it is a kind of "Our Thing" conspiracy, but not nearly as appealing, as folkloric, as the Mafia in Sicily, or the 'Ndrangheta in Calabria (now the most powerful Italian crime syndicate), or the Camorra in Naples, or the Sacro Corona Unita in Calabria, for in Italy the criminal world has geographically distinct components. Everyone in MESA knows everyone else; the maneuvering, the politicking, the fear that the truth-revealers are in hot pursuit, and perhaps someday soon Congress, will pull back the curtain, and take away all that government money that the Khalidis and the Dabashis of MESA want to be lavished as research grants to members of the group, or to the institutions that employ them, so that MESA might more easily spread its anti-Israel and anti-American message, and convince Americans to ask "what have we done to make them hate us?" and make us believe that the Muslim threat emanates from "only a handful of extremists."

"Mesa Nostra" is my little invention. It communicates the louche nature of the enterprise. It has little to do with real scholarship. Ask yourself this: could Joseph Schacht, the great authority on Islamic law, or Arthur Jeffery, an authority on Islam, on Muhammad, and on aspects of the lexicon of the early Qur'an, both of them once stars in Columbia's Middle Eastern firmament, have been hired today — at Columbia, or indeed, anywhere that the plotters of Mesa Nostra rule the roost? No, they could not.

The Arabs have poured money into various Georgetown Centers for Arab and Middle Eastern studies (because Washington is where the power is, that's where the service officers are trained). Particularly effective in spreading soothing propaganda for Islam in Washington has been the Prince Alwaleed Bin Talal Center for Muslim-Christian Understanding.

They have also endowed professorial chairs: the most prestigious of all is the "Custodian of the Two Holy Mosques" professorship at Harvard Law School. Do the Arabs get their money's worth? They do, indeed they do. And the Middle East Studies Association — MESA — sits at the center of the academic spider web.

So that's why I call it "Mesa Nostra." Everybody should.

CHAPTER TWENTY-SEVEN

Karen Armstrong:
The Coherence of Her Incoherence

AREN ARMSTRONG, long famous for her description of Muhammad as the consummate "peacemaker" who "brought together the warring tribes of Arabia," in the early 2000s, right after 9/11, assumed the mantle not of the Prophet, but of the Prophet's defender. In a 2005 article in *The Guardian*, she retells in her inimitable fashion the story of European Christendom's relations with Islam and with Muslims. In her retelling, the Muslims are innocent victims, and more than innocent victims, she likens them again and again to the Jews, the people persecuted most relentlessly through time and space. The Muslims are also, according to Armstrong, the people who provided, in that bright shining moment of European history known as Islamic Spain, the only real tolerance and humanity to be found anywhere in Europe before the modern era. It is a tough job to make that case, given that Muslims raided up and down European coasts, destroying villages and murdering villagers, and seizing still others who were brought back alive to North Africa to serve as slaves (the men), and sex slaves (the women). In fact, more than one million Christian Europeans were seized and brought back to Muslim lands. That's a lot to overlook, but Karen Armstrong proves equal to the task. And her real objective is to make Europeans ashamed of themselves for showing any signs of wariness or suspicion about the millions of Muslims who now live in Europe, having come among the indigenous Infidels to settle, but not to settle down.

It is curious to see how often in this article Karen Armstrong makes references to examples of historic mistreatment of the Jews. For in her previous books she has exhibited a palpable distaste for Israel, and has attempted on every occasion to pretend that the claims of the "three Abrahamic faiths" to Jerusalem are identical in the importance that each attaches to the city (but as a city Jerusalem is not holy in Islam, and never was), and she is fond, in her discussion of "fundamentalisms"— always presented in the plural — to make reference to the one or two examples of what she calls "Jewish terrorism." She fails to consider whether or not the assassination of Yitzhak Rabin by a Jewish political opponent, or the mental collapse of Dr. Baruch Goldstein which led him, acting entirely alone and on impulse, to wreak his solitary revenge on those whose Jewish victims Goldstein treated every day as a doctor, until he could no longer stand it, snapped, and proceeded to massacre 27 Muslims at a mosque in Hebron, really can be compared to the many thousands of planned acts, many of them fortunately foiled, and others not, that are part of the worldwide jihad against completely innocent Infidels, within Muslim lands, and without.

Here is how Armstrong begins her 2005 article in *The Guardian*:

> In 1492, the year that is often said to inaugurate the modern era, three very important events happened in Spain. In January, the Catholic monarchs Ferdinand and Isabella conquered the city of Granada, the last Muslim stronghold in Europe; later, Muslims were given the choice of conversion to Christianity or exile. In March, the Jews of Spain were also forced to choose between baptism and deportation. Finally, in August, Christopher Columbus, a Jewish convert to Catholicism and a protégé of Ferdinand and Isabella, crossed the Atlantic and discovered the West Indies. One of his objectives had been to find a new route to India, where Christians could establish a military base for another crusade against Islam. As they sailed into the new world, western people carried a complex burden of prejudice that was central to their identity.

This first paragraph is a scandal, consisting almost entirely of baseless assertions, incredible omissions, and complete fabrications. But it is not inexplicable. For Karen Armstrong history does not exist. It is putty in the hands of the person who writes about history. You use it to make a point, to do good as you see it. And whatever you need to twist or omit is justified by the purity of your intentions — and Karen Armstrong always has the purest of intentions. She knows that we in the "white Western world" (as some like to call it) fail to understand others.

She knows of our deep need to create "the Other" — a psychic need felt exclusively, and with great intensity, apparently, only by us, the white Christian peoples, and never by anyone else.

Though Western civilization, a product that was formed from the inheritance of both classical antiquity and of Christianity (which itself has a strong Hebraic element, so that it should more accurately be called Judeo-Christianity, a word about which some are still self-conscious), has far outstripped any rival in its achievements, both collective and by individuals, in art and science, in political and economic thought, in social and economic development, and has really never needed to create the "Other" (the entire business of "Othering" is a recent ideological fashion which by this point is getting long in the seminar and call-for-papers tooth).

Indeed, it is Islam which, though Karen Armstrong does not see it, because she knows nothing about Islam (which doesn't keep her from writing about it, endlessly), has the strongest claim to being based on the need of its Believers for "the Other." It is in Islam that emphasis is placed constantly on the only division that matters: that between Believer (to whom all loyalty is owed by other Believers, and for whom all transgressions may be forgiven, except that of disloyalty to Islam) and the Unbeliever, or Infidel (who must be opposed, and subjugated if such an Infidel refuses to accept Islam or stands in the way of its spread). That Armstrong fails to see this is extraordinary; it is everywhere in Qur'an, hadith, and sira. But she is on a mission: to make us feel guilty about our treatment of Muslims in the past (hence the harping on the Crusades, and the failure to provide what prompted those Crusades — the Muslim conquest of the Holy Land and refusal to allow Christians to make their wonted pilgrimages — and to make us believe that there is no difference between the Crusades, which were limited in both time and space, and jihad, which goes on forever, and everywhere, until the whole world submits to Islam. She wants to evoke Western guilt that should not exist at all, so that we will, today, be inhibited from responding appropriately to Muslim atrocities.

"In 1492, the year that is often said to inaugurate the modern era..." Who says that the year 1492 inaugurated the modern era? And what does the phrase "the modern era" mean in any case? The year 1492 was chosen by this lover of symmetries and the "three monotheisms" (now said to be studying Buddhism as the latest stop in her Spiritual Search) because in that year, in Spain, Jews and Christians and Muslims each acted, or were acted upon, in ways that Karen Armstrong finds useful to both misstate, and exploit. She will not mention what happened before 1492. She will not tell us about the Muslim invasion and conquest of Spain, or about the 700 years of the Reconquista, nor will she tell us when the Jews first came to Spain, long before the Muslim invasion, even before the Visigoths arrived. She will not point out that the Jews were inoffensive victims, and unlike the Muslims, never invaded, never conquered, never held the Christians of Spain in thrall, never posed a threat to the body politic.

In 1492, "the Catholic monarchs conquered Granada, the "last Muslim stronghold in Europe." What then should we call all those lands in southern and eastern Europe that the Ottomans were at that very moment busy conquering and seizing, including Constantinople, the richest, most populous, most important city in all of Christendom for 800 years (taken by the Turks on a Tuesday – May 29, 1453), and the Balkans (including the then-vast Serbian lands), and the lands that are modern-day Albania, Greece, Rumania, Bulgaria, and they continued to press northward and westward, later seizing much of Hungary and threatening Vienna twice. Were these not parts of Europe, and was not a good deal of Europe, including what had been for a millennium the most important city in Christendom, Constantinople, firmly in Muslim hands forty years before Granada fell? Yet Armstrong claims Granada was "the last Muslim stronghold in Europe."

But it would not do for Armstrong to remind readers that while the Muslim invaders and conquerors of Spain lost their last "stronghold" in Granada, other Muslim invaders and conquerors were busy at the other end of Europe, seizing lands and imposing on the non-Muslims populations they had conquered the *devshirme* (the forced levy of Christian boys in the Balkans to serve as soldiers and bureaucrats for the Ottoman Sultan) as well as imposing on them the jizyah (the capitation tax on non-Muslims) and all the other disabilities that, wherever Muslims conquered, were imposed, as part of a clearly elaborated system, and not merely the whim of a sole ruler, that affected all non-Muslims.

Now having begun with that year 1492, Armstrong has a bit of a problem. It was in that year that Jews were forced to be baptized or to leave. But though Granada had fallen, nothing then happened to the Muslims. In fact, they were treated with the same gentleness that all the Mudejares (Spanish Muslims) who had been defeated, in successive campaigns, were always treated by the Christian victors.

Henry Lea, the pioneering historian of the Inquisition, who was hardly looking for ways to exculpate Christianity, describes the generos-

ity with which the defeated Muslims were treated in Granada, and after
the prior victories:

> It was the Jews against whom was directed the growing intolerance
> of the fifteenth century and, in the massacres that occurred, there
> appears to have been no hostility manifested against the Mudejar-
> es. When Alfonso de Borja, Archbishop of Valencia (afterwards
> Calixtus III), supported by Cardinal Juan de Torquemada, urged
> their [the Mudejars] expulsion on Juan II of Aragon, although he
> appointed a term for their exile, he reconsidered the matter and left
> them undisturbed. So when, in 1480, Isabella ordered the expul-
> sion from Andalusia of all Jews who refused baptism and when, in
> 1486, Ferdinand did the same in Aragon, they both respected the
> old capitulations and left the Mudejares alone. The time-honored
> policy was followed in the conquest of Granada, and nothing could
> be more liberal than the terms conceded to the cities and districts
> that surrendered. The final capitulation of the city of Granada was a
> solemn agreement, signed November 25, 1491, in which Ferdinand
> and Isabella, for themselves, for their son the Infante Juan and for
> all their successors, received the Moors of all places that should
> come into the agreement as vassals and natural subjects under the
> royal protection, and as such to be honored and respected. Religion,
> property, freedom to trade, laws and customs were all guaranteed,
> and even renegades from Christianity among them were not to be
> maltreated, while Christian women marrying Moors were free to
> choose their religion. For three years, those desiring expatriation
> were to be transported to Barbary at the royal expense, and refu-
> gees in Barbary were allowed to return. When, after the execution
> of this agreement, the Moors, with not unnatural distrust, wanted
> further guarantees, the sovereigns made a solemn declaration in
> which they swore by God that all Moors should have full liberty
> to work on their lands, or to go wherever they desired through the
> kingdoms, and to maintain their mosques and religious observanc-
> es as heretofore, while those who desired to emigrate to Barbary
> could sell their property and depart.[1]

It was not until 1502, after difficulties ensued between Spanish
authorities, including the famous Cardinal Ximenes (he of the Com-
plutensian Polyglot) and the Muslims (Mudejares) that they were given
the choice of expulsion or conversion. And a great many of them pretended to convert and remained in Spain — far more Muslims were

---

1   Henry Charles Lea, *A History of the Inquisition of Spain*, 1906-1907.

capable of engaging in dissimulation of their faith than were the hapless Jews, who were expelled, in 1492, virtually overnight. It was much later, after several revolts, that the remaining Muslims were finally expelled in 1609.

But Armstrong manages to smuggle in that first, rather ineffective expulsion of 1502: "later [i.e. in a different year altogether] Muslims were given the choice of Christianity or exile." She does not add, and may not know, that Muslims in Spain after the fall of Granada were not under any danger of expulsion, and it was only when they showed signs of refusing to integrate as expected (and it was assumed that over time they would share the Christian faith, though at first nothing was done to demand such a sign), that the Spanish rulers toughened their stance. She may not know, either, that Muslims in a Spain now everywhere ruled by Christians asked members of the ulema in North Africa (in present-day Morocco) to determine whether they might continue to live under non-Muslim rule, and were told that it was not licit; it was important for them not to be ruled by non-Muslims, and they must, therefore, return to the Muslim-ruled lands of North Africa. Such details provide a rather different slant on what Karen Armstrong offers — she takes the real tragedy, the overnight expulsion of the hapless and inoffensive Jews, and attempts to make the reader think that the Muslims were equally inoffensive, equally harmless, and treated with equal ferocity, as the Jews. But they were not equally inoffensive, not equally harmless, and not treated with equal ferocity.

First comes the fall of Granada to the Christians in 1492. Then, second in time, and certainly in Karen Armstrong's indignation, came the expulsion of the Jews: "In March, the Jews of Spain were also forced to choose between conversion and exile." Note how that "also" is dropped in, as if the real event, the main event, was the nonexistent (in 1492) expulsion of the Moors, which she had taken care to slip into her discussion of the Fall of Granada, so that she could diminish the significance of the expulsion of the Jews.

But the Muslims were invaders and conquerors, who had been been resisted for 700 years of the Reconquista, and were expelled merely across the Straits of Gibraltar from whence they had come, to live again among fellow Muslims, under Muslim rule. Armstrong never says that. Nor does she point out, as she would if she were trying to distinguish the quite different treatments of Jews and Muslims, that the Jews of Spain never invaded, never conquered, never represented a threat to the political or social order. And when they were expelled they were not to find refuge, like the Muslims did in North African lands ruled by co-religionists, but again, to be scattered, to Ottoman domains and to Christian ones, chiefly Salonika and Amsterdam, to be treated indifferently, or kindly, or with contumely, or worse.

Under Muslim rule, despite their sometimes horrendous treatment, as recorded by Maimonides in his "Epistle to the Yemen" (Maimonides fled Islamic Spain), the Jews managed to make important cultural contributions as translators (along with Christians), as physicians, and as poets (the name Judah Halevi comes to mind). They were perfectly willing to live in Spain under Christian rule. They did nothing to deserve their expulsion. But Karen Armstrong has sympathy for the Jews only insofar as that sympathy can be transferred to the real objects of her pity, the Muslims, and she will do nothing to cause readers to see the difference in the two cases, one of clear mistreatment (the Jews), the second a matter of political prudence. (The Muslims continued to rise in scattered revolts against the Christians during the 16th century.) It took more than a century for the Spanish rulers and clergy, to realize that many of the Muslims, though conquered, were not about to abandon Islam and convert to Christianity; some pretended to, but those called the "Moriscos" continued to be secret Muslims, and therefore potentially subversive or rebellious. It had taken 700 years for the Reconquista. Why should the Spanish Christians, now that they were militarily victorious everywhere, take a chance that these "secret Muslims" might never again rise in revolt? Between 1609 and 1614 the Moriscos were finally expelled from Spain.

Both Jews and Moors were expelled from Spain, but however determined Armstrong may be to convince us (most unconvincingly) that these were identical historical events, both prompted by the demonization of "the Other" (a phenomenon which apparently results from the peculiar psychic deficiency of Christian Europe) they were not identical. The phrase "the expulsion of the Jews and the Moors" — as if they were identical both in time and in severity — comes trippingly off the tongue but remains an offense to history and the truth.

The third great event in that fateful year 1492, after the conquest of Granada, which Armstrong wrongly calls the "last stronghold" of Islam in Europe (overlooking the fact that the Ottomans were firmly ensconced in Constantinople and were busy expanding Muslim rule in the Balkans), and the two "identical" expulsions of what she insists were identically unthreatening Muslims and Jews, was the voyage of Columbus: "In August, Christopher Columbus, a Jewish convert to Catholicism and a protégé of Ferdinand and Isabella, crossed the Atlantic and discovered the West Indies."

Note how casually Armstrong drops in her astonishing remark: Columbus was a "a Jewish convert to Catholicism." She treats it as a given, and finds no need to offer sources or evidence.

Armstrong offers no authority for her statement. But why should she? Her purpose here is twofold. What better way to establish, in her vulgar, "some-of- my-best-friends-and-discoverers-of-the-New-World-are-Jewish" way, than to claim Columbus for the Jews (of course, assuming that people still honor Columbus for his deeds of derring-do, which would exclude all those who despise Columbus as the First Settler-Colonialist). At the same time, she can have this "Jewish" Columbus be depicted as part of a larger enterprise, for now he, that "Jewish convert to Catholicism," has embraced the putative aggressive military plans of Ferdinand and Isabella. But Ferdinand and Isabella had no plans of conquest in the New World which, of course, they did not know existed. They were interested only in finding new trade routes to Asia, the previous routes having been blocked by the Muslim conquest of Constantinople in 1453. According to Armstrong, finding an alternate route to Asia for trade was not what Los Reyes Católicos (Ferdinand and Isabella) hoped Columbus would find, but rather, the best route to "India, where Christians could establish a military base for another crusade against Islam." This is completely a product of Armstrong's imagination. She would have us believe that it was those aggressive and bloodthirsty Christians — Columbus and his backers — who were still hankering to make war against the peaceful Muslims. To repeat: Columbus was only looking for a new trade route from Europe to the East.

Having been transformed into a "Jewish convert to Catholicism," Columbus can more conveniently be depicted by Armstrong as a Pentagon Proto-Neo-Con, Jewish-but-also-Christian-fundamentalist, off on his voyage to "establish a military base" for "another crusade against Islam." Like a Pentagon official, negotiating for American bases in the New World.

"A military base for another crusade against Islam" — what can we say? Armstrong appears to believe that the Crusades, which were limited in space to the recapture of the Holy Land, and in time to 200 years (1090-1290, roughly), in fact, were some kind of central and permanent imperative, just the way the jihad — though it goes unmentioned in all of Armstrong's copious published vaporings on Islam — remains a permanent and central feature of Islamic teaching. But she is wrong. There was no ongoing effort in 1492 to embark on a new Crusade. Not a word about it, from Columbus, from his financial backer Luis Santangel, or from Los Reyes Católicos themselves.

And had such a thought occurred to someone, what kind of sense would it have made, militarily, to try to attack Muslims in the Holy Land from India? Europeans may not have known how far India was from Europe by sea, but they knew that it was very far from the Holy Land (in fact, Columbus thought it was much closer to Europe — that was his optimistic miscalculation). By 1492, the southeastern part of Europe itself had been for many decades under constant military assault by the powerful Ottoman armies. A few decades before, the first city of Christendom had fallen to the Ottoman Turks, to the Muslims. How, with such constant dangers, could anyone even think of launching a new Crusade from India? How would tens of thousands of men be transported there, stationed there, and then transported again to the Holy Land? How would they make their way safely through the vast Muslim-controlled lands of Persia, of Mesopotamia, of Syria, in order to reach the Holy Land in order to fight the Saracens?

Armstrong's nonsense perhaps has to do with some rude and indigestible bits of history that she dimly recalls, about the story of Prester John, the mythical Christian king of a mythical Christian kingdom, placed first, in European imaginations, in India, and later transferred to Ethiopia — a fable, designed to hearten European Christians who were always fearful of Muslim assaults, facing the constant threat of Arab raiding parties by sea, up and down European coasts, and the Turkish land armies of the mighty Ottoman Sultan. It was comforting to think that Prester John would join forces with Europe's Christians to push back the Muslim armies.

Armstrong's every word adds to the absurdity. There is no evidence for Armstrong's assertions about Columbus himself, or about what motivated him. History is putty in her hands, we said earlier. But the word putty does not do her infantile approach to history justice. History is for Karen Armstrong not so much putty as Playdoh. She can roll it about, she can pull it apart, she can twist and turn it with the same delight exhibited by a two-year-old when a solid block of Playdoh is finally softened up for use by grown-up hands. But the two-year-old is an innocent at play, and even if he leaves a momentary mess, he has done no real harm. Karen Armstrong is not innocent, and manages to do a great deal of harm, careless or premeditated harm, to history. Too many people read that she has written a few books, and assume, on the basis of nothing at all, that "she must know what she is talking about" – and some of her nonsense sticks. And though a few scholars have dealt devastatingly with her claims, it is Armstrong who produces these best-sellers, and this is how the vast public, in debased democracies, learns its history today. It is hearsay as history — "Karen Armstrong says" or "John Esposito says."

And that is only her first paragraph.

CHAPTER TWENTY EIGHT

The Scholar of the House:
Khaled Abou El Fadl

D EVOTEES OF THE genre know the pleasure to be derived from reading Hamid Dabashi's eulogy to Edward Said, with its echoes, for the connoisseur, of Dzhambul's 1936 "Song About Stalin" — the first verse of which you can find, if you wish, in *Ogonyok*, No. 14, March 14, 1990. The "Song About Stalin" goes thus in rough translation:

> Stalin-Sun! For our happiness, may you live [forever] in the Kremlin,
> We bring offerings to you — our songs, our hearts, and our flowers.
> In the whole wide world, on this earthly sphere of Man,
> No one is more important for All Humanity [or: the Folk] than You.

Now, with those lines dew-fresh in your memory, quickly return to and peruse Dabashi's celebration of Edward Said (*Al Jazeera*, Sept. 25, 2013). You will certainly detect the influence of the "Song About Stalin" on Dabashi's "Ode to Edward Said" as surely as you would, in "Hyperion," that of Milton on Keats (two names that do not naturally come to mind when Said and Dabashi are mentioned).

> Close proximity to a majestic mountain is a mixed blessing — one is at once graced by the magnanimity of its pastures and the bounty of its slopes, and yet one can never see where one is sitting, under the shadow of what greatness, the embracing comfort of what assurance. The splendor of mountains — Himalayas, Rockies, Alborz — can only be seen from afar, from the safe distance of only a visual, perceptive, appreciative, awe-inspiring grasp of their where-

abouts.

A very happy few — now desolate and broken — have had the rare privilege of calling Edward Said a friend, fewer a colleague, even fewer a comrade, only a handful a neighbor — the closer you came to Edward Said the more his intimate humanity, ordinary simplicity, the sweet, endearing, disarmingly embracing character — his being a husband, a father, a father-in-law, an uncle, a cousin — clouded and colored the majesty that he was. Our emails and voice-mails are still full of his precious words, his timely consolations, anecdotal humor, trivial questions, priceless advice — all too dear to delete, too intimate to share. We were all like birds flying around the generosity of his roof, tiny dandelions joyous in the shade of his backyard, minuscule creatures pasturing on the bounteous slopes of the mountain that he was.

The prince of our cause, the mighty warrior, the Salah al-Din of our reasoning with mad adversaries, source of our sanity in despair, solace in our sorrow, hope in our own humanity, is now no more.

In his absence now it is possible to remember the time when you were and he was not part of your critical consciousness, your creative disposition, your presence in the world — when he did not look over your shoulder watching every single word you wrote.

If remembering the time that you were but he was not integral to you is not to be an exercise in archeological futility, then it has to account for the distance, the discrepancy, between the bashful scholasticism of the learning that my generation of immigrant intellectuals received and the confidence and courage with which we can stand up today in face of outrageous fortune — hand in hand with our brothers and sisters across races and nations, creeds and chaos — and say, "NO!"

Today, there is a solidarity of purpose among a band of rebels and mutineers — gentiles are among us and Jews, Christians and pagans, Hindus and Muslims, atheists we are and agnostics, natives and immigrants — who speak truth to power with the voice of Edward Said the echo of our chorus. How we came here — where we are, hearing with his ears, seeing with his eyes, talking with his tongue — is a question not for making an historical record but for taking moral courage.

Now in the moment of his myth, when Edward Said has left us to our own devices and joined the pantheon of mythic monuments, is precisely the time to have, as he once said, a Gramscian inventory of our whereabouts — once with, and now without him. Today the world is at once poorer in his absence and yet richer through his memory — and precisely in that paradox dwell the seeds of our dissent, the promise of our future, the solemnity of our oath at the sacred site of his casket.

Yes, I thought you'd like that. The Moment Of Our Myth.

Not to be outdone, Abou El Fadl, now that appetizing thing, a full professor, has also produced a work of extravagant praise. But unlike Hamid Dabashi on Edward Said, Abou El Fadl chooses to lavish praise on…Abou El Fadl. You can find it as his website searchforbeauty.org (formerly scholarofthehouse.org). It's worth a read. I've given below about as much of his self-praise as anyone can be expected to stand:

> Dr. Khaled Abou El Fadl is one of the world's leading authorities on Shari'ah, Islamic law and Islam, and a prominent scholar in the field of human rights. He is the Omar and Azmeralda Alfi Distinguished Professor of Law at the UCLA School of Law where he teaches International Human Rights; Islamic Jurisprudence; Law and Terrorism; Islam and Human Rights; Political Asylum and Refugee Law; The Trafficking of Human Beings: Law and Policy; and Political Crimes and Legal Systems. He was also formerly the Chair of the Islamic Studies Interdepartmental Program at UCLA.

> Among his many honors and distinctions, Dr. Abou El Fadl was awarded the University of Oslo Human Rights Award, the Leo and Lisl Eitinger Prize in 2007, and named a Carnegie Scholar in Islamic Law in 2005. He was previously appointed by President George W. Bush to serve on the U.S. Commission for International Religious Freedom, and also served as a member of the board of directors of Human Rights Watch. He works with human rights organizations such as Amnesty International and the Lawyers' Committee for Human Rights (Human Rights First) as an expert in a wide variety of cases involving human rights, terrorism, political asylum, and international and commercial law. In 2017 and 2005, he was also listed as one of LawDragon's Top 500 Lawyers in the Nation. In 2013, he was recognized among "The 50 Smartest People of Faith" by TheBestSchools.org, and was awarded the "American Muslim Achievement Award" in 2014. He has been ranked among "The Power 500 List of the World's Most Influential Arabs" and "The

World's 500 Most Influential Muslims."

A prolific scholar and prominent public intellectual, Dr. Abou El Fadl is the author of numerous books and articles on various topics in Islam and Islamic law. He has lectured on and taught Islamic law throughout the United States and Europe in academic and non-academic environments for over twenty years. His work has been translated into numerous languages including Arabic, Persian, French, Norwegian, Dutch, Ethiopian, Russian, Vietnamese and Japanese, among others.

Dr. Abou El Fadl is most noted for his scholarly approach to Islam from a moral point of view. He writes extensively on universal themes of humanity, morality, human rights, justice, and mercy, and is well known for his writings on beauty as a core moral value of Islam. He is one of the foremost critics of puritan and Wahhabi Islam. Dr. Abou El Fadl has appeared on most major national and international media channels, and has published widely in such publications as the *New York Times, Washington Post, Wall Street Journal, Los Angeles Times, Al-Jazeera English, Huffington Post, Boston Review* and many others.

His latest book is entitled, *Reasoning with God: Reclaiming Shari'ah in the Modern Age*, considered to be his magnum opus and intellectual autobiography. His other books include: *The Great Theft: Wrestling Islam from the Extremists; Speaking in God's Name: Islamic Law, Authority and Women; Rebellion and Violence in Islamic Law; And God Knows the Soldiers: The Authoritative and Authoritarian in Islamic Discourses; Islam and the Challenge of Democracy; The Place of Tolerance in Islam; and The Search for Beauty in Islam: A Conference of the Books*. His book, *The Great Theft*, was the first work to delineate the key differences between moderate and extremist Muslims, and was named one of the Top 100 Books of the year by Canada's *Globe and Mail* (Canada's leading national newspaper). His book, *The Search for Beauty in Islam: A Conference of the Books*, is a landmark work in modern Muslim literature.[1]

Why bring up Dabashi on Said, over two decades after the latter's death in 2003? Only because I never dared hope to find something else that would supply the kind and degree of pleasure you obtain from Dabashi's immortal work. But I have, in the Ode to Khaled Abou El Fadl as composed by Khaled Abou El Fadl. It would be churlish not to

---

1 See: https://www.searchforbeauty.org/

share it.

Khaled Abou El Fadl is simply a specific example of a more general phenomenon: Every Man His Own Hero. In pre-Internet days, hundreds of millions of Chinese (some of them now the proud parents and grandparents of single-minded capitalists) held aloft Chairman Mao's Little Red Book. Tens of millions of Russians in bad old Soviet days put Stalin's "Short Course" on their bookshelves, even though it was hardly the stuff that would qualify, nowadays, for Oprah's Book Club. In Libya, Qaddafi flogged his "Green Book," containing the Wisdom of Muammar Qaddafi; once upon a time, thousands read it, for the book was the talk and the toast of the town, if the town was in Tripolitania.

Now, with the Internet, disinterested "Friends and Supporters" of virtually anyone can offer that anyone's words, hailed as a Spiritual and All-Purpose Guide to Just About Everything. It is not merely that Everyman can now blog here, and post there, over and over again. Now Everyman Can Appear on the Worldwide Web as The Glorious Helmsman of Humanity, courtesy of his self-effacing "Friends and Supporters." On the Internet, at a dedicated website, you can be not only King or Queen of the Universe, and not just for a day but from here on out, and even from beyond the grave (your website will outlast you). Everyman can now count himself a king of infinite space, even if bound in his own gigabyte nutshell, in mysterious Googlelandia, or in some particular place TBA.

In offering so many different aspects of Dr. Khaled Abou El Fadl's Life and Works, at his new website, searchforbeauty.org, was simply ahead of its time. It would be hard to choose which section of his website is most impressive. There is the biographical "About Dr. Khaled Abou El Fadl." There is the scholarly "Bibliography of Khaled Abou El Fadl." There is the epistolary "Letters to Dr. Abou El Fadl." There is "Dr. Abou El Fadl In the Media." There are "Khutbahs by Dr. Abou El Fadl." And there is even "Recommended Reading" — "recommended" by none other than Dr. Khaled Abou El Fadl, many of whose own books are among those he found most to recommend. But that is not cause for carping. It would be silly indeed for someone, especially a world-famous scholar like Dr. Abou El Fadl, to write a book that, afterwards, he felt he could not recommend.

Indeed, Khaled Abou El Fadl's refreshing absence of humility, rightly understood, is truly humble. Was it not Golda Meir who once cut short someone engaging in pro-forma self-deprecation: "Don't be so humble, you're not that great"? Dr. Khaled Abou El Fadl has clearly been "not so humble;" it logically follows, therefore, that he is likely to be very great.

Not the least of Dr. Khaled Abou El Fadl's services was the list he compiled of what he called "The Worst Books About Islam," books so bad that Dr. Khaled Abou El Fadl hoped no one would waste his time even opening one of them. That list included, among much else, Professor John Wansbrough's *Qur'anic Studies*, Ibn Warraq's anthology of scholarly articles, entitled *The Quest for the Historical Muhammad*, and Joseph Schacht's *The Origins of Muhammadan Jurisprudence*.

Wansbrough and Schacht have long been admired by Western scholars of Islam: the first as a pioneer in the study of early Islam and the teacher of both Patricia Crone and Michael Cook; the second as one of the most scrupulous and authoritative students of Islamic law in the Western world. But neither Wansbrough nor Schacht was a Muslim. And by now it should be obvious that Muslims insist we cannot rely on any non-Muslim scholar's supposed "understanding" of Islam, no matter how many languages that scholar may know, or how many decades of tireless and, on the surface, disinterested study he may have devoted to the matter. The simplest of seminarians at Al-Azhar, the most grizzled Afghani poppy farmer, by virtue of being a Muslim, necessarily understands Islam in a way that no non-Muslim, no matter how learned, possibly can.

This should not be confused with the whole business of "Orientalism." Dr. Khaled Abou El Fadl is no Edward Said, who has been receiving so many palpable hits that his likeness is beginning to look like St. Sebastian. Khaled Abou El Fadl realizes that Schacht and Wansbrough and Crone and Luxenberg and Ibn Warraq may well have had nothing to do with the "imperialism project." He needs, other Muslims need, to find an objection broader and deeper and sturdier now that burnt offerings are no longer made with quite the same frequency on the altar at the Temple of Said.

No, Khaled Abou El Fadl's objection is much more profound. It is just that non-Muslims obviously cannot be expected to feel, deeply, the profound richness and variety and multiplicity of Islam. Khaled Abou El Fadl realizes the permanent impossibility of any non-Muslim making any valid generalizations about Islam ever — or indeed, of saying anything at all about Islam from "the outside," as richly various and variously rich as Islam is, so different in its theory and practice, depending on the time, depending on the space. There are practically as many Islams as there are Muslims, according to El Fadl, and non-Muslims — who seem disturbingly confident that they can make pronouncements on matters they know nothing about — should never forget it. Especially when they are about to say something negative, as they do so often nowadays, simply because they need that old whipping-boy — the Other. Ever since the Communists retired from the scene, the West, and especially America, have been grooming Islam to fill that role.

Dr. Khaled Abou El Fadl knows that non-Muslims cannot talk about "Islam" because "Islam," as one thing, does not exist, but only as many things, and only Muslims can talk truthfully, without rancor or hidden agendas, about those things which seem never to overlap or add up to one thing. One particular kind of non-Muslim — the kind that speaks Arabic, and has an Arab name, and calls himself an Arab, but happens to be Christian — may sometimes be exempted from the ban, because the genetic makeup of such people, their Arab DNA, permits a special insight into the nature of Islam. But Schacht, Wansbrough, Snouck Hurgronje and a thousand other scholars did not possess that precious Arab strand of recombinant DNA. The entire corpus of their work, as a result, is fatally vitiated.

Ibn Warraq, whose *The Quest for the Historical Muhammad* makes the list compiled by Khaled Abou El Fadl of "The Worst Books on Islam," suffers from a different, equally fatal handicap. Although Ibn Warraq was raised as a Muslim and began attending a madrasa at the age of six (the very age at which Dr. Khaled Abou El Fadl began to attend his own elementary classes in Qur'an at Al-Azhar), Ibn Warraq fell away from Islam, and ultimately renounced it. And now he spends his time writing about Islam, as if he understood it.

But a mysterious phenomenon, of which Muslims have long been aware but which is insufficiently appreciated by non-Muslims, is that of the complete mental disarray, accompanied by severe memory loss, that results from the shock to the apostate's system. It's akin to whirling about in a centrifuge in a dark laboratory, with a mad scientist rubbing his gleeful hands as he watches you whirl, and whirl. And the name of that mad scientist is Shaytan — Satan.

Apostasy from Islam is a truly wrenching experience, often proving fatal. For in leaving Islam, one is giving up all chance for Eternal Happiness and throwing away the Total Explanation of the Universe, which gives daily life the only coherence it may be said to possess. Imagine being supplied with the Secret of the Universe, but failing to appreciate it, and then throwing it away. That is what, Muslims assure us, apostates from Islam do.

Naturally there are consequences. Whatever they may once have known, or thought they knew, about Islam before, the very act of apostasy renders them incapable of recalling anything of value about the faith that for so long sustained them. Their apostasy renders them incapable of understanding or speaking about Islam. Their so-called "testimony" about Islam is thus essentially worthless. That is true of Ibn Warraq as well as of Anwar Sheikh and Ali Sina and Ayaan Hirsi Ali and so many others. The minute they become apostates, they no longer know what they are talking about when they talk about Islam. And as apostates, of course they concentrate only on negative aspects that they fabricate about Islam.

A comparison may be instructive. One marketing trick of Ibn Warraq, and of other ex-Muslims, is the assumption of an alias, designed to make it seem that they are in some danger. Dr. Khaled Abou El Fadl, in contrast, does not use an alias despite the "many threats" he claims to have received, and has repeatedly told us about only with great reluctance. He is determined, he says, to continue his heroic refusal to kowtow to the "Wahhabists" who are giving Islam such a bad name in some quarters.

Dr. Khaled Abou El Fadl has been just as brave in speaking truth to powerful non-Muslims. It was he who fearlessly argued that "jihad" means "interior struggle" and not "Holy War," and that there could not possibly be any kind of "Holy War" in Islam. It was Dr. Khaled Abou El Fadl who, just after 9/11, forthrightly expressed his immediate thoughts, which were to worry about harm that might come to Muslims as a result of this attack. That could not have been an easy and popular thing to say in America just after the attacks of 9/11. The cowardly, of course, would only offer some words of sympathy and solidarity with American non-Muslims; Khaled Abou El Fadl was not about to play the taqiyya hypocrite. He is a Muslim, and he worries only about his fellow Muslims. Whether dealing with those threatening Wahhabists, or their mirror-image, the threatening Infidels, he will not trim his sails. "Ich kann nicht anders" — "I can do no other" — is as much his motto as it is anyone's.

At the Secular Islam site, Ibn Warraq offers his articles on Islam to the entire universe, or at least the universe of those who happen to stumble upon his website, free of charge, there for the taking. At his previous website, scholarofthehouse.org, Khaled Abou El Fadl, or rather his Friends and Supporters, did things differently. Visitors, at least at first, had nothing inflicted on them. Instead, in the original version of scholarofthehouse.org, they were politely offered his articles, his lectures, his interviews, all demurely on sale. Only those who demonstrated a real interest, by sending in the appropriate sum, would read or hear in detail what Khaled Abou El Fadl wished to say on a great many subjects. He obviously did not believe in inflicting his views on the entire world, but on sharing them with a self-selected group of paying guests.

Perhaps that marks the difference between a coarse apostate such as Ibn Warraq, with his anthologies of pseudo-scholarship (just look at a list of the "scholarly" contributors to his other books, such as *The Origins of the Koran* and *What the Koran Really Says*), and the refined Islamic luminescence that was and is Khaled Abou El Fadl. He is not only a scholar of the house, but one who was doing his best to ensure that his house in due time should have many mansions.

This has all changed now. Originally, there were so many things on sale at this website devoted to Dr. Khaled Abou El Fadl. These included collections of his articles (for $60) and whole series of his recorded lectures on this or that aspect of Islam, which could be ordered on either audiocassette or CD. The first item at the previous website, www.scholarofthehouse.org, was "What's New" — new articles, new interviews, new Qur'anic commentaries, brave new books by Dr. Khaled Abou El Fadl, each with the price helpfully appended.

Should you, for example, have in years past wanted to buy Dr. Khaled Abou El Fadl's commentary on Surah 103: Al-Asr, that would have cost you $8.00; for the same price, you could have purchased his discussion of Sura 111: Al-Lahab. A lecture, "Islam and Democracy," went for $4.00, while an Unedited Interview on "Islamic Democracy" was a bargain at $8.00. And if you were moved to send a contribution to support those who operate the website by gathering, and posting, and selling Dr. Khaled Abou El Fadl's work, information about how to do that in the most expeditious manner was also conveniently available.

All this is gone from his website now. Could this change have been made in reaction to a previous version of this very article, which I published at *Jihad Watch* in 2005? It was immediately after this that the website of Dr. El Fadl was first taken off-line, only to reappear in a completely different guise a few months later.

At the website, under the "Our Mission" rubric, the "Friends and Supporters" of Dr. Khaled Abou El Fadl noted that "Dr. Abou El Fadl is neither involved in nor responsible for any of the activities related to this website, including the naming of the site, the conducting of any matters of business, or the making of any decisions regarding its policies. Dr. Abou El Fadl does not gain any profit from the sales generated from the website."

But before the buying apparatus was removed, someone must have been making some money from the sale of Dr. Abou El Fadl's articles, and the 10-part lecture series (on audiocassettes and CD) on Marriage and Divorce, and on the gallimaufry of taped lectures, interviews, writings, and opinions on this and on that. The halo of the hagiographic sanctified the brazenly commercial enterprise at this website dedicated so flatteringly, even djambullishly, to the Thought and Greatness of One Man.

This raises an awkward question. Could it be that these "Friends and Supporters" were trying to make money from the genius of Dr. Khaled Abou El Fadl while purporting to honor him, and were using the website only to flog his wares and keep the cash for themselves? Meanwhile, the trusting and unworldly Dr. Khaled Abou El Fadl himself, that "inexhaustible fountain of fertilacious fertility whose riveting rivulets water the oasis where the roses and bulbuls of Gulistan bloom and twitter both day and night, even in the endless tract-housing wastes of the American intellectual desert," as Hamid Dabashi might put it, apparently received not a penny for his thoughts — at least not those of his thoughts that were available for sale at scholarofthehouse.org.

What kind of "Friends and Supporters" are these, anyway? Dr. Khaled Abou El Fadl has a right to know.

CHAPTER TWENTY-NINE

Constructing "The Other"

I T HAS BECOME a peculiar sort of conventional wisdom among those of a particular intellectual and ideological bent — the idea that each generation of Americans seems to identify a particular enemy, contrived to fit ideologies or economic necessities. Americans must always find "The Other" whom they can then hate and fear.

"The Other" was, of course, Edward Said's favorite topic. He kept talking about the need of the West to create the Islamic "Other," but said nothing about the fact that the Original, the Ur, the Other of All Others, was the one that was created by Islam to sustain Believers. The most perduring "Other" is the Infidel, who must be hated no matter what good he "appears" to do, what kindness he "appears" to offer — such as those hapless American soldiers in Iraq who wondered why everyone tried to kill them as they built schools, hospitals, electricity grids, and roads.

But no one is concerned about that. Everyone know that the real "Other"— constructor, the real villain of the "Other" piece here, is not the Islamic world but the West — the need for white, European, racist, colonialist Europe/America to "construct" that "Other" that it can then despise. For without that "Other" to hate, that miserable, racist, dysfunctional, poverty-stricken, ruinous, chaotic, violent, worthless bunch of countries and peoples who ridiculously call themselves the West, or, even more absurdly, "Western civilization," and who have given the world absolutely nothing of value, would scarcely be able to justify their own chaotic and confused existence. After all, just compare its ridiculous accomplishments with the scientific achievements and immortal works of art produced over 1350 years everywhere that Islam has planted itself.

It was not enough for the West to have constructed "the Other" of Hitler and the Nazis, and to have caused World War II thereby, with all the enormous suffering that could have been avoided. It was not enough for that West to have constructed "the Other" of Lenin and Stalin and the Politburo, and to have deliberately inveigled the Red Army into Eastern Europe to seize control for local Communists so that, all over the West, people would be filled with quite unnecessary alarm and dread.

No, now they are at it again, having somehow tricked a few misguided people, a handful of Muslim extremists who were putty in the hands of the CIA and Mossad, to here and there plan their pathetic little attacks (with, admittedly, one or two actually succeeding — to the great delight, you can be sure, of the master puppeteers in Langley and Tel Aviv). And what about all these so-called "plots" that those behind this sinister undertaking claim to have discovered, with all that fanfare, all over Europe, or all these people picked up and charged with "terrorism" all over the United States? What is that if not a sustained effort at scaring people, all cooked up to make them think there is a problem with Islam?

Yes, I know what you are going to argue. You will say that they never actually mentioned Islam. All they talked about is the "war on terror." Exactly. Exactly the point I was trying to make. It was precisely the refusal of Western governments to blame the teachings of Islam in any way, to even go out of their way never to mention Islam, that was the most diabolical part of it.

It was the old "don't put beans up your nose" strategy. By failing so noticeably and so obviously to mention Islam, the government was actually doing everything it could to make people focus on precisely that — Islam. For people are not fools. Or rather, you can only fool those people in some ways, and not in others. By now, everyone in the West knows that their own governments are not to be trusted, that they are run often by the very foolish people who foolishly try to fool them. But they can't do it. The fools who rule are even bigger fools than the fools they rule over, who cannot be so easily fooled as the ruling fools think.

And that is why, you see, when the ruling Western elites engaged, for the third time in less than a century, in "constructing the Other"— first the Nazis, then the Communists — they then fixed on the helpless, innocent Muslims as the third Other, the pretend-threat to Western civilization that would justify spending hundreds of billions on defense, and in creating a hysterical quasi-police state to conduct the so-called "war on terror." And the diabolical Westerners believe they have hit on the very best way to construct that Other: that is, precisely, not to construct it! When the political and media elites in Europe take care not to name Islam or Muslims as the sources of Western distress and malaise, the hundreds of millions who have grown to distrust their leaders will instead do the opposite, and focus precisely on the subject of Islam and Muslims.

Have I made everything clear?

Good. I thought I would.

CHAPTER THIRTY

Does Poverty Breed Jihad?

THIS CONSTANT refrain about young Muslims turning to "militant Islam" or "Islamism" or some such because of poverty can be answered in two ways.

The first way is to point out that the extensive studies by sociologists of the backgrounds of many hundreds, or even thousands, of Muslim terrorists have all concluded that on the whole, they are much better off and much better educated than the average Muslim. The terrorists have included the scions of both what may be described as among the First Families of Egypt (Ayman al-Zawahiri's grandfather's brother was Azzam Pasha, the first Secretary of the Arab League); and Saudi Arabia (the Bin Laden family is, after the Al-Saud, possibly the richest family in Saudi Arabia), as well as urban planners (Mohamed Atta), successful computer engineers ("Mike" Hawash), mild-mannered accountants, and so on.

So the idea that poverty is the problem, which simply helps everyone avoid looking squarely at the theory and practice of Islam over 1400 years, can easily be shown to be nonsense.

The second way, however, is to pretend, for a minute, that "poverty" might have something to do with it — that when Muslims are poor, they necessarily find solace in Islam and become "immoderate" Muslims. Suppose that were true? What would that mean? Are Infidels supposed to guarantee a particular standard of living to all Muslims living in the West, not to mention elsewhere, so that they never feel sufficiently put upon, do not feel that they are falling behind in their own standard of living? Would that make sense? Is that the Infidel man's new burden?

And what about other kinds of setbacks? What about the Muslim

203

who is rejected by an Infidel woman he is courting, and feels slighted as a result, and resentful, and…well, you know. What about the Muslim who loses his job, and is mad at his Infidel boss, and…well, yet again, you know. The problem is this: there are a thousand reasons why people feel bad, in how they suffer in one way or another. We who are not Muslim do not have at hand a ready grid for the universe which teaches us to blame and hate the "Other." We who are not Muslim do not have at hand a prism, constructed from the verses of Qur'an, and the Hadith stories, and the supposed facts of Muhammad's supposed existence — a prism through which Muslims can view the universe, and again, blame the Infidel for all their discontents.

And so what are we Infidels to do? Spend the rest of our lives making sure that no Muslims are unhappy, or recognizing that the source of their enmity towards us — the ideology of Islam — cannot be changed, but we can nonetheless work to deprive Muslims of the means of doing us harm. To fight terrorism, all terror groups, and those who support them (such as CAIR, and Students for Justice in Palestine) should be banned, their financing cut off, while those who have not only supported but planned or carried out acts of terrorism should be imprisoned or killed.. Muslim states that threaten the West with conventional combat (as Erdogan has taken to doing, despite Turkey being a member of NATO), should be subject to weapons embargoes, and whenever possible, have their arsenals destroyed, as Israel has been doing to the weapons left in Syria by Assad's fleeing army.

Demography is now the most effective means to spread Muslim power across the globe. The West must end all Muslim migration to Infidel lands, now that it is clear that a large Muslim presence everywhere in Europe is both deleterious and dangerous, and deport as many Muslims as possible, beginning with those who have committed crimes. Muslim economic migrants should be forced to fulfill a work requirement in order to receive welfare benefits, and the benefits themselves should be greatly decreased, and cease altogether after, say, the first two years of a Muslim immigrant's presence in the country. Campaigns of counter-da'wa need to be carried on, especially in prisons, where Muslims have been adept at converting fellow prisoners to their faith. Europeans need to keep steadily and whole in mind that the large-scale presence of Muslims in their countries has created a situation for the indigenous non-Muslims that is much more unpleasant, expensive, and physically dangerous, than would be the case without that large-scale presence. A war between Islam and the West, or more exactly,, between Islam and all the rest, has already begun, but only one side has yet recognized it. The West, however, has amazing powers of recuperation, and should start to fight for its survival now.

And we should create the conditions where Muslims themselves, through simple observation, can learn or be forced to learn that what is wrong with their societies, politically, economically, socially, and intellectually, is entirely owed to the teachings of Islam itself. The Soviet Union collapsed because the system was found to have failed. It could not make the lives of its people better. The outside world, chiefly the United States, helped create the conditions in which that failure was impossible for Soviet citizens to ignore or explain away. The same thing can be done, much more slowly and with much more difficulty, with Islam — showing its own followers that, for example, it is inshallah-fatalism that keeps them from having developed successful economies, and it is the spirit of submission to authority, and blind obedience, that makes despotism such a natural part of Islam. If Muslims wish not merely to buy with money from the sale of oil and natural gas the goods and services of the Infidel world, but to be able to produce those goods and services themselves, they will have to limit the hold of Islam on Muslim minds, as Ataturk attempted. We non-Muslims should openly discuss how Islam suppresses skeptical inquiry, stunts mental growth, and hinders both artistic expression and the pursuit of science.

CHAPTER THIRTY-ONE

Islamophobia? Really?

THE WORD "Islamophobia" must be held up for inspection and its users constantly asked precisely how they would define that word. They should be put on the defensive for waving about what is clearly meant to be a scare-word that will silence criticism.

So let us ask them, which of the following criticisms of Islam is to be considered "Islamophobia:"

1. Muhammad is a role-model for all time. Muhammad married Aisha when she was six and had sexual intercourse with her when she was nine. I find appalling that Muslims consider this act of Muhammad to be that of the man who is in every way a role-model, and hence to be emulated. In particular, I am appalled that virtually the first act of the Ayatollah Khomeini, a very orthodox and learned Shi'a theologian, was to lower the marriageable age of girls in Iran to nine — because, of course, that was Aisha's age when Muhammad had sexual relations with her. Khomeini himself married his wife when she was fifteen.

2. I find appalling that Islam provides a kind of Total Regulation of the Universe, so that its adherents are constantly asking for advice as to whether or not, for example, they can wear their hair in a certain way, grow their beards in a certain way, wish an Infidel a Merry Christmas (absolutely not!).

3. I find appalling the religiously-sanctioned doctrine of taqiyya — a doctrine that has its sources in the Qur'an itself (3:28 and 16:106). Taqiyya is the religiously-sanctioned dissimulation about the faith of Islam, and about the beliefs held by its adherents. It has its origins in the need of Shi'a Muslims to hide their faith from their much-more-popu-

lous rivals, the Sunnis.

4. I find appalling many of the acts which Muhammad committed, including his personally taking part in the massacre of 600-900 members of the Qurayza, his inspiring the assassination of at least three of those who mocked him, including Abu Afak, a 120-year-old Jewish poet, Asma bint Marwan, a female poet, and Ka'b ibn al-Ashraf, a Jewish poet, by in each case asking aloud "who will rid me of this person" and his loyal followers, taking the obvious hint, did as he desired.

5. I find appalling the hatred expressed throughout the Qur'an, the hadith, and the sira for Infidels — all Infidels. They are described as "the most vile of created beings" (98:6) and the Qur'an is full of commands to wage violent jihad against them, merely for the crime of not being Muslims.

6. I find nauseating the historic imposition of the jizya, a capitation tax on Infidels, the requirement that they wear identifying garb on their clothes and dwellings, that they not be able to build or repair houses of worship without the permission of Muslim authorities, that they must ride donkeys sidesaddle and dismount in the presence of Muslims, that they have no legal recourse against Muslims for they are not equal at law — and a hundred other things, designed to insure their permanent, as the canonical texts say, "humiliation." A practice from the past, you say? Or a practice that in many ways can still be detected, in the shabby treatment of non-Muslims all over the Muslim world, from the mistreatment of Copts, Assyrians, Chaldeans, Maronites, Armenians, Jews, Hindus, Buddhists, who are still living in Muslim countries, to the disguised jizyah of the Bumpitura system in Malaysia, which forces non-Muslims to hire and share profits with Muslim employees who may have contributed nothing to the financial wellbeing of a particular firm. Some Muslims even seem to regard the welfare benefits they receive in the West as a form of jizyah.

7. I find appalling the mass murder of 60-70 million Hindus over 250 years of Mughal rule, and the destruction of tens of thousands of Hindu (and Buddhist) artifacts, temples, and temple complexes, many of the them listed in two fat volumes edited by Sita Ram Goel.

8. I find the long history of the persecution in Iran of the Zoroastrians, which has led to their decrease in population to a mere 15,000, out of an Iranian population of 85 million, something to deplore. The great scholar of Zoroastrianism, Mary Boyce, offers piquant details of that persecution, including the deliberate torture and killing of dogs (which are revered by Zoroastrians), even by small Muslim children

who are taught to so behave, in order to make Zoroastrians miserable.

9. I find the record of Muslim intellectual achievement singularly unimpressive, and I attribute this to the failure to encourage free and skeptical inquiry, which is necessary for, among other things, the development of modern science. I find convincing the argument that there continued to be some intellectual activity in non-Muslim lands for a few centuries after their initial conquest by Muslims, as long as the Christians and Jews (in the Middle East) were still a significant and fructifying influence, and that when that ceased to be, such activity came to an abrupt end.

10. I deplore the prohibition on sculpture or on paintings of living things. I deplore the horrific vandalism and destruction of Christian, Jewish, Zoroastrian, Hindu, and Buddhist sites, from the thousands of temples, right up to today, with the destruction of the Bamiyan Buddhas in Afghanistan, pre-Islamic archeological sites vandalized all over Iraq, and in Europe itself, churches and statues in public are now the object of Muslim attacks and destruction.

11. I deplore that part of Muslim jurisprudence which renders all treaties between Infidels and Muslims worthless from the viewpoint of the Infidels, though worth a great deal from the viewpoint of the Muslims, for they are only signing a "hudna," a truce-treaty rather than a true peace-treaty, and because they must ultimately go to war against the Infidel, or press their jihad against the Infidel in other ways. Given the model of the Treaty of al-Hudaibiyya that Muhammad concluded with the Meccans, an agreement that was to have lasted ten years but which he broke after 18 months, no Infidel state or people can ever put their trust in a treaty that Muslims make with Infidels.

12. I deplore the speech of former Malaysian Prime Minister Mahathir Mohammad, so roundly applauded several years ago, in which he called for the "development" not of human potential, not of art and science, but essentially of weapons technology and the harnessing and encouraging of Muslim "brain power" for the sole purpose of defeating the Infidels in war.

13. I deplore the fact that Muslims are taught, and clearly many have taken to heart, the idea that they should offer their loyalty only to fellow Muslims, the umma al-islamiyya, and never to Infidels or to the Infidel nation-state to which they have sworn an oath of allegiance — apparently such an oath must always be an act of perjury, because such Muslim loyalty to a non-Muslim polity is impossible.

14. I deplore the ululations of pleasure over acts of terrorism, the

passing out of candies, the evident delight shown by celebrating crowds in Cairo, Ramallah, Khartoum, Beirut, Damascus, Baghdad, and of course all over Saudi Arabia, when news of the World Trade Center attacks became known. Only in Iran, with a populace increasingly disaffected from Islam, was the attack greeted with silence. I attribute statements of exultation about the "Infidels" deserving such an attack to the fact that Muslims are taught to view the world as in a state of permanent war between the Believers and the Infidels.

15. On that score, I deplore that mad division of the world between dar al-Islam and dar al-harb, and the requirement that there be uncompromising hostility between the two until the final triumph of the former, and the permanent subjugation and incorporation into it of the latter.

16. I deplore the sexual inequality and mistreatment of women, which I can show has a clear basis in the canonical Islamic texts, and is not simply, *pace* Shirin Ebadi and other quasi-"reformers," a "cultural" matter.

17. I deplore the fact that Infidels living in Muslim lands feel, with justice, insecure, but that Muslims treat the Infidel countries in which they now live, and their indigenous inhabitants, too, with disdain, arrogance, and endless demands for the indigenous non-Muslims to yield to what Muslims want — whether it be to have crucifixes removed in public places, or to change the laws of laicity in France so that hijabs may be worn in schools and government offices, or to demand that "hate speech" laws be expansively interpreted in order to shut down criticism of Islam.

18. I deplore the emphasis in Islam on the collective, and the hatred for the autonomy of the individual. In particular, I believe that someone born into Islam has a perfect right to leave Islam if he or she chooses — and that there should be no punishment for this free exercise of conscience, much less the murderous punishment so often inflicted.

19. I deplore the fact that while Muslims claim that Islam is a "universalist" religion, it has been a vehicle for Arab imperialism, causing those conquered and Islamized in some cases to forget, or become indifferent or even hostile to, their own pre-Islamic histories. The requirement that the Qur'an be read in Arabic (one of the first things Ataturk did was commission both a Turkish Qur'an and a Turkish tafsir, or commentary), that Muslims turn toward Mecca, in Arabia, five times a day in prayer, that at least once in every Muslim's life, if he has the means to do so, he should go on the Hajj to Mecca, and the belief many Muslims

hold that the ideal form of society can be derived from the Sunna of 7th century Arabia, and that their own societies are worth little by comparison, imposes an Arab cultural and linguistic imperialism that convinces those conquered non-Muslims, now sporting Arab names, that they, too, just like their conquerors, are Arabs.

20. I deplore the attacks on ex-Muslims who, if they publicize their apostasy, often must live in fear. I deplore the attacks on Salman Rushdie and his translators, including the murder of his Japanese translator, the attempts on the life of Ayaan Hirsi Ali, and the absence of serious debate about the nature of Islam and of its reform — except as a means to further beguile and distract Infidels who are becoming more wary and harder to bamboozle.

21. I deplore the emptiness of the "Tu Quoque" arguments directed at Christians and Jews, based on a disingenuous quotation of passages — for example, from Leviticus — that are completely ignored and have not been invoked for two thousand years, and I deplore the rewriting of history so that Christianity can be blamed for atrocities with which it had nothing to do, so that a Muslim professor can tell an American university audience that "the Ku Klux Klan used to crucify (!) African-Americans, everyone standing around during the crucifixion singing Christian hymns(!)."

The KKK hung — lynched — its victims. It never crucified its victims. Crucifixion remained a practice inflicted by Muslim Arabs. Nor did the KKK lynch mobs sing "Christian hymns." This is a story made-up so as to be able to charge that Christians, too, can be accused of the same barbarity, based on Christian doctrine, as that we accuse Muslims of, based on their texts and teachings.

22. I deplore the phony appeals of the "we all share one Abrahamic faith" and "we are the three monotheisms" when, to my mind, a Christian or a Jew has far less to fear from any practicing polytheistic Hindu or Buddhist than from fellow monotheists who are Muslim.

23. I deplore the fact that Islam is based on the idea of world-conquest, not of accommodation, and that its adherents do not believe in Western pluralism except insofar as this can be used as an instrument, temporarily most useful, to protect the position of Islam until its adherents have firmly established themselves in the Bilad al-Kufr, the Lands of the Infidels.

24. I deplore the view, in Islam, that it is not a saving of an individual soul that is involved when one conducts da'wa or the Call to Islam, but rather, something that appears to be much more like signing some-

one up for the Army of Islam. The recruit need not have read all the fine print; he need not know Islamic tenets; he need not even have read or know what is in the sira and hadith or much of the Qur'an; he need only recite a single sentence. That does not show a deep concern for the nature of the conversion (sorry, "reversion").

25. I deplore the sentiment that "Islam is to dominate and not to be dominated." I deplore the sentiment "War is deception" as uttered by Muhammad. I deplore Muhammad's remark that "I have been made victorious through terror." I am appalled at what has happened over 1350 years in vast swaths of territory formerly filled with Christians, Jews, Zoroastrians, Hindus, and Buddhists, much of which is now today almost monotonously Islamic. I do not think Islam welcomes any true diversity, if by that is meant the possibility of full equality for non-Muslims.

26. I deplore the fact that slavery is permitted in Islam, that it is discussed in the Qur'an, and that it was suppressed in 19th century Arabia only through the exertion of British naval power in the Gulf; that it was formally done away with in Saudi Arabia only in 1962; that it still exists in Mali, and the Sudan, and even Mauritania, where Arabs enslave black Africans; that it may still exist, away from prying Western eyes, deep in the Arabian interior. Certainly the treatment of the Thai, Filipino, Indian and other female house workers in Arab households in the Gulf amounts to slavery. Muhammad, the Perfect Man, bought, sold, and traded slaves. It is no accident that there has never been a Muslim William Wilberforce.

I could go on, and am prepared to adduce history, and quotations from the canonical texts. And so are the many thousands of Infidels who have looked into Islam, or in their own countries had a close look at the Muslim populations, recently arrived, which have made their own existences, as non-Muslims, far more unpleasant, expensive, and dangerous than they would otherwise be.

If this is "Islamophobia," then please show me exactly why it is irrational (i.e., not based on facts or observable behavior, or a study of history) to dislike or even hate Islam. If you cannot show that, then perhaps that word should not be invoked. But if you do invoke it, be prepared to have copious quotations from Qur'an and hadith and sira constantly presented to audiences so that they may judge Islam for themselves, without the "guidance" of apologists for Islam, both Muslim and non-Muslim.

PART IV

What Is To Be Done?

CHAPTER THIRTY-TWO

What Can the French Do?

THE FRENCH STATE cannot any longer tolerate "the lost lands of the Republic," that is, the 750 No-Go areas where Muslims now rule, and impose, through violence if necessary, their own rules on all those who enter those areas. It must realize that it is losing territory to those who do not wish the indigenous people, or the state, of France well, do not respect its laws or mores, but hope through demographic jihad to ultimately conquer the entire country.

What can the French do?

First, they can put a stop to Muslim immigration. From now on, no legal immigration from any Muslim country should be permitted. As for illegal Muslim migrants, the government must devote much greater resources of both police and magistrates into locating illegal Muslim migrants and promptly deporting them back to their countries of origin. Too many Muslims who have been ordered to leave the country have stayed on for years (and are still in France), secure in the knowledge that the French police lack the resources to track them down. Any deportation order should be immediately enforced, not giving Muslims time to disappear into one of the No-Go areas.

Second, in order to make immigration to France much less attractive, the government can stop providing welfare benefits to immigrants during the first five years of their residence in France. That means those — overwhelmingly Muslim maghrebins — who arrive expecting at once to batten on every benefit the generous French welfare state offers, including free or subsidized housing, free medical care, free education, unemployment payments, family allowances, and more, will instead have to go immediately to work, and continue to work for five years before becoming eligible to receive any benefits paid for by French tax-payers. That will certainly make those would-be immigrants think twice about choosing to go to France.

Third, the police and the army must physically conquer the No-Go areas, taking them back one-by-one. This means both police and sol-diers must enter these areas and search for Muslim criminals, especially drug traffickers, robbers, and burglars who hide out in the No-Go areas. The French police have to increase their permanent presence in order to enforce the laws, especially those that Muslims in No-Go areas have flouted. For example, they must make sure that in schools and other public institutions, hijabs and other outward signs of religious identi-fication (including Jewish kippahs and Sikh turbans) are not worn, for they violate the French state's principle of laïcité. The niqab is banned in all public places, but in the No-Go areas, niqabs are much in evidence. The authorities must now enforce that ban everywhere.

The French must make sure it is understood by Muslims in France that the laws of the state must be obeyed everywhere in the Hexagon. But such enforcement in the schools should not be left to the teachers and principals, who are most immediately vulnerable to threats from Muslim parents, but by the police, who should arrest any Muslim par-ents who violently object to the no-hijab policy, or to the teaching of certain subjects (such as Christianity in France, the French Revolution, and the Holocaust) and judges must not hesitate to impose large fines and even jail time on those who make threats to the teaching staff.

Fourth, whenever there is violent unrest by Muslims both in and outside the No-Go areas — as, for example, pro-Hamas demonstrations demanding that the French government halt all military sales to Israel, or anti-police demonstrations prompted by the death of a Muslim delin-quent who died in a car crash while fleeing the police, or non-Muslims savagely beaten for "violating the Sharia" by eating ice cream during Ra-madan, instead of ignoring these mini-uprisings as too dangerous to handle, not just the police, but the army must be out in force, and used to patrol the No-Go areas and to suppress rioters. Muslims must not be allowed anymore to think that the French government's writ does not run in heavily Muslim areas. Those rounded up by the army should be checked against a database: any who have been convicted of a crime or crimes should be subject to immediate deportation.

If this is done often enough — arresting Muslim malefactors in No-Go areas, and then deporting them from France, enforcing the hi-jab bans in schools, and the niqab bans in all public places — Muslims will realize that the French government is no longer going to tolerate the mixture as before. Like the police, the army should also patrol in No-Go areas as a sign that the French government has returned in force to make sure that its laws, and not the Shari'a, are observed. It will take time, and even occasional violence by the state, to undo the triumphalist sense Muslims now have that, bit by bit, they are taking over France. It won't happen without casualties, among both Muslims, and the police-men and soldiers tasked with disabusing them of their current belief that France is theirs to inherit. But the French no longer have a choice.

CHAPTER THIRTY-THREE

War for the Soul of Islam?

T HE EGYPTIAN government is corrupt. Egyptian leaders batten on the $1.5 billion in American aid, not to mention whatever they manage to wheedle out of the Europeans. But the poor, who exist everywhere, or others who were not poor but outraged at the corruption, did not merely say that Hosni Mubarak and company are "corrupt." That is what non-Muslims would say. No — when President Mubarak was overthrown, the demonstrators said that Mubarak and his Family-and-Friends fellow thieves were "infidels" or were in the pockets of "infidels" or in league with them. All discontent, all political life, can be reduced to the categories that Islam so conveniently provides, and it is based on the endless war between the Believer and the Infidel.

It is no different in Saudi Arabia. Are the thousands of "princes" of the Al-Saud family helping themselves to the country's oil wealth? Of course they are. Is it sickening? Of course it is. But the problem is seen, by those sickened by that appropriation, and the decadent pursuits (which are "decadent" only in Islamic terms) of those princes, as demonstrating the "un-Islamic" nature of the Al-Saud.

Muslims view the world through the prism of Islam. It provides a Total Explanation of the Universe, which covers every possible detail of life. It would be impossible to find a category of injustice that cannot be defined in terms of Islam. Corruption is unjust, and therefore, for those who wish to fight it, it must necessarily be un-Islamic. On the other hand, violently spreading Islam, fighting the Infidels if they resist, and treating them terribly according to the principles of the sharia when and where they submit or are conquered, is also Islamic.

So what should we do? Those now making policy seem to want to believe any number of things, none of them true. Some want to believe that Islam is fundamentally decent, save for the fundamentalists, whose definition keeps changing and expanding — from a "tiny handful of extremists" to "the Wahhabis" to the "Wahhabis and the Salafists" to "10-15% of all Muslims" to…well, the latest effort is to convince us that there is "war going on within Islam itself." This is nonsense — there are some Muslims who are of a secularist bent, but they are hardly making war on the other, traditional Muslims. These secular Muslims are just trying to survive as best they can, and to stop the further encroachments of Islam where it has temporarily been constrained, as it was in Turkey under Kemalist rulers, or even in Iraq under the Ba'athists.

There is no "war for the soul of Islam." There is instead the 1400-year war of Islam against, not the West — but all the rest. That war can die down, when the financial wherewithal for conducting the war diminishes. It can die down, when there are no battlefield triumphs to swell Muslim hearts with pride and to embolden Muslim troops. It can die down, as money and access to arms diminish, or Muslims lose the freedom to move to Infidel lands to conduct, behind enemy lines, the kind of non-military warfare that undermines Infidel morale and even spreads Islam, through campaigns of da'wa, among the most vulnerable types within Infidel society: the economically marginal; the psychically marginal; the prisoners seeking for an Instant Community of Brothers able to protect them behind bars; and the spoiled and confused flotsam and jetsam that are products of Western social collapse, such as John Walker Lindh and Adam Gadahn, and all the other weak-minded Americans and Europeans who converted to Islam and joined the jihad.

Unless this is understood, Infidels will no doubt keep transferring enormous sum to the Muslim oil states of the Middle East. But the oligopolistic power wielded by the Arab oil states has dissipated, thanks to such technical developments as fracking, which has made the US not just energy-independent but an oil exporter, and as well to the rapid world-wide increase in alternative sources of energy, such as solar, wind, and nuclear energy, and finally, demand for oil has been reduced by the increasing electrification of car fleets. The colossal sums from the sale of oil that Saudi Arabia has enjoyed until now are steadily decreasing. Crown Prince Mohammed bin Salman has allocated more than a trillion dollars to his NEOM megaproject. All of this means that there is less of that money that used to be spent around the world by the Saudi government to pay for mosques, madrasas, and salaries for imams. And the entire Western world should be in a crash program to support drilling on lands, including those heretofore off-limits to such drilling, and off-shore as well, and subsidizing the rapid development of renewable sources — solar, wind, geothermal, and hydropower — not only for environmental reasons, but to diminish the colossal revenues from the sale of oil and natural gas that are currently going to the rich Arab states of the Gulf — especially Saudi Arabia.

What must the world's non-Muslims now do to prevent the spread of Islam, especially in Europe?

1. Limit the ability of Muslim states or groups to acquire major weaponry. Above all, by diplomacy or most likely by military force, prevent Iran from acquiring nuclear weapons. In addition, do not provide Saudi Arabia with nuclear reactors, as the Trump Administration is apparently considering. The same machines that can enrich uranium to low levels for fuel can enrich it to high levels for bombs.

2. Pour hundreds of billions of dollars into building still more solar and wind farms all over Europe and North America. This can be presented as prompted by environmental concerns, but those investments will also greatly, and quickly, diminish the oil revenues of Muslim countries. With less money, those countries will have to pull back on building mosques and madrasas world-wide, nor will they be willing to pay the salaries of tens of thousands of imams in the Infidel lands.

3. Work in Europe and in North America to educate people about the tenets of Islam, the attitudes and atmospherics of Islam, and the history of both jihad-conquest, and of the imposition of dhimmi status on subjugated non-Muslims, over 1400 years.

4. Do nothing that would inadvertently narrow the natural fissures within the Islamic world, between Arabs and non-Arabs, or between Sunni and Shi'a. One obvious example is Algeria, where the Berbers resent the cultural and linguistic imperialism of the majority Arabs, as shown by the Berber riots in Tizi-Ouzou, where demands were made for the Berber language, Tamazight, to receive official recognition and to be taught in schools in Berber areas of the country. Another is Iraq, where the Kurds hope to obtain still greater autonomy from the Arab-dominated government in Baghdad. In Syria, the Sunni jihadists who now rule in Damascus will never be reconciled with the Alawites in Laatakia, who supported Bashar Assad's anti-Sunni despotism. The Kurds pose a separatist threat in all four countries where they live: in Syria, in Iraq in Iran, and in Turkey. The Americans should take it upon themselves to supply the Kurds in both Iraq and Syria with weapons with which to

defend themselves against attempts by Arab governments to end their autonomy. That will create a constant turmoil in those countries. From the point of view of Infidels, that is a good thing.

5. By denying further aid to the poorer Muslim countries, such as Egypt and Jordan, the West will force those countries to go hat in hand to the rich oil states of the Gulf, which is likely to cause bad blood between the donors, who don't relish paying for their poorer cousins, and the aid recipients, for whom such aid — no matter how much — will never be enough.

6. The Western powers should do all they can to become energy-independent. First, through domestic oil and gas drilling including in government-owned lands, where such drilling has until now been prohibited. Fear of nuclear reactor accidents — Three Mile Island, Chernobyl — needs to be overcome, and modern, safe nuclear reactors, those built not by Russia but by France, which has the longest experience in harnessing nuclear energy for peaceful purposes, need to be built by the hundreds, or even thousands. Governments should encourage the move to electric vehicles by offering greater subsidies to buyers of such vehicles. These measures will take away much of the power of OPEC states to collect, as they have in the past, oligopolistic rents. Less revenues for those states means less money for building mosques and madrasas all over the West, less money for weapons with which to threaten the West, including Israel, less money to buy influence with foreign politicians, less money to pay for academic centers of Islamic studies in the West that churn out not scholars but Defenders of the Faith — that faith being Islam — on the model of the Prince Alwaleed Bin Talal Center for Muslim-Christian Understanding affiliated with Georgetown University.

Again, here is a sentence that needs to be memorized. Its truth cannot be denied. And that sentence is as follows:

The presence of large numbers of Muslims within the lands of the Infidels has created a situation for the indigenous Infidels that is far more unpleasant, expensive, and physically dangerous than it would be without the presence of large numbers of Muslims.

There are not many people in France, Italy, Spain, Germany, the U.K., Belgium, Sweden, Denmark and other places who could deny the truth of that statement. Even when they do not know quite what to do, even if they are among those who still hope that they will be able to integrate many of the Muslim migrants into their societies, they know that a terrible mistake was made by their leaders in allowing tens of millions of them to settle in their countries in the first place.

Save for the hirelings — those on the take from Arabs, the band of ex-diplomats, ex-intelligence agents, estate agents selling mansions and messuage in Mayfair and Belgravia to assorted rich Gulf Arabs, corrupt journalists, and academic recipients of Saudi, U.A.E., and Kuwaiti largesse such as John Esposito — as well as the members of the wandering tribe of antisemites, who find themselves quite naturally on the side of Muslims, everyone knows that that sentence is true.

CHAPTER THIRTY-FOUR

What We have Lost, and Stand to Lose

W HAT HAVE WE lost because of Islam? A short list:
Security: At every airport, subway station, bus station, at every sports event, at every public lecture, in every office building, at every museum, at every large gathering and many small gatherings all over this country (particularly those that are specifically Christian or Jewish or Hindu, and certainly all those that are devoted to discussing the menace of Islam), there are now security guards, security checks, long waits that use up, at airports alone, billions of man-hours that were never used up in such fashion before 9/11. Why? All because of the threat not of "terrorism" in general, but rather of Muslim terrorism in particular, none of which would have been necessary in the absence of Muslim terrorist threats. Since 9/11, there have been over 48,000 separate attacks by Muslim terrorists.

Freedom to travel over much of the world: How many of us now realize that it will be difficult or dangerous from now on to visit all of the sites of classical antiquity that can be found in North Africa, or the Middle East, or in Turkey, because these lands are in the grip of increasingly restive and aggressive Muslims, not all of whom are content merely to take the dollars of Western tourists. Think of how many attacks there have been, prompted in the minds of the perpetrators by the tenets, the doctrines, the attitudes, of Islam, against Swiss tourists at Luxor (68 stabbed to death, and many decapitated), against tourists at the Valley of the Kings, in Egypt, or against visitors to the island of Djerba in Tunisia, or Western guests at a luxury hotel in Marrakesh, Morocco. There are 57 Muslim states. How many of them are perfectly safe for non-Muslims to visit today?

This is not just a matter of tourism, but of a non-Islamic cultural patrimony that is located in lands ruled by Muslims. Only the desire for tourist dollars (and in Egypt some non-Islamic national pride, in those pyramids, mummies, mastabahs, and canopic jars) have kept the relics of the pre-Islamic past, the "Time of Ignorance" or jahliyya, in Muslim countries from falling into disrepair and worse, no matter how significant they remain in the view of Western man. This indifference, or even hostility, toward their own pre-Islamic past that Muslims are taught to feel, has brought about an attendant impoverishment of their own societies and themselves.

Freedom to think: How many of those born into Islam over the last 1400 years might have, but for Islam, made some kind of mark on the world, something in art, science, moral philosophy? Something, anything. Instead, what we have is pitiful, compared not only to the Western world, but to the civilizations of the East, and of pre-Columbian America. All of North Africa, all of the Middle East and many other places that became subject to Islam, saw their peoples deprived of many means of artistic expression. Their ability to engage in free and skeptical inquiry that is necessary for the pursuit of science, has been permanently dampened.

Freedom of conscience: the right, which took centuries to develop in the West, but does not hold in Muslim lands, to believe or not believe whatever you wish. Apostasy may not always and everywhere in Muslim lands be punished by death, but it is certainly punished by death in some places, and the penalty is threatened everywhere. It is often carried out by vigilantes, as in the case of Farag Foda, the Egyptian writer. Think of Ali Dashti, tortured to death at the age of 84 by officials in the Islamic Republic of Iran for writing *Twenty-Three Years*, a study critical of Muhammad. Think of the celebrated Egyptian writer, the blind Taha Hussein, and his employment travails that resulted from his daring to express in print his view that the Qur'an was not a reliable historical source. Think of the Kuwaiti Hussein Qambar Ali (known during his conversion to Christianity as Robert Hussein), who after an Islamic court declared him to be an "apostate" was threatened with death. And even in the United States, those who wish to leave Islam are often very quiet about it, afraid of social ostracism from Muslims, and worse, much worse.

Islam offers Believers a Total Regulation of Life, dividing existence into what is halal (licit) and haram (illicit) — from what you eat and what you wear to exactly how you wash, and every other conceivable aspect of life. This makes people into zombies, following rules that often make no sense, that are ludicrous, but must be followed. Shall I give some of the embarrassing details, about the odd number of stones, and so on, that you must use to wipe yourself, or would you prefer that I spared all of us that sort of thing? Just go to any Muslim website where questions are asked as to whether a Muslim can do this or can't do that. Why follow these rules? Oh, because Allah Knows Best. Q.E.D. That is all ye know on earth, and all ye need to know.

Then there is the equally extraordinary belief that the Qur'an contains everything, all of science, all of knowledge, absolutely everything, if only we have the wit or understanding to detect it. If there is a surer way to stunt the mental growth of hundreds of millions, I can't imagine what it might be.

Those of us who are not Muslims should thank God we were not born into this crazy and violent creed. It is no great achievement to have avoided Islam by not being born a Muslim. It is a great achievement, given how fearsome the consequences can be, to be born into Islam and then to reject it.

It is a negative achievement, an astounding feat of mental self-immolation, to be born a non-Muslim and then to actually wish to become a Muslim. There are those on their Spiritual Search who simply ran out of places to look, or decided to stop at the next inn or caravanserai, the one with Arabic script and the hubble-bubble pipe, and the calligraphy on the green-colored walls.

But is a hubble-bubble pipe and Kufic calligraphy worth those mind-forged manacles in exchange?

CHAPTER THIRTY-FIVE

Victory is not Inevitable

THERE IS NOTHING inevitable about the defeat of the worldwide jihad. In fact, if one looks at the emptying out of non-Muslim populations within the last century, one finds that the non-Muslims living in North Africa, the Middle East, Turkey, and Iran, consisting of Christians and Jews, has gone steadily down. And the non-Muslim percentage of the population in Pakistan and Bangladesh, in Malaysia and Indonesia, consisting mainly of Hindus (as well as Sikhs, Buddhists, and Christians) has also steadily diminished. The desire to convert to Islam in order to avoid the onerous status of dhimmi, the forced expulsions (as of Hindus from Pakistan and Bangladesh), mass murders, and even genocide, as with the Armenians in Turkey, have all helped to explain this demographic change.

Meanwhile, everywhere in the Lands of the Infidels, tens of millions of Muslims have been allowed to settle deep inside what they regard as enemy lines. And once inside, Muslim women have been steadily outbreeding the indigenous non-Muslims, with much higher fertility rates. The percentage of Muslims in the populations of France, of Germany, of Italy, and in many other countries steadily, unstoppably, rises.

If demography is destiny, and if nothing is done to halt both Muslim immigration, and to discourage the astounding overbreeding by Muslims — in France the fertility rate for Muslims is 2.9, while for non-Muslims it is 1.9, below replacement level. The Muslim percentage of the population inexorably increases. In Italy (with a negative birthrate), in Spain, in England, in Germany, the same kind of results obtain. Anyone can do the simple calculation. And as the number of Muslims increases, Western politicians rush to appease them to win their votes, both by increasing the benefits available to them, and by supporting an open-door policy on immigration. They are thinking of their own welfare, heedless of the welfare of their country.

A few years ago, a prominent leader of the Socialist Party in France sent out word to his underlings that they should forget entirely about "the Jews" and Israel, and concentrate entirely on winning the Muslim vote, which can only be won by adopting Muslim demands on welfare benefits, on foreign policy, and in meeting Muslim demands for changes in the laws, customs, and manners to be observed within the Infidel land in which they happen to have settled. Much the same kind of cravenness by politicians can be observed in Great Britain, where in local elections, and not only in London with Mayor Sadiq Khan, politicians vie in their desire to appease and please Muslim voters.

Those who would like to register their fear and dismay, and their desire to make their country less welcoming to Muslims, who do not, and cannot, wish the resident Infidels well, have only the Reform UK party led by Nigel Farage in Britain, the National Rally party in France led by Marine Le Pen and Jordan Bardella, the Alternative für Deutschland party led by Alice Weidel in Germany, and the Party for Freedom led by Geert Wilders in the Netherlands to wholeheartedly support. By successfully demonizing the leaders of these anti-immigrant, or more exactly anti-Muslim immigrant, parties, the left has made it harder elsewhere in Europe to find and promote articulate, respectable political figures able both to instruct and to warn (as to the immutable nature, and menace, of Islam and its adherents) the mass of common people who have been betrayed by their elites.

There is a widespread inability, among those American and European elites, to understand the timeframe in which events in Europe are taking place, and how late things are for the Americans (and the Europeans) to come to their senses. When members of our media and political elites go to Europe, they live in luxurious hotels, and meet their well-heeled analogues far from any No-Go areas that look like Algiers or Marrakesh. They are cushioned by their own ignorance of languages — so that, for example, even reading *Le Monde* or *Le Figaro* or the *Corriere della Sera* or *El Pais* is impossible — and information arrives filtered through the pollyannish English-language press and television. Thus they are less alarmed than they should be by the Islamization of Europe.

Western Europe could still be saved from this Islamization, but only if a slew of anti-immigrant leaders, knowledgeable about the faith, are elected, unafraid to help their populations come to their senses about Islam, and those leaders need to be supported in this effort by a muscular United States. A great deal of time and money has been wasted on the debacles in Iraq and Afghanistan, when the real battle against Islamic domination should be fought in the countries of the West where the threat of both violent and demographic jihad steadily grows. The task requires containing, constraining, dividing, and demoralizing the forces of Islam. There is still time — just.

CHAPTER THIRTY-SIX

And To Think I Could See It On Mulberry Street

S HOULD EURABIA become a fully realized entity, what would become of European art? It's never too early to start planning.

Memo to Max Hollein, director of the Met:

Begin raising money now for that special "Louvre" wing of the Metropolitan that you are going to have to build in 30 years, Actually, it will not be a wing — I'm afraid you are going to have to have a space almost as big as the Louvre itself, taking up many acres of Central Park. After all, once Muslims are in a position to make their demands met, we know what will happen to the statues and paintings of living beings in the Louvre, don't we? And not just in the Louvre, but those figurative paintings and statues in the Musée Guimet, the Musée Nissim Camondo, the Musée Rodin, the Musée Fabre, the Musée de Cluny, and all the rest, will need to be taken out of the country so as to avoid their destruction by Muslims who consider these art works to be haram, forbidden.

Just before World War II the Americans (and to a much lesser extent the British) received the cream of German and Austrian art historians, who staffed our academic departments of art history: Erwin Panofsky, Jakob Rosenberg, Rudolf Wittkower, E. H. Gombrich, Ernst Kitzinger, Gisela Richter, George Hanfmann, Rudolf Arnheim and so many others, who helped train, and raise the standards of, several generations of American art historians. And now, should Europe be sufficiently Islamized, European art historians will now be followed to America, nearly a century after their arrival, by the art in its museums.

Are we Americans lucky, or what?

Let's take this idea for a walk, shall we?

The New Rijksmuseum might best be placed where there once stood Nieuw Amsterdam. Close to New York City, but not in it. Mamaroneck, Oyster Bay, Scarsdale are close by, so that you can take in the works of all those Dutchmen — Hals, Rembrandt, Ruisdael, and even Vermeer, all just a few train stops outside Manhattan.

The New Prado, possibly as a tribute to the general Hispanidad, would best be placed either in Miami, or possibly in Texas, or New Mexico. The wild West will come to mean a bit more than sagebrush and the Durango Kid. A little hint of Philip II, with pride of place given to Bosch's *Garden of Earthly Delights* that, if it remained in the Prado, would surely be destroyed by Muslim connoisseurs. So let those Prado paintings find their refuge in Albuquerque, or Santa Fe, or Santa Barbara.

The New National Gallery, that will house works from the National Gallery in London, should be close to Washington, but not in it. So it's to be Virginia, definitely upperclass Virginia. But where? Southside Virginia, say at the plantation at Brookneal formerly owned by Ambassador David K. E. Bruce? Or possibly in the riding country, the land of Three-Day Eventing, and the admirers of Charles Chenevix French. Yes, possibly Upperville would be just the place for the New National Gallery. And docents, winsome female docents, all of them, please, definitely FFV (First Families of Virginia). And if you insist, a handful of interns as well from the Main Line, and the wilder shores of Oyster Bay, Long Island.

The New Uffizi? Here we have a problem. I'll leave this one up to you, dear reader. Where do you want to place all those sculptures, and those paintings so offensive to Muslim sensibilities, like Botticelli's *Primavera* (Venus on a Half-Shell) or the *Madonna del Parto* by Piero della Francesca, or the statue of David by Michelangelo, or his *Pietà*, sure to be among the first pieces of sculpture Muslims would want to have destroyed?

There are many other museums — the Vatican Museum, the Fitzwilliam Museum in Cambridge and the Ashmolean in Oxford, the Ducal Museum in Urbino, the museums in Arezzo, Piero's frescoes in Sansepolcro, the Gemäldegalerie, and on and on. Hundreds of museums, hundreds of thousands of art works needing to be rescued from wanton Muslim destruction.

Even if that nightmare scenario were to come true, and future curators in Europe will be forced to follow the late Sheikh Qaradawi's handy guide as to what is haram and what halal, a great deal of Western art can be shipped out, made safe, rescued for posterity. But none of this has to be. It is not too late to halt and even reverse the Muslim presence in Europe.

Perhaps we can come to some arrangement with Europe's Muslims. After all, Italy does contain two-thirds of the Western world's art treasures. Without Italy, Western civilization is unthinkable (that can't be said for any other country, I'm afraid). So let's offer to let Muslims continue to live in the rest of Europe, but Italy must be spared and kept free from Islam. And we Americans will guarantee its security (as, for other reasons, we will guarantee that other essential component of the spiritual heritage of the Western world, Israel).

But if the Muslims prove implacable, then we will have to bring over the contents of the Uffizi, and whatever statues of Michelangelo, Donatello, and others are to be found all over the country, in the Piazza della Signoria in Florence, in the Piazza Farnese, in the Piazza Navona, in all the Piazze Romane, everywhere and offer them a refuge here. Possibly all those Americans now putting their tax-deductible dollars to work in the "Save Venice" Campaign, forgetting that the real sea that may swamp not just Venice but all of Italy, consists of adherents of a grim ideology that commands the destruc- tion of most Western art works (the attempted destruction of Joseph's Tomb in Israel and the successful blowing up of the Bamiyan Buddhas in Afghanistan were simply the most notable recent examples of 1400 years of Muslim destruction of Christian, Jewish, Hindu, and Buddhist artifacts and monuments).

Hanover Street and the North End in Boston being what they now are, one would have to opt for the New Uffizi to be placed in New York, in Little Italy and, most fittingly, on Mulberry Street. Yes, Gennaro, there is a Santa Claus — and everyone in New York can now visit the Uffizi without leaving the city.

And someday someone will write a children's book about all the art treasures of Europe, kept from harm, as in some fabulous fable, by being housed in new museums built expressly for them, in America, the country with a big heart and a big wallet. It will be a simple book, with pictures of some of the sculptures and paintings, carefully labelled and designed to introduce young children to the wonders of the fine arts. And that future book will be called:

"And To Think that I Saw It On Mulberry Street."

Oops. I think that title's been taken.

As Joe E. Brown once said, nobody's perfect.

CHAPTER THIRTY-SEVEN

What's at Stake

S OME TIME AGO I observed that "without Europe the West becomes bereft" – and was almost immediately asked to explain. Here goes, by way of explanation:

The British Museum.
The Louvre.
The Prado.
The National Gallery.
The Uffizi.
The Rijksmeum.
Alte Pinakothek.
The Vatican Museum.
The Library at Chatsworth.
The Concertgebouw.
The canals of Venice.
Murano.
The Piazza della Signoria.
Florence.
Umbria.
Todi.
The Dulwich Gallery.
Paris.
Ile St. Louis
Toledo.
The Tivoli Gardens.
The Boboli Gardens.

The Jardin des Plantes.
Las Ramblas in Barcelona.
The Judería in Cordoba.
The Portuguese Synagogue in Amsterdam.
Trinity College Great Court.
Rome.
Pushkin's house and library in St. Petersburg.
Musée Guimet. Muséee of Nissim Camondo. Jeu de Paume.
The Luxembourg Gardens
Versailles.
Tolstoy's house at Yasnaya Polyana.
Linnaeus's house in Uppsala.
Uppsala.
Tsarskoe Selo.
The Dulwich Gallery.
Dickens's House.
Samuel Johnson's House.
Oxford.
Cambridge.
The National Railway Museum in York.
The islands of Lewis and Harris.
Chartres.
The cathedral at Chartres
The birthplace of Hans Christian Andersen in Odense.
Stratford-on-Avon.
Swans on the Avon River.
Swan Upping.
The Thames.
The Seine.
The Ebro.
The Tiber.
The Danube.
The Palazzo of the D'Este family in Ferrara.
The Palazzo Pubblico in Siena.
The Pinacoteca in Siena.
The Ducal Palace in Urbino
Spoleto.
San Gimignano.
The Villa Lante.
The caves of Lascaux.

The caves of Altamira.
St. Sulpice.
The Piazza Farnese.
Piazza del Popolo.
Piazza di Spagna.
The Piazza Navona.
The Spanish Steps.
The house of Gogol at 47, via Sistina, Rome.
The house of Keats (now called the Keats-Shelley House) in Rome.
The Protestant Cemetery in Rome
Via Condotti.
Via del Babuino.
The obelisk in the Piazza Minerva.
The fountain in the Piazza Navona.
La Barcaccia.
Trinità dei Monti.
Musée de Cluny.
Mont Saint-Michel.
Ile de Ré.
Musée Andre-Jacquemart.
The lavender fields in Senanque.
The Bibliothèque Nationale.
The Colosseum.
The Parthenon.
Arezzo.
The street of alfarrabistas in Lisbon.
Lisbon.
The White Horse of Uffington.
The mist on Malvern Hill.
Tintern Abbey.
The gardens at Chiswick.
Lac Leman.
The Castle of Chillon.
Prague.
The Jewish cemetery at Prague.
Cracow.
Buda.
Pest.

And all the rest.

The King James version of the Bible. The Wyclif version. And the Tyndale. But not the New Revised. Wynkyn de Worde. Sir Kenelm Digby. Sir John Maundeville. Bosworth Field. Agincourt.

And lest we forget, let's name a few of those writers whose works would be banned in an Islamized Europe, starting with the English writers: Geoffrey Chaucer, Edmund Spenser, William Shakespeare, Christopher Marlowe, John Milton, John Dryden, Alexander Pope, James Boswell, Samuel Johnon, John Keats, Lord Byron and Robert Burns; and the Italian writers: Jacopone da Todi, Dante, Petrarch, Boccaccio, Ariosto, Tasso, Leopardi, Alessandro Manzoni, Giuseppe AlleMontale, and Ungaretti; the French writers Charles d'Orleans, François Villon, Michel de Montaigne, Rabelais, Jean Racine, Pierre Corneille, André Chenier, Victor Hugo, Charles Baudelaire, Gustave Flaubert, Arthur Rimbaud, Paul Verlaine, Marcel Proust and Georges Perec; the Polish writers Wislawa Szymborska, Zbigniew Herbert. and Czeslaw Milosz, the Russian writers Gavrila Derzhavin, and Ivan Krylov, and Alexander Pushkin, Nikolai Gogol, Fyodor Tiutchev, Afanasy Fet, Andrey Bely, Vladislav Khodasevich, Vladimir Nabokov; and so on, all banned for the thoughts they deigned to express that would be anathema in a Europe ruled by Islam.

Have I left anyone out? Yes. Ten of thousands.

So add your own entries to my lists above. Don't forget to include the names of famous writers, musicians, painters, philosophers, and scientists, whom I just remembered, and embarrassingly must admit to having left out. I listed Shakespeare and Dante and Pushkin, but overlooked such people as Mozart, and Bach, and Beethoven, and Isaac Newton, and Spinoza, and Hume, and Rembrandt, and Piero della Francesca, and Cezanne and Balthus, and — unforgivably, Michelangelo and Leonardo.

Goodness, this could go on forever.

You don't care? Those Europeans deserve what they get?
Surely you jest.

Index

241

N

www.ingramcontent.com/pod-product-compliance
Lightning Source LLC
Chambersburg PA
CBHW050647270326
41927CB00012B/2918